INTERNATIONAL FERRY WAGONS

First Edition

Andrew Marshall

Published by Metro Enterprises Ltd., 48 Southcliffe Drive, Baildon, Shipley, West Yorkshire, BD17 5QX.

ISBN 0 947773 20 7

SECTION 1 - NOTES & INTRODUCTION

INTRODUCTION

This book is the third in a series of three volumes intended to cover all privately owned wagons registered to run on BR. Vehicles covered in this volume are all privately owned International Ferry Wagons registered to run on British Rail. Also included in this volume for the sake of a complete review of the Ferry Wagon scene are Ferry Wagons owned by the various railway administrations, including BR.

NUMBERING SYSTEM

The numbering scheme currently in use for wagons which cross international frontiers was devised by the International Union of Railways (UIC) and introduced as and from 1st October 1968. A number of changes with regard to Privately Owned vehicles took place in the early 1980's and former numbers are quoted in this volume where appropriate. The review of this scheme presented here is not intended to be exhaustive, but contains sufficient detail as is necessary to be relevant to the wagons featured in this book.
Each vehicle is allocated a 12 digit number, which is broken down as follows:

DIGITS 1 & 2 - EXCHANGE CODE

Digits 1 & 2 indicate whether a vehicle is bogie or fixed-axle, whether or not the gauge of the wagon is fixed or variable, the International Organisation under whose jurisdiction the wagon comes and limits on usage as follows:

01	Common user non bogie fixed gauge Railway Owned wagons in the Europ, OPW or Interfrigo pools.
03	Common user non bogie fixed gauge Privately Owned wagons in the Interfrigo pool.
04	Common user non bogie variable gauge Privately Owned wagons in the Interfrigo pool.
06	Common user non bogie variable gauge Leased Privately Owned wagons in the Interfrigo pool.
21	Non common user non bogie fixed gauge Railway Owned wagons to RIV or PPW standard designs.
23	Non common user non bogie fixed gauge Privately Owned wagons to RIV or PPW standard designs.
24	Non common user non bogie variable gauge Privately Owned wagons to RIV or PPW standard designs.
31	Non common user bogie fixed gauge Railway Owned wagons to RIV or PPW standard designs.
33	Non common user bogie fixed gauge Privately Owned wagons to RIV or PPW standard designs.
34	Non common user bogie variable gauge Privately Owned wagons to RIV or PPW standard designs.
43	Two axle Privately Owned wagons not to RIV or PPW standard designs, worked internationally by special agreement.
83	Bogie Privately Owned wagons not to RIV or PPW standard designs, worked internationally by special agreement.

Europ Pool	Western European Railways wagon pool.
Interfrigo	European Railways refrigerated van pool.
OPW	Eastern European Railways wagon pool.
RIV	Reglomento Internazionale Vagoni } International wagon
PPW	Prawila Polsowanij Wagonami } standardisation regulations

These digits are known as the Exchange Code as they indicate whether or not a wagon is suitable for exchange between two systems and under what restrictions.

DIGITS 3 & 4 - HOME NETWORK

Digits 3 & 4 indicate the home network of the vehicle as follows:

44 Budapesti Helyi Erdekū Vasut (BHEV). (Budapest Suburban Railway)
54 Ceskoslovenské Státni Dráhy (CSD). (Czechoslovak State Railways)
55 Magyar Államvasutak (MÁV). (Hungarian State Railways)
70 British Rail (BR).
71 Rede Nacionale de los Ferrocarriles Españoles (RENFE). (Spanish National Railways)
72 Zajednica Jugoslovenskih Zeleznica (JZ). (Yugoslav Railways)
74 Statens Järnvägar (SJ). (Swedish State Railways)
80 Deutsche Bundesbahn (DB). (German Federal Railway)
81 Österreichische Bundesbahnen (ÖBB). (Austrian Federal Railways)
83 Ente Ferrovie dello Stato (FS). (Italian Railways)
85 Schweizerische Bundesbahnen (SBB/CFF). (Swiss Federal Railways)
87 Société Nationale des Chemins de Fer Français (SNCF). (French National Railways)
88 Société Nationale des Chemins de Fer Belges (SNCB/NMBS). (Belgian National Railways)

DIGITS 4 to 8 - PRECISE WAGON TYPE.

Numbers are divided into ten groups as follows:

2xxx Non standard vans.
4xxx Non standard flats.
5xxx Standard opens & sliding or tilting roof wagons.
6xxx Non standard opens.
7xxx Tank wagons.
8xxx Refrigerated vans.
9xxx Special vehicles.

Within each group, the last three digits specify the precise type of wagon. As will be appreciated, the multiplicity of these type codes prevents them from being listed here due to considerations of space.

DIGITS 9 to 11 - VEHICLE SERIAL NUMBER

These are the individual number of the vehicle.

DIGIT 12 - COMPUTER CHECK DIGIT

This digit allows the various railway computers to verify that there has been no error in the recording of the previous eleven digits, and is calculated as the result of a mathematical equation of these eleven digits. This latter digit is not shown in this publication, but may be calculated easily by multiplying alternate digits by 2 & 1 respectively and then deducting the total from the next whole ten.

For example:	3	3	8	0	4	6	6	7	0	0	0
Multiply by:	2	1	2	1	2	1	2	1	2	1	2
Totals	6	3	16	0	8	6	12	7	0	0	0

Summation 6+3+1+6+0+8+6+1+2+7+0+0+0 = 40, 40-40 = 0, therfore check digit is 0.

Vehicles are listed in this publication in order of the home network digits, with the Exchange Codes being listed in the type headings.

BRAKES

All International Ferry Wagons are equipped with air brakes or through pipe. The type of brake equipment fitted to each vehicle is indicated by the BR TOPS code shown in the type heading. A list of the TOPS brake codes applicable to this publication is shown inside the rear cover.

DESIGN CODES

This is a six character code used by BR to describe precisely each type of vehicle. The first two characters are letters to describe the use of the wagon, and also form the first two letters of the three letter TOPS code allocated to the wagon. A list of relevant codes to this volume is given on the inside rear cover. The next character in the case of a Ferry Wagon is always E. The final three characters indicate the reference number of the specific design to which the wagon has been built. These start at 001 as the first issued reference and work upwards. Many wagons were recoded early in 1990. Old and new codes are given where appropriate.

DETAIL DIFFERENCES

Differences between wagons within batches are shown in this volume by use of letters as notes as appropriate.

WEIGHTS

All are given in metric tonnes. The maximum axle load permitted on BR is 25.5 tonnes, so the maximum weight for a two axle wagon is 51 tonnes and for a bogie wagon 102 tonnes.
Tare Weight - this is the weight of an empty wagon, given to the nearest 10 kg.
Gross Laden Weight (GLW) - this is the maximum permitted weight of a wagon and its cargo, to keep it within the axle load limit or within the limit of its suspension.
The carrying capacity of any wagon is therefore the Gross Laden Weight minus the Tare Weight.

MAXIMUM SPEED

Is given in Miles Per Hour (mph). This regulates the type of train into which a vehicle can be formed. No train is permitted to run any faster than the maximum speed restriction of the slowest wagon in the train. Due to the types of suspension fitted, some wagons are allowed to run at faster speeds when loaded, whilst others are permitted to run faster when empty.
Class 4 trains are permitted to run up to 75 mph
Class 6 trains are permitted to run up to 60 mph
Class 7 trains are permitted to run up to 45 mph
Class 8 trains are permitted to run up to 35 mph
Class 9 trains are permitted to run up to 25 mph if unfitted, or up to 35 mph if partially fitted.

LENGTH

Is given in metric units then imperial units. Lengths quoted are the overall length of the wagon over buffers/couplings.

BOGIE AND SUSPENSION TYPES

The type of runnig gear fitted to each type of wagon is given in the heading for each type of wagon, where known.

ACKNOWLEDGEMENTS

As information on the vehicles listed in this book is not available from BR sources, the author would like to thank the many wagon owners, builders, hirers and enthusiasts who have provided information to assist in the compilation of this volume. Any further information which readers may be able to contribute, or any constructive comment will be welcomed, and should be sent to the author at the publishers address shown on the title page.

SECTION 2 - WAGON DETAILS

Information to hand as at October 1990 is incorporated in this section.

44 2197 000-026 INSULATED VAN IMB

Builder: Ganz, Hungary.
Design Code: IME420 (a IME636)
Owner: BHEV.
Tare Weight: 15.00 t.
Gross Laden Weight: 45.00 t.
Maximum Speed: 60 mph.
Length:
Suspension Type: Double Link.
Exchange Code: 21.
Notes: IME636 are coded IMX. Not currently working on British Rail.

44 2197 000 a
44 2197 001
44 2197 002
44 2197 003
44 2197 004
44 2197 005
44 2197 006
44 2197 007
44 2197 008
44 2197 009 a
44 2197 010
44 2197 011
44 2197 012 a
44 2197 013
44 2197 014
44 2197 015
44 2197 016
44 2197 017
44 2197 018
44 2197 019
44 2197 020
44 2197 021
44 2197 022
44 2197 023
44 2197 024
44 2197 025
44 2197 026

54 2380 000-099 LARGE VAN ILB

Builder: Ceskoslovenské Vagónky, Poprad, Czechoslovakia.
Design Code: ILE353.
Owner: CSD.
Tare Weight: 14.50 t.
Gross Laden Weight: 40.00 t.
Maximum Speed: 60 mph.
Length: 14020 mm (46 ft. 0 in.)
Suspension Type: Double Link.
Exchange Code: 21.
Notes: Not currently working on British Rail.
Previous Number Series: 21 54 2140 502-9/13-9/22-9/32-9/42-9/52-9/62-9/ 72-9/83-9/92-9/602/4-9/12-9/22-7.

54 2380 000
54 2380 001
54 2380 002
54 2380 003
54 2380 004
54 2380 005
54 2380 006
54 2380 007
54 2380 008
54 2380 009
54 2380 010
54 2380 011
54 2380 012
54 2380 013
54 2380 014
54 2380 015
54 2380 016
54 2380 017
54 2380 018
54 2380 019
54 2380 020
54 2380 021
54 2380 022
54 2380 023
54 2380 024
54 2380 025
54 2380 026
54 2380 027
54 2380 028
54 2380 029
54 2380 030
54 2380 031
54 2380 032
54 2380 033
54 2380 034
54 2380 035
54 2380 036
54 2380 037
54 2380 038
54 2380 039
54 2380 040
54 2380 041
54 2380 042
54 2380 043
54 2380 044
54 2380 045
54 2380 046
54 2380 047
54 2380 048
54 2380 049
54 2380 050
54 2380 051
54 2380 052
54 2380 053
54 2380 054
54 2380 055
54 2380 056
54 2380 057
54 2380 058
54 2380 059
54 2380 060
54 2380 061
54 2380 062
54 2380 064
54 2380 065
54 2380 066
54 2380 067
54 2380 068
54 2380 069
54 2380 070
54 2380 071
54 2380 072
54 2380 073
54 2380 074
54 2380 075
54 2380 076
54 2380 077
54 2380 078
54 2380 079
54 2380 080
54 2380 081
54 2380 082
54 2380 083
54 2380 084
54 2380 085
54 2380 086
54 2380 087
54 2380 088

54 2380 089	54 2380 092	54 2380 095	54 2380 098
54 2380 090	54 2380 093	54 2380 096	54 2380 099
54 2380 091	54 2380 094	54 2380 097	

55 8480 000-098 REFRIGERATED VAN IIX

Builder: VEB Waggonbau Dessau, East Germany.
Design Code: IIE183 (a IIE620). **Owner:** Interfrigo.
Tare Weight: 16.50 t. **Gross Laden Weight:** 36.00 t.
Maximum Speed: 60 mph. **Length:** 11740 mm (38 ft. 6 in.)
Suspension Type: Double Link. **Exchange Code:** 01.
Notes: IIE620 are coded IIB. 001-005 are the only wagons currently to work on British Rail.
Previous Number Series: 12 55 8097 000-098.

55 8480 000	55 8480 025	55 8480 050	55 8480 075
55 8480 001 a	55 8480 026	55 8480 051	55 8480 076
55 8480 002 a	55 8480 027	55 8480 052	55 8480 077
55 8480 003 a	55 8480 028	55 8480 053	55 8480 078
55 8480 004 a	55 8480 029	55 8480 054	55 8480 079
55 8480 005 a	55 8480 030	55 8480 055	55 8480 080
55 8480 006	55 8480 031	55 8480 056	55 8480 081
55 8480 007	55 8480 032	55 8480 057	55 8480 082
55 8480 008	55 8480 033	55 8480 058	55 8480 083
55 8480 009	55 8480 034	55 8480 059	55 8480 084
55 8480 010	55 8480 035	55 8480 060	55 8480 085
55 8480 011	55 8480 036	55 8480 061	55 8480 086
55 8480 012	55 8480 037	55 8480 062	55 8480 087
55 8480 013	55 8480 038	55 8480 063	55 8480 088
55 8480 014	55 8480 039	55 8480 064	55 8480 089
55 8480 015	55 8480 040	55 8480 065	55 8480 090
55 8480 016	55 8480 041	55 8480 066	55 8480 091
55 8480 017	55 8480 042	55 8480 067	55 8480 092
55 8480 018	55 8480 043	55 8480 068	55 8480 093
55 8480 019	55 8480 044	55 8480 069	55 8480 094
55 8480 020	55 8480 045	55 8480 070	55 8480 095
55 8480 021	55 8480 046	55 8480 071	55 8480 096
55 8480 022	55 8480 047	55 8480 072	55 8480 097
55 8480 023	55 8480 048	55 8480 073	55 8480 098
55 8480 024	55 8480 049	55 8480 074	

55 8580 000-099 REFRIGERATED VAN IIX

Builder: VEB Waggonbau Dessau, East Germany.
Design Code: IIE621 (a IIE622). **Owner:** Interfrigo.
Tare Weight: 16.50 t. **Gross Laden Weight:** 36.00 t.
Maximum Speed: 75 mph. **Length:** 11740 mm (38 ft. 6 in.)
Suspension Type: Double Link. **Exchange Code:** 01.
Notes: IIE622 are coded IIB. 55 8580 001-005 are currently the only wagons to work on British Rail.
Previous Number Series: 12 55 8298 000-099.

55 8580 000	55 8580 004 a	55 8580 008	55 8580 012
55 8580 001 a	55 8580 005 a	55 8580 009	55 8580 013
55 8580 002 a	55 8580 006	55 8580 010	55 8580 014
55 8580 003 a	55 8580 007	55 8580 011	55 8580 015

55 8580 016
55 8580 017
55 8580 018
55 8580 019
55 8580 020
55 8580 021
55 8580 022
55 8580 023
55 8580 024
55 8580 025
55 8580 026
55 8580 027
55 8580 028
55 8580 029
55 8580 030
55 8580 031
55 8580 032
55 8580 033
55 8580 034
55 8580 035
55 8580 036
55 8580 037
55 8580 038
55 8580 039
55 8580 040
55 8580 041
55 8580 042
55 8580 043
55 8580 044
55 8580 045
55 8580 046
55 8580 047
55 8580 048
55 8580 049
55 8580 050
55 8580 051
55 8580 052
55 8580 053
55 8580 054
55 8580 055
55 8580 056
55 8580 057
55 8580 058
55 8580 059
55 8580 060
55 8580 061
55 8580 062
55 8580 063
55 8580 064
55 8580 065
55 8580 066
55 8580 067
55 8580 068
55 8580 069
55 8580 070
55 8580 071
55 8580 072
55 8580 073
55 8580 074
55 8580 075
55 8580 076
55 8580 077
55 8580 078
55 8580 079
55 8580 080
55 8580 081
55 8580 082
55 8580 083
55 8580 084
55 8580 085
55 8580 086
55 8580 087
55 8580 088
55 8580 089
55 8580 090
55 8580 091
55 8580 092
55 8580 093
55 8580 094
55 8580 095
55 8580 096
55 8580 097
55 8580 098
55 8580 099

70 2795 300-349 LARGE BOGIE VAN KVA

Builder: Linke-Hofmann-Busch, Salzgitter, West Germany, 1985-86.
Design Code: KVE593 (Ex PIE593). **Owner:** VTG.
Tare Weight: 26.50 t. **Gross Laden Weight:** 90.00 t.
Maximum Speed: 60 mph. **Length:** 22200 mm (72 ft. 10 in.)
Bogie Type: LHB 82. **Exchange Code:** 83.
Notes: 12 wagons are on hire to Perrier Water, the others being available for general hire.

70 2795 300
70 2795 301
70 2795 302
70 2795 303
70 2795 304
70 2795 305
70 2795 306
70 2795 307
70 2795 308
70 2795 309
70 2795 310
70 2795 311
70 2795 312
70 2795 313
70 2795 314
70 2795 315
70 2795 316
70 2795 317
70 2795 318
70 2795 319
70 2795 320
70 2795 321
70 2795 322
70 2795 323
70 2795 324
70 2795 325
70 2795 326
70 2795 327
70 2795 328
70 2795 329
70 2795 330
70 2795 331
70 2795 332
70 2795 333
70 2795 334
70 2795 335
70 2795 336
70 2795 337
70 2795 338
70 2795 339
70 2795 340
70 2795 341
70 2795 342
70 2795 343
70 2795 344
70 2795 345
70 2795 346
70 2795 347
70 2795 348
70 2795 349

70 2795 350-364 SLIDING DOOR VAN KVA

Builder: Waggon Union, Siegen, West Germany, 1987-88.
Design Code: KVE678 (Ex PIE678). **Owner:** Transfesa.
Tare Weight: 26.30 t. **Gross Laden Weight:** 80.00 t.
Maximum Speed: 60 mph. **Length:** 22140 mm (72 ft. 8 in.)
Bogie Type: Y21CSC. **Exchange Code:** 83.
Notes: Used on various workings to and from Europe.

70 2795 350	70 2795 354	70 2795 358	70 2795 362
70 2795 351	70 2795 355	70 2795 359	70 2795 363
70 2795 352	70 2795 356	70 2795 360	70 2795 364
70 2795 353	70 2795 357	70 2795 361	

70 2797 000-029 LARGE BOGIE VAN KVA

Builder: BREL Shildon, UK, 1979.
Design Code: KVE483 (Ex PIE483). **Owner:** Danzas.
Tare Weight: 26.00 t. **Gross Laden Weight:** 80.00 t.
Maximum Speed: 60 mph. **Length:** 21100 mm (69 ft. 6 in.)
Bogie Type: Y25CS2. **Exchange Code:** 33.
Previous Number Series: 21 70 0298 000-029.
Notes: Used on various workings to and from Europe.

70 2797 000	70 2797 008	70 2797 016	70 2797 023
70 2797 001	70 2797 009	70 2797 017	70 2797 024
70 2797 002	70 2797 010	70 2797 018	70 2797 025
70 2797 003	70 2797 011	70 2797 019	70 2797 026
70 2797 004	70 2797 012	70 2797 020	70 2797 027
70 2797 005	70 2797 013	70 2797 021	70 2797 028
70 2797 006	70 2797 014	70 2797 022	70 2797 029
70 2797 007	70 2797 015		

70 4289 000-027 AUTIC PIA

Builder: Société Nouvelle des Ateliers, France, 1981.
Design Code: PIE735 (a PIE738). **Owner:** Tiphook.
Tare Weight: 27.16 t. **Gross Laden Weight:** 38.96 t.
Maximum Speed: 75 mph (a 60 mph). **Length:** 27000 mm (89 ft. 6 in.)
Suspension Type: Double Link. **Exchange Code:** 43.
Notes: Work between various locations on British Rail as they are not yet allowed to visit Europe. On hire to MAT Transauto. Currently in the course of being renumbered into this series.

70 4289 000	(RLS92 + RLS 92)	70 4289 014	(RLS92 + RLS 92)
70 4289 001 a	(RLS92 + RLS 92)	70 4289 015	(RLS92 + RLS 92)
70 4289 002	(RLS92 + RLS 92)	70 4289 016	(RLS92 + RLS 92)
70 4289 003	(RLS92038 + RLS 92039)	70 4289 017	(RLS92 + RLS 92)
70 4289 004	(RLS92 + RLS 92)	70 4289 018	(RLS92 + RLS 92)
70 4289 005	(RLS92 + RLS 92)	70 4289 019	(RLS92 + RLS 92)
70 4289 006	(RLS92 + RLS 92)	70 4289 020	(RLS92 + RLS 92)
70 4289 007	(RLS92 + RLS 92)	70 4289 021	(RLS92 + RLS 92)
70 4289 008	(RLS92 + RLS 92)	70 4289 022	(RLS92 + RLS 92)
70 4289 009	(RLS92 + RLS 92)	70 4289 023	(RLS92 + RLS 92)
70 4289 010	(RLS92 + RLS 92)	70 4289 024	(RLS92 + RLS 92)
70 4289 011	(RLS92 + RLS 92)	70 4289 025	(RLS92 + RLS 92)
70 4289 012	(RLS92 + RLS 92)	70 4289 026	(RLS92 + RLS 92)
70 4289 013	(RLS92 + RLS 92)	70 4289 027	(RLS92 + RLS 92)

70 4424 001-005 KGA

2 AXLE CONTAINER FLAT

Builder: Simotra, France, 1984.
Design Code: KGE578 (Ex PIE578).
Tare Weight: 12.00 t.
Maximum Speed: 60 mph.
Suspension Type: Double Link.
Notes: All currently stored.

Owner: STS.
Gross Laden Weight: 40.00 t.
Length: 14140 mm (46 ft. 5 in.)
Exchange Code: 23.

70 4424 001
70 4424 002
70 4424 003
70 4424 004
70 4424 005

70 4746 100-179 KHA

BOGIE COVERED STEEL

Builder: Arbel-Fauvet, Douai, France, 1987-88.
Design Code: KHE684 (Ex PIE684).
Tare Weight: 23.50 t.
Maximum Speed: 60 mph.
Bogie Type: Y25LS.

Owner: Tiphook.
Gross Laden Weight: 90.00 t.
Length: 20590 mm (67 ft. 10 in.)
Exchange Code: 33.

Notes: Some currently stored. Others are used on various workings from Lackenby and Eastgate, and between Huntly and Irivine.

70 4746 100
70 4746 101
70 4746 102
70 4746 103
70 4746 104
70 4746 105
70 4746 106
70 4746 107
70 4746 108
70 4746 109
70 4746 110
70 4746 111
70 4746 112
70 4746 113
70 4746 114
70 4746 115
70 4746 116
70 4746 117
70 4746 118
70 4746 119
70 4746 120
70 4746 121
70 4746 122
70 4746 123
70 4746 124
70 4746 125
70 4746 126
70 4746 127
70 4746 128
70 4746 129
70 4746 130
70 4746 131
70 4746 132
70 4746 133
70 4746 134
70 4746 135
70 4746 136
70 4746 137
70 4746 138
70 4746 139
70 4746 140
70 4746 141
70 4746 142
70 4746 143
70 4746 144
70 4746 145
70 4746 146
70 4746 147
70 4746 148
70 4746 149
70 4746 150
70 4746 151
70 4746 152
70 4746 153
70 4746 154
70 4746 155
70 4746 156
70 4746 157
70 4746 158
70 4746 159
70 4746 160
70 4746 161
70 4746 162
70 4746 163
70 4746 164
70 4746 165
70 4746 166
70 4746 167
70 4746 168
70 4746 169
70 4746 170
70 4746 171
70 4746 172
70 4746 173
70 4746 174
70 4746 175
70 4746 176
70 4746 177
70 4746 178
70 4746 179

70 4746 180-199 KHA

BOGIE COVERED STEEL

Builder: Arbel-Fauvet, Douai, France, 1988.
Design Code: KHE696 (Ex PIE696).
Tare Weight: 23.50 t.
Maximum Speed: 60 mph.
Bogie Type: Y25LS.
Notes: All currently stored.

Owner: Tiphook.
Gross Laden Weight: 90.00 t.
Length: 20590 mm (67 ft. 10 in.)
Exchange Code: 33.

Autic 43 70 4289 007 at Hoo Junction on 5th August 1990. *(R. Wallace)*

Bogie Covered Steel 33 70 4746 115 at Wakefield on 16th July 1988. *(R. Wallace)*

70 4746 180
70 4746 181
70 4746 182
70 4746 183
70 4746 184
70 4746 185
70 4746 186
70 4746 187
70 4746 188
70 4746 189
70 4746 190
70 4746 191
70 4746 192
70 4746 193
70 4746 194
70 4746 195
70 4746 196
70 4746 197
70 4746 198
70 4746 199

70 4798 000-099 BI-MODAL KOA

Builder: Rautaruukki, Oulu, Finland, 1990.
Design Code: KOE736.
Owner: Tiphook.
Tare Weight: 28.00 t.
Gross Laden Weight: 65.00 t.
Maximum Speed: 75 mph.
Length: 16250 mm (53 ft. 4 in.)
Bogie Type: Sambre et Meuse VNH1.
Exchange Code: 83.
Notes: Production version of TIPH96500, of which only the first wagon has been delivered at time of writing. 000-039 are to be hired to Charterail for use by Pedigree.

70 4798 000
70 4798 001
70 4798 002
70 4798 003
70 4798 004
70 4798 005
70 4798 006
70 4798 007
70 4798 008
70 4798 009
70 4798 010
70 4798 011
70 4798 012
70 4798 013
70 4798 014
70 4798 015
70 4798 016
70 4798 017
70 4798 018
70 4798 019
70 4798 020
70 4798 021
70 4798 022
70 4798 023
70 4798 024
70 4798 025
70 4798 026
70 4798 027
70 4798 028
70 4798 029
70 4798 030
70 4798 031
70 4798 032
70 4798 023
70 4798 034
70 4798 035
70 4798 036
70 4798 037
70 4798 038
70 4798 039
70 4798 040
70 4798 041
70 4798 042
70 4798 043
70 4798 044
70 4798 045
70 4798 046
70 4798 047
70 4798 048
70 4798 049
70 4798 050
70 4798 051
70 4798 052
70 4798 053
70 4798 054
70 4798 055
70 4798 056
70 4798 057
70 4798 058
70 4798 059
70 4798 060
70 4798 061
70 4798 062
70 4798 063
70 4798 064
70 4798 065
70 4798 066
70 4798 067
70 4798 068
70 4798 069
70 4798 070
70 4798 071
70 4798 072
70 4798 073
70 4798 074
70 4798 075
70 4798 076
70 4798 077
70 4798 078
70 4798 079
70 4798 080
70 4798 081
70 4798 082
70 4798 083
70 4798 084
70 4798 085
70 4798 086
70 4798 087
70 4798 088
70 4798 089
70 4798 090
70 4798 091
70 4798 092
70 4798 093
70 4798 094
70 4798 095
70 4798 096
70 4798 097
70 4798 098
70 4798 099

70 5899 000-074 KIB

BOGIE COIL STEEL HOOD

Builder: Linke-Hofmann-Busch, Salzgitter, West Germany 1979-80.
Design Code: KIE485 (Ex PIE485) [a KIE732]
Owner: VTG.
Tare Weight: 27.50 t.
Gross Laden Weight: 88.00 t.
Maximum Speed: 60 mph.
Length: 14540 mm (47 ft. 9 in.)
Bogie Type: LHB 78.
Exchange Code: 33.
Notes: Used on various workings to and from Lackenby, and from various locations to and from Europe.
Previous Number Series: 21 70 0599 000-074, except 33 70 5698 019/26/31/35/36/38/48/49/56/70/72/74.

70 5899 000 a	70 5899 019 a	70 5899 038 a	70 5899 057
70 5899 001	70 5899 020	70 5899 039 a	70 5899 058
70 5899 002	70 5899 021 a	70 5899 040 a	70 5899 059
70 5899 003 a	70 5899 022 a	70 5899 041 a	70 5899 060
70 5899 004 a	70 5899 023	70 5899 042 a	70 5899 061
70 5899 005 a	70 5899 024	70 5899 043 a	70 5899 062 a
70 5899 006 a	70 5899 025	70 5899 044 a	70 5899 063
70 5899 007	70 5899 026	70 5899 045 a	70 5899 064 a
70 5899 008 a	70 5899 027	70 5899 046	70 5899 065
70 5899 009	70 5899 028	70 5899 047 a	70 5899 066 a
70 5899 010	70 5899 029	70 5899 048	70 5899 067
70 5899 011	70 5899 030	70 5899 049	70 5899 068 a
70 5899 012	70 5899 031	70 5899 050	70 5899 069
70 5899 013	70 5899 032	70 5899 051	70 5899 070
70 5899 014	70 5899 033 a	70 5899 052	70 5899 071
70 5899 015	70 5899 034	70 5899 053	70 5899 072
70 5899 016	70 5899 035	70 5899 054 a	70 5899 073
70 5899 017	70 5899 036	70 5899 055 a	70 5899 074
70 5899 018 a	70 5899 037 a	70 5899 056	

70 5899 075-104 KIA

BOGIE COIL STEEL HOOD

Builder: Linke-Hofmann-Busch, Salzgitter, West Germany, 1985.
Design Code: KIE585 (Ex PIE585). **Owner:** VTG.
Tare Weight: 24.70 t. **Gross Laden Weight:** 90.00 t.
Maximum Speed: 60 mph. **Length:** 14540 mm (47 ft. 9 in.)
Bogie Type: LHB 78. **Exchange Code:** 33.
Notes: Used on various workings to and from Lackenby, and from various locations to and from Europe.

70 5899 075	70 5899 083	70 5899 091	70 5899 098
70 5899 076	70 5899 084	70 5899 092	70 5899 099
70 5899 077	70 5899 085	70 5899 093	70 5899 100
70 5899 078	70 5899 086	70 5899 094	70 5899 101
70 5899 079	70 5899 087	70 5899 095	70 5899 102
70 5899 080	70 5899 088	70 5899 096	70 5899 103
70 5899 081	70 5899 089	70 5899 097	70 5899 104
70 5899 082	70 5899 090		

70 6094 044-057 OPEN TUBE OIX

Builder: British Rail, Faverdale, 1961.
Design Code: OIE247. **Owner:** British Rail.
Tare Weight: 13.66 t. **Gross Laden Weight:** 40.00 t.
Maximum Speed: 60 mph. **Length:** 11000 mm (36 ft. 1 in.)
Suspension Type: Double Link. **Exchange Code:** 21.
Notes: Also carry BR numbers B733234/236/239/243/246/247. Based on the Southern Region and used for the conveyance of Ferry Wagon spares to and from Europe.

70 6094 044	70 6094 049	70 6094 056	70 6094 057
70 6094 046	70 6094 053		

70 6094 432 — OPEN HIGH — KLA

Builder: Ateliers de Joigny, France, 1956.
Design Code: KLE671 (Ex PIE671)
Tare Weight: 10.50 t.
Maximum Speed: 45 mph.
Suspension Type: BR Parabolic Spring.
Notes: Currently stored.
Previous Number: 23 87 5756 432.
Owner: Tiphook.
Gross Laden Weight: 45.00 t.
Length: 10000 mm (32 ft. 10 in.)
Exchange Code: 43.

70 6094 432

70 6790 000-099 — BOGIE BOX — JRA

Builder: Arbel-Fauvet, Douai, France, 1988-89.
Design Code: JRE703 (Ex PIE703).
Tare Weight: 22.18 t.
Maximum Speed: 60 mph.
Bogie Type:
Owner: Tiphook.
Gross Laden Weight: 90.00 t.
Length: 14460 mm (47 ft. 5 in.)
Exchange Code: 33.
Notes: 002/5/7/8/11/12/16/17/21-23/25/27/31/32/37/41/42/44/45/47/49 are currently on hire to Bardon Hill Quarries. The remainder are either stored or working in Europe.

70 6790 000
70 6790 001
70 6790 002
70 6790 003
70 6790 004
70 6790 005
70 6790 006
70 6790 007
70 6790 008
70 6790 009
70 6790 010
70 6790 011
70 6790 012
70 6790 013
70 6790 014
70 6790 015
70 6790 016
70 6790 017
70 6790 018
70 6790 019
70 6790 020
70 6790 021
70 6790 022
70 6790 023
70 6790 024
70 6790 025
70 6790 026
70 6790 027
70 6790 028
70 6790 029
70 6790 030
70 6790 031
70 6790 032
70 6790 033
70 6790 034
70 6790 035
70 6790 036
70 6790 037
70 6790 038
70 6790 039
70 6790 040
70 6790 041
70 6790 042
70 6790 043
70 6790 044
70 6790 045
70 6790 046
70 6790 047
70 6790 048
70 6790 049
70 6790 050
70 6790 051
70 6790 052
70 6790 053
70 6790 054
70 6790 055
70 6790 056
70 6790 057
70 6790 058
70 6790 059
70 6790 060
70 6790 061
70 6790 062
70 6790 063
70 6790 064
70 6790 065
70 6790 066
70 6790 067
70 6790 068
70 6790 069
70 6790 070
70 6790 071
70 6790 072
70 6790 073
70 6790 074
70 6790 075
70 6790 076
70 6790 077
70 6790 078
70 6790 079
70 6790 080
70 6790 081
70 6790 082
70 6790 083
70 6790 084
70 6790 085
70 6790 086
70 6790 087
70 6790 088
70 6790 089
70 6790 090
70 6790 091
70 6790 092
70 6790 093
70 6790 094
70 6790 095
70 6790 096
70 6790 097
70 6790 098
70 6790 099

70 6905 000-049 BOGIE HOPPER KPA

Builder: Arbel-Fauvet, Douai, France, 1988.
Design Code: KPE700 (Ex PIE700). **Owner:** Tiphook.
Tare Weight: 22.50 t. **Gross Laden Weight:** 90.00 t.
Maximum Speed: 60 mph. **Length:** 16570 mm (54 ft. 5 in.)
Bogie Type: Y25. **Exchange Code:** 83.
Notes: On hire to Tarmac, working between Whatley and Hothfield, and Corby and Cliffe Hill. Others on hire to RMC, working between Buxton and Birmingham and on hire to Bardon Hill Quarries, used on various workings to and from Bardon Hill.

70 6905 000	70 6905 013	70 6905 026	70 6905 038
70 6905 001	70 6905 014	70 6905 027	70 6905 039
70 6905 002	70 6905 015	70 6905 028	70 6905 040
70 6905 003	70 6905 016	70 6905 029	70 6905 041
70 6905 004	70 6905 017	70 6905 030	70 6905 042
70 6905 005	70 6905 018	70 6905 031	70 6905 043
70 6905 006	70 6905 019	70 6905 032	70 6905 044
70 6905 007	70 6905 020	70 6905 033	70 6905 045
70 6905 008	70 6905 021	70 6905 034	70 6905 046
70 6905 009	70 6905 022	70 6905 035	70 6905 047
70 6905 010	70 6905 023	70 6905 036	70 6905 048
70 6905 011	70 6905 024	70 6905 037	70 6905 049
70 6905 012	70 6905 025		

70 6905 100-199 BOGIE HOPPER KPA

Builder: Arbel-Fauvet, Douai, France, 1988.
Design Code: KPE702 (Ex PIE702). **Owner:** Tiphook.
Tare Weight: 22.99 t. **Gross Laden Weight:** 90.00 t.
Maximum Speed: 60 mph. **Length:** 16570 mm (54 ft. 5 in.)
Bogie Type: Y25. **Exchange Code:** 83.
Notes: Most wagons are currently stored, but 166-168 & 181-199 are currently working in Europe.

70 6905 100	70 6905 120	70 6905 140	70 6905 160
70 6905 101	70 6905 121	70 6905 141	70 6905 161
70 6905 102	70 6905 122	70 6905 142	70 6905 162
70 6905 103	70 6905 123	70 6905 143	70 6905 163
70 6905 104	70 6905 124	70 6905 144	70 6905 164
70 6905 105	70 6905 125	70 6905 145	70 6905 165
70 6905 106	70 6905 126	70 6905 146	70 6905 166
70 6905 107	70 6905 127	70 6905 147	70 6905 167
70 6905 108	70 6905 128	70 6905 148	70 6905 168
70 6905 109	70 6905 129	70 6905 149	70 6905 169
70 6905 110	70 6905 130	70 6905 150	70 6905 170
70 6905 111	70 6905 131	70 6905 151	70 6905 171
70 6905 112	70 6905 132	70 6905 152	70 6905 172
70 6905 113	70 6905 133	70 6905 153	70 6905 173
70 6905 114	70 6905 134	70 6905 154	70 6905 174
70 6905 115	70 6905 135	70 6905 155	70 6905 175
70 6905 116	70 6905 136	70 6905 156	70 6905 176
70 6905 117	70 6905 137	70 6905 157	70 6905 177
70 6905 118	70 6905 138	70 6905 158	70 6905 178
70 6905 119	70 6905 139	70 6905 159	70 6905 179

70 6905 180	70 6905 185	70 6905 190	70 6905 195
70 6905 181	70 6905 186	70 6905 191	70 6905 196
70 6905 182	70 6905 187	70 6905 192	70 6905 197
70 6905 183	70 6905 188	70 6905 193	70 6905 198
70 6905 184	70 6905 189	70 6905 194	70 6905 199

70 7190 200-201 TANK TIX

Builder: Rolls-Royce, UK, 1965.
Design Code: TIE296.
Tare Weight: 13.00 t.
Maximum Speed: 60 mph.
Suspension Type: Double Link.
Notes: Currently stored.
Previous Number Series: 21 70 0780 200-201.

Owner: STS.
Gross Laden Weight: 40.00 t.
Length: 9368 mm (30 ft. 9 in.)
Exchange Code: 23.

70 7190 200	70 7190 201

70 7190 203-222 TANK TIB

Builder: Powell Duffryn, Cardiff, UK, 1964.
Design Code: TIE288.
Tare Weight: 12.30 t.
Maximum Speed: 60 mph.
Suspension Type: Double Link.
Notes: Currently stored.
Previous Number Series: 21 70 0780 203-222.

Owner: STS.
Gross Laden Weight: 40.00 t.
Length: 9372 mm (30 ft. 9 in.)
Exchange Code: 23.

70 7190 203	70 7190 209	70 7190 212	70 7190 221
70 7190 205	70 7190 210	70 7190 218	70 7190 222
70 7190 208	70 7190 211	70 7190 220	

70 7190 400-408 TANK TIX

Builder: Charles Roberts, Wakefield, UK, 1964.
Design Code: TIE291.
Tare Weight. 14.25 t.
Maximum Speed: 60 mph.
Suspension Type: Double Link.
Notes: Currently stored.
Previous Number Series: 21 70 0780 400-408.

Owner: Tiger Rail.
Gross Laden Weight: 40.00 t.
Length: 8863 mm (29 ft. 1 in.)
Exchange Code: 23.

70 7190 400	70 7190 402	70 7190 404	70 7190 407
70 7190 401	70 7190 403	70 7190 405	70 7190 408

70 7277 353-372 LPG TANK TIX

Builder: Charles Roberts, Wakefield, UK, 1962.
Design Code: TIE313.
Tare Weight: 20.00 t.
Maximum Speed: 60 mph.
Suspension Type: Double Link.

Owner: Tiger Rail.
Gross Laden Weight: 40.00 t.
Length: 8889 mm (29 ft. 2 in.)
Exchange Code: 23.

Notes: 353-358/372 are currently stored. 362-366 are on hire to ICIO, working from

Haverton Hill to and from Europe.
Previous Number Series: 21 70 0780 353-372.

70 7277 353	70 7277 356	70 7277 362	70 7277 366
70 7277 354	70 7277 357	70 7277 363	70 7277 372
70 7277 355	70 7277 358	70 7277 365	

70 7286 410-417 TANK TIX

Builder: Charles Roberts, Wakefield, UK, 1964.
Design Code: TIE391.
Owner: Tiger Rail.
Tare Weight: 15.45 t.
Gross Laden Weight: 40.00 t.
Maximum Speed: 60 mph.
Length: 8864 mm (29 ft. 1 in.)
Suspension Type: Double Link.
Exchange Code: 23.
Notes: All stored except 411, which is on hire to ICIO, working from Haverton Hill to and from Europe.

70 7286 410	70 7286 412	70 7286 415	70 7286 417
70 7286 411	70 7286 413	70 7286 416	

70 7390 027-031 TANK TIA

Builder: C.F.P.M., Bobigny, France, 1979.
Design Code: TIE494.
Owner: STS.
Tare Weight: 11.90 t.
Gross Laden Weight: 40.00 t.
Maximum Speed: 60 mph.
Length: 9090 mm (30 ft. 3 in.)
Suspension Type: Double Link.
Exchange Code: 23.
Notes: Work between Baglan Bay and Purfleet, except 028 & 031 which are currently working in Belgium.
Previous Number Series: 21 70 0785 027-031.

70 7390 027	70 7390 029	70 7390 030	70 7390 031
70 7390 028			

70 7390 399-406 TANK TIA

Builder: Charles Roberts, Wakefield, UK, 1964.
Design Code: TIE704.
Owner: Tiger Rail.
Tare Weight: 13.28 t.
Gross Laden Weight: 40.00 t.
Maximum Speed: 35 mph.
Length: 8863 mm (29 ft. 1 in.)
Suspension Type: Double Link.
Exchange Code: 23.
Notes: On hire to ICIO. Used on workings between Haverton Hill and Europe.
Previous Number Series: 23 70 7190 399-406.

70 7390 399	70 7390 406

70 7390 409-415 TANK TIA

Builder: Procor, Wakefield, UK, 1979.
Design Code: TIE656 (a TIE705).
Owner: Associated Octel.
Tare Weight: 15.00 t.
Gross Laden Weight: 40.00 t.
Maximum Speed: 60 mph.
Length: 8860 mm (29 ft. 1 in.)
Suspension Type: Double Link.
Exchange Code: 23.

Notes: Used on various workings between Ellesmere Port and Europe.
Previous Number Series: 23 70 0785 409-415.

70 7390 409 a	70 7390 411	70 7390 413	70 7390 415
70 7390 410	70 7390 412	70 7390 414 a	

70 7390 635-671 TANK TIB

Builder: Metro-Cammell, Birmingham, UK, 1964.
Design Code: TIE661. **Owner:** TSL.
Tare Weight: 12.30 t. **Gross Laden Weight:** 40.00 t.
Maximum Speed: 60 mph. **Length:** 9068 mm (29 ft. 9 in.)
Suspension Type: Double Link. **Exchange Code:** 23.
Notes: On hire to Whyte Chemicals, working to and from Europe.
Previous Number Series: 21 70 0080 635-671.

70 7390 635	70 7390 653	70 7390 659	70 7390 671
70 7390 647			

70 7392 000-007 TANK TIA

Builder: Norbittt-Pickering, Wishaw, UK, UK, 1954(a 1957).
Design Code: TIE162. **Owner:** ICI Mond.
Tare Weight: 18.90 t. **Gross Laden Weight:** 35.00 t.
Maximum Speed: 60 mph. **Length:** 8560 mm (28 ft. 1 in.)
Suspension Type: Double Link. **Exchange Code:** 23.
Notes: Used on workings between Runcorn and Europe.
Previous Number Series: 21 70 0785 000-007.

70 7392 000	70 7392 002	70 7392 004 a	70 7392 007
70 7392 001	70 7392 003 a	70 7392 006	

70 7392 021-026 TANK TIA

Builder: Norbitt-Pickering, Wishaw, UK, 1954.
Design Code: TIE461. **Owner:** ICI Mond.
Tare Weight: 18.40 t. **Gross Laden Weight:** 35.00 t.
Maximum Speed: 60 mph. **Length:** 8559 mm (28 ft. 1 in.)
Suspension Type: Double link. **Exchange Code:** 23.
Notes: Used on workings between Runcorn and Europe.
Previous Number Series: 21 70 0785 021-026.

70 7392 021	70 7392 023	70 7392 025	70 7392 026
70 7392 022	70 7392 024		

70 7392 400-405 TANK TIX

Builder: Waggonfabrik Uerdingen, Krefeld, West Germany, 1958-59.
Design Code: TIE113. **Owner:** BPIG.
Tare Weight: 14.80 t. **Gross Laden Weight:** 32.00 t.
Maximum Speed: 60 mph. **Length:** 9660 mm (31 ft. 9 in.)
Suspension Type: Double Link. **Exchange Code:** 23.
Notes: Work between Rotterdam and Grangemouth.

Previous Number Series: 21 70 0785 400-405.

70 7392 400
70 7392 401
70 7392 403
70 7392 404
70 7392 405

70 7397 101-139 TANK TIB

Builder: Rootes Pressings, Linwood, UK, 1964-66.
Design Code: TIE339 (a TIE341). **Owner:** STS.
Tare Weight: 15.00 t (a 13.00 t). **Gross Laden Weight:** 40.00 t.
Maximum Speed: 60 mph. **Suspension Type:** Double Link.
Length: 9165 mm (30 ft. 1 in.), a 9194 mm (30 ft. 2 in.)
Exchange Code: 23.
Notes: 125/126/129 are owned by CAIB. Used on various workings to and from Europe.
Previous Number Series: 21 70 0785 101-139.

70 7397 101
70 7397 103
70 7397 104
70 7397 105
70 7397 106
70 7397 107
70 7397 108
70 7397 109
70 7397 111
70 7397 112
70 7397 115
70 7397 116
70 7397 117
70 7397 121
70 7397 122
70 7397 123
70 7397 125 a
70 7397 126 a
70 7397 127 a
70 7397 128 a
70 7397 129 a
70 7397 130 a
70 7397 131 a
70 7397 132 a
70 7397 133 a
70 7397 134 a
70 7397 135 a
70 7397 136 a
70 7397 137 a
70 7397 138 a
70 7397 139 a

70 7398 063-065 TANK TIB

Builder: Waggonfabrik Uerdingen, Krefeld, West Germany, 1977. (a Ringhofer, West Germany, 1977; b Familleureux, France, 1977).
Design Code: TIE445. **Owner:** VTG.
Tare Weight: 15.00 t. **Gross Laden Weight:** 40.00 t.
Maximum Speed: 60 mph. **Length:** 8740 mm (28 ft. 8 in.)
Suspension Type: Double Link. **Exchange Code:** 23.
Notes: Used on various workings to and from Amlwch.

70 7398 063
70 7398 064 a
70 7398 065 b

70 7490 000-001 TANK TIB

Builder: Charles Roberts, Wakefield, UK, 1974.
Design Code: TIE344. **Owner:** Dow Chemicals.
Tare Weight: 15.50 t. **Gross Laden Weight:** 35.00 t.
Maximum Speed: 60 mph. **Length:** 8862 mm (29 ft. 1 in.)
Suspension Type: Double Link. **Exchange Code:** 23.
Previous Number Series: 21 70 0785 243-244.
Notes: Used on various workings to and from Europe.

70 7490 000
70 7490 001

70 7490 002 TANK TIB

Builder: Charles Roberts, Wakefield, UK, 1964.
Design Code: TIE727. **Owner:** Associated Octel.

Tare Weight: 16.50 t.
Gross Laden Weight: 40.00 t.
Maximum Speed: 60 mph.
Length: 8863 mm (29 ft. 1 in.)
Suspension Type: Double Link.
Exchange Code: 23.
Notes: Used on workings between Ellesmere Port and Europe.
Previous Number Series: 21 70 0785 250.

70 7490 002

70 7490 050-051 TANK TIX

Builder: Charles Roberts, Wakefield, UK, 1966.
Design Code: TIE320.
Owner: Hauser.
Tare Weight: 15.50 t.
Gross Laden Weight: 40.00 t.
Maximum Speed: 60 mph.
Length: 8864 mm (29 ft. 1 in.)
Suspension Type: Double Link.
Exchange Code: 23.
Notes: Used on workings between Haverton Hill and Europe.
Previous Number Series: 21 70 0785 050-051.

70 7490 050
70 7490 051

70 7490 240-251 TANK TIA

Builder: Charles Roberts, Wakefield, UK, 1961.
Design Code: TIE245.
Owner: Associated Octel.
Tare Weight: 16.00 t.
Gross Laden Weight: 40.00 t.
Maximum Speed: 60 mph.
Length: 8407 mm (27 ft. 7 in.)
Suspension Type: Double Link.
Exchange Code: 23.
Notes: Used on workings between Ellesmere Port and Europe.
Previous Number Series: 21 70 0780 240-251.

70 7490 240
70 7490 241
70 7490 242
70 7490 243
70 7490 244
70 7490 245
70 7490 246
70 7490 247
70 7490 248
70 7490 249
70 7490 250
70 7490 251

70 7490 253-294 TANK TIB

Builder: Charles Roberts, Wakefield, UK, 1964.
Design Code: TIE628(a TIE727).
Owner: Associated Octel.
Tare Weight: 16.50 t.
Gross Laden Weight: 40.00 t.
Maximum Speed: 60 mph.
Length: 8863 mm (29 ft. 1 in.)
Suspension Type: Double Link.
Exchange Code: 23.
Notes: TIE727 are coded TIA. Used on workings between Ellesmere Port and Europe.
Previous Number Series: 21 70 0785 253-294.

70 7490 253
70 7490 257
70 7490 258 a
70 7490 262
70 7490 263 a
70 7490 264
70 7490 266 a
70 7490 267
70 7490 268
70 7490 269
70 7490 270
70 7490 273
70 7490 274
70 7490 275
70 7490 277
70 7490 279
70 7490 281 a
70 7490 282
70 7490 283
70 7490 284 a
70 7490 287 a
70 7490 288 a
70 7490 289 a
70 7490 290 a
70 7490 291
70 7490 293 a
70 7490 294

70 7490 295-298 TANK TIB

Builder: C. Roberts, Wakefield, UK, 1970.
Design Code: TIE385. **Owner:** VTG.
Tare Weight: 15.65 t. **Gross Laden Weight:** 39.95 t.
Maximum Speed: 60 mph. **Length:** 8864 mm (29 ft. 1 in.)
Suspension Type: **Exchange Code:** 43.
Notes: Used on various workings to and from Amlwch.
Previous Number Series: 26 70 0785 295-8.

70 7490 295 70 7490 296 70 7490 297 70 7490 298

70 7490 357-360 TANK TIB

Builder: Procor, Wakefield, UK, 1975.
Design Code: TIE385. **Owner:** VTG.
Tare Weight: 15.65 t. **Gross Laden Weight:** 39.95 t.
Maximum Speed: 60 mph. **Length:** 8864 mm (29 ft. 1 in.)
Suspension Type: **Exchange Code:** 43.
Notes: Used on various workings to and from Amlwch.
Previous Number Series: 26 70 0785 357-60.

70 7490 357 70 7490 358 70 7490 359 70 7490 360

70 7490 406-408 TANK TIB

Builder: Procor, Wakefield, UK, 1978.
Design Code: TIE628(a TIE727). **Owner:** Associated Octel.
Tare Weight: 16.50 t. **Gross Laden Weight:** 40.00 t.
Maximum Speed: 60 mph. **Length:** 8863 mm (29 ft. 1 in.)
Suspension Type: Double Link. **Exchange Code:** 23.
Notes: TIE727 is coded TIA. Used on workings between Ellesmere Port and Europe.
Previous Number Series: 21 70 0785 406-408.

70 7490 406 70 7490 407 a 70 7490 408

70 7490 409-418 TANK TIA

Builder: Charles Roberts, Wakefield, UK, 1964.
Design Code: TIE705(a TIE725). **Owner:** Tiger Rail.
Tare Weight: 12.90 t. **Gross Laden Weight:** 40.00 t.
Maximum Speed: 35 (a 45) mph. **Length:** 8863 mm (29 ft. 1 in.)
Suspension Type: Double Link. **Exchange Code:** 23.
Notes: On hire to ICIO. Used on various workings between Haverton Hill and Europe.
Previous Number Series: 23 70 7286 409-418.

70 7490 409 70 7490 414 70 7490 418 a

70 7492 367-370 TANK TIB

Builder: Charles Roberts, Wakefield, UK, 1962.
Design Code: TIE567. **Owner:** ICI Organics Division.

Tare Weight: 20.00 t.
Gross Laden Weight: 20.00 t.
Maximum Speed: 60 mph.
Length: 8889 mm (29 ft. 2 in.)
Suspension Type: Double Link.
Exchange Code: 23.
Notes: Used on workings between Haverton Hill and Europe.
Previous Number Series: 23 70 7277 367-370.

70 7492 367	70 7492 368	70 7492 369	70 7492 370

70 7498 005-009 TANK TIB

Builder: Waggonfabrik Uerdingen, Krefeld, West Germany, 1977 (a Ganz-Mávag, Budapest, Hungary, 1977).
Design Code: TIE445.
Owner: VTG.
Tare Weight: 15.00 t.
Gross Laden Weight: 40.00 t.
Maximum Speed: 60 mph.
Length: 8740 mm (28 ft. 8 in.)
Suspension Type: Double link.
Exchange Code: 23.
Notes: Used on various workings to and from Amlwch.

70 7498 005	70 7498 008	70 7498 009 a

70 7499 300-301 TANK TIA

Builder: Charles Roberts, Wakefield, UK, 1967.
Design Code: TIE599.
Owner: Tiger Rail.
Tare Weight: 15.50 t.
Gross Laden Weight: 46.00 t.
Maximum Speed: 60 mph.
Length: 10667 mm (35 ft. 0 in.)
Suspension Type: Parabolic Springs.
Exchange Code: 43.
Notes: On hire to Shell Chemicals. Used on various workings to and from Stanlow.

70 7499 300	70 7499 301

70 7890 100-126 TIA
CHINA CLAY SLURRY TANK

Builder: Société ANF-Industrie, Blanc-Misseron, France, 1989.
Design Code: TIE708.
Owner: Tiger Rail.
Tare Weight: 21.40 t.
Gross Laden Weight: 90.00 t.
Maximum Speed: 60 mph.
Length: 15240 mm (50 ft. 0 in.)
Bogie Type: Y25.
Exchange Code: 33.
Notes: On hire to English China Clays. Work between Burngullow and Irvine. To be recoded TIE734 on completion of modifications.

70 7890 100	70 7890 107	70 7890 114	70 7890 121
70 7890 101	70 7890 108	70 7890 115	70 7890 122
70 7890 102	70 7890 109	70 7890 116	70 7890 123
70 7890 103	70 7890 110	70 7890 117	70 7890 124
70 7890 104	70 7890 111	70 7890 118	70 7890 125
70 7890 105	70 7890 112	70 7890 119	70 7890 126
70 7890 106	70 7890 113	70 7890 120	

70 7890 200-204 TANK TIA

Builder: Ateliers de Joigny, France, 1989.

Bogie Coil Steel Hood 33 70 5899 001 at Walton Old Yard on 21st May 1989. *(R. Wallace)*

Bogie Box 33 70 6790 022 at Hoo Junction on 26th March 1989. *(R. Wallace)*

Design Code: TIE715.
Owner: CAIB.
Tare Weight: 23.11 t.
Gross Laden Weight: 80.00 t.
Maximum Speed: 60 mph.
Length: 15240 mm (50 ft. 0 in.)
Bogie Type: Y25.
Exchange Code: 33.
Notes: On hire to ISC. Work between Avonmouth and Yugoslavia.

70 7890 200	70 7890 202	70 7890 203	70 7890 204
70 7890 201			

70 7892 000-023 BOGIE TANK TIB

Builder: Fauvet-Girel, Douai, France, 1969.
Design Code: TIE387 (a TIE497).
Owner: STS.
Tare Weight: 33.52 t.
Gross Laden Weight: 80.00 t.
Maximum Speed: 60 mph.
Length: 18900 mm (62 ft. 0 in.)
Bogie Type: Y25C.
Exchange Code: 33.
Notes: TIE497 are coded TIA. On hire to ICIO. Used on various workings to and from Haverton Hill.

70 7892 000	70 7892 006	70 7892 012 a	70 7892 018 a
70 7892 001	70 7892 007	70 7892 013 a	70 7892 019 a
70 7892 002	70 7892 008	70 7892 014 a	70 7892 020 a
70 7892 003	70 7892 009	70 7892 015 a	70 7892 021 a
70 7892 004	70 7892 010	70 7892 016 a	70 7892 022 a
70 7892 005	70 7892 011	70 7892 017 a	70 7892 023 a

70 7892 024-046 BOGIE TANK TIB

Builder: Waggon Union, Siegen, West Germany, 1979-81.
Design Code: TIE467.
Owner: VTG.
Tare Weight: 30.01 t.
Gross Laden Weight: 80.00 t.
Maximum Speed: 60 mph.
Length: 18900 mm (62 ft. 0 in.)
Bogie Type: Talbot.
Exchange Code: 33.
Notes: Used on various workings to and from Europe.
Previous Number Series: 33 80 7892 024-034/011/012/104-023.

70 7892 024	70 7892 031	70 7892 036	70 7892 041
70 7892 025	70 7892 032	70 7892 037	70 7892 042
70 7892 026	70 7892 033	70 7892 038	70 7892 043
70 7892 028	70 7892 034	70 7892 039	70 7892 044
70 7892 030	70 7892 035	70 7892 040	70 7892 046

70 7895 001-022 BOGIE TANK TIB

Builder: Waggon Union, Siegen, West Germany, 1980-81.
Design Code: TIE467.
Owner: VTG.
Tare Weight: 30.01 t.
Gross Laden Weight: 80.00 t.
Maximum Speed: 60 mph.
Length: 18900 mm (62 ft. 0 in.)
Bogie Type: Talbot.
Exchange Code: 33.
Notes: Used on various workings to and from Europe.
Previous Number Series: 33 80 7895 001-022.

70 7895 001	70 7895 003	70 7895 005	70 7895 007
70 7895 002	70 7895 004	70 7895 006	70 7895 008

70 7895 009	70 7895 015	70 7895 019	70 7895 021
70 7895 013	70 7895 016	70 7895 020	70 7895 022
70 7895 014	70 7895 018		

70 7895 151-165 BOGIE TANK TIB

Builder: Linke-Hofmann-Busch, Salzgitter, West Germany, 1986 (a Franz Kaminski, West Germany, 1985-86).
Design Code: TIE554.
Owner: VTG.
Tare Weight: 21.40 t.
Gross Laden Weight: 80.00 t.
Maximum Speed: 60 mph.
Length: 14400 mm (47 ft. 3 in.)
Bogie Type:
Exchange Code: 33.
Notes: On hire to ICIO and English China Clays. Used on workings between Haverton Hill and Europe (ICIO) and between Quidhampton and Scotland (ECC).

70 7895 151	70 7895 155 a	70 7895 159 a	70 7895 163 a
70 7895 152	70 7895 156 a	70 7895 160 a	70 7895 164 a
70 7895 153	70 7895 157 a	70 7895 161 a	70 7895 165 a
70 7895 154	70 7895 158 a	70 7895 162 a	

Tank 23 70 7197 215 at Radstock on 28th June 1986. *(R. Wallace)*

70 7895 200-204 BOGIE TANK TIA

Builder: Arbel-Fauvet, Douai, France, 1968.
Design Code: TIE680 (a TIE688).
Owner: STS.
Tare Weight: 21.00 t.
Gross Laden Weight: 80.00 t.
Maximum Speed: 60 mph.
Length: 15240 mm (50 ft. 0 in.)
Bogie Type: Y25C.
Exchange Code: 33.
Notes: On hire to English China Clays. Used between Burngullow and Sittingbourne.
Previous Number Series: 83 70 7895 000-004.

70 7895 200	70 7895 202	70 7895 203	70 7895 204 a
70 7895 201			

70 7899 021-060 BOGIE TANK TIA

Builder: Arbel-Fauvet, Douai, France, 1987.
Design Code: TIE686 (a TIE685, b TIE692).
Owner: Tiphook.
Tare Weight: 26.80 t (a 24.38, b 24.73).
Gross Laden Weight: 80.00 t.
Maximum Speed: 60 mph.
Length: 18900 mm (62 ft. 0 in.) a b 18290 (60 ft 0 in).
Bogie Type: Y25Ls.
Exchange Code: 33.
Notes: 027-034/042-045/051 are currently working in Europe. The remainder are on hire to ICI. Used on workings between Purfleet and Duxford.

70 7899 021	70 7899 031	70 7899 041 a	70 7899 051 b
70 7899 022	70 7899 032	70 7899 042 a	70 7899 052 b
70 7899 023	70 7899 033	70 7899 043 a	70 7899 053 b
70 7899 024	70 7899 034	70 7899 044 a	70 7899 054 b
70 7899 025	70 7899 035	70 7899 045 a	70 7899 055 b
70 7899 026	70 7899 036	70 7899 046 a	70 7899 056 b
70 7899 027	70 7899 037	70 7899 047 a	70 7899 057 b
70 7899 028	70 7899 038	70 7899 048 a	70 7899 058 b
70 7899 029	70 7899 039	70 7899 049 a	70 7899 059 b
70 7899 030	70 7899 040	70 7899 050 a	70 7899 060 b

70 7996 001-003 BOGIE SODIUM TANK TIA

Builder: Standard Wagon, Heywood, UK, 1985.
Design Code: TIE581.
Owner: Associated Octel.
Tare Weight: 34.30 t.
Gross Laden Weight: 80.00 t.
Maximum Speed: 60 mph.
Length: 17190 mm (56 ft. 5 in.)
Bogie Type: Y25CS2.
Exchange Code: 33.
Notes: Used on workings between Ellesmere Port and Biebesheim.

70 7996 001	70 7996 002	70 7996 003

70 9192 002-022 TWIN SILO CEMENT KKB

Builder: Cadoux, Paris, France, 1985 (a Simotra, France, 1986).
Design Code: KKE589 (Ex PIE589) [a KKE664 (Ex PIE664).
Owner: STS.
Tare Weight: 11.00 t (a 10.50 t).
Gross Laden Weight: 40.00 t.
Maximum Speed: 60 mph.
Length: 8960 mm (29 ft. 5 in.)

Suspension Type: Double Link and Parabolic Spring.
Exchange Code: 23 (a 43).
Notes: KKE664 are coded KKA. 002 is currently stored. On hire to Tunnel Cement. Used between Tring and Southampton.

70 9192 002	70 9192 008 a	70 9192 013 a	70 9192 018 a
70 9192 003 a	70 9192 009 a	70 9192 014 a	70 9192 019 a
70 9192 004 a	70 9192 010 a	70 9192 015 a	70 9192 020 a
70 9192 005 a	70 9192 011 a	70 9192 016 a	70 9192 021 a
70 9192 006 a	70 9192 012 a	70 9192 017 a	70 9192 022 a
70 9192 007 a			

70 9280 000-029 JIA

COVERED BOGIE HOPPER

Builder: CFMF, Bobigny, France, 1983.
Design Code: JIE538 (Ex PIE538). **Owner:** Scottish Malt Distillers.
Tare Weight: 22.25 t. **Gross Laden Weight:** 80.00 t.
Maximum Speed: 60 mph. **Length:** 18290 mm (60 ft. 0 in.)
Bogie Type: Y25CS2. **Exchange Code:** 33.
Notes: Used on various workings based at Whitemoor.

70 9280 000	70 9280 008	70 9280 016	70 9280 023
70 9280 001	70 9280 009	70 9280 017	70 9280 024
70 9280 002	70 9280 010	70 9280 018	70 9280 025
70 9280 003	70 9280 011	70 9280 019	70 9280 026
70 9280 004	70 9280 012	70 9280 020	70 9280 027
70 9280 005	70 9280 013	70 9280 021	70 9280 028
70 9280 006	70 9280 014	70 9280 022	70 9280 029
70 9280 007	70 9280 015		

70 9280 030-081 JIA

COVERED BOGIE HOPPER

Builder: Fauvet-Girel, Douai, France, 1983-84.
Design Code: JIE561 (Ex PIE561)[a JIE 570 (Ex PIE570)]
Owner: TSL.
Tare Weight: 21.80 t(a 22.30 t). **Gross Laden Weight:** 80.00 t (a 88.00 t).
Maximum Speed: 75 mph. **Length:** 18290 mm (60 ft. 0 in.)
Bogie Type: Y25CS2 (a Y25L). **Exchange Code:** 33.
Notes: Used on various workings based on Whitemoor.

70 9280 030	70 9280 043	70 9280 056	70 9280 069
70 9280 031	70 9280 044	70 9280 057	70 9280 070
70 9280 032	70 9280 045	70 9280 058	70 9280 071
70 9280 033	70 9280 046	70 9280 059	70 9280 072
70 9280 034	70 9280 047	70 9280 060	70 9280 073
70 9280 035	70 9280 048	70 9280 061	70 9280 074
70 9280 036	70 9280 049	70 9280 062	70 9280 075
70 9280 037	70 9280 050	70 9280 063	70 9280 076
70 9280 038	70 9280 051	70 9280 064	70 9280 077
70 9280 039	70 9280 052	70 9280 065	70 9280 078
70 9280 040	70 9280 053	70 9280 066	70 9280 079
70 9280 041	70 9280 054	70 9280 067	70 9280 080
70 9280 042	70 9280 055	70 9280 068	70 9280 081 a

70 9292 200-214 BOGIE TANK TIA

Builder: Arbel-Fauvet, Douai, France, 1987-88.
Design Code: TIE689.
Owner: Tiphook.
Tare Weight: 24.80 t.
Gross Laden Weight: 90.00 t.
Maximum Speed: 60 mph.
Length: 18900 mm (62 ft. 0 in.)
Bogie Type: Y25LS.
Exchange Code: 33.
Notes: All currently working in Europe, with the exception of 203, which is stored in Glasgow.

70 9292 200
70 9292 201
70 9292 202
70 9292 203
70 9292 204
70 9292 205
70 9292 206
70 9292 207
70 9292 208
70 9292 209
70 9292 210
70 9292 211
70 9292 212
70 9292 213
70 9292 214

70 9382 000-058 JIB
COVERED BOGIE HOPPER

Builder: Fauvet-Girel, Douai, France, 1974-75.
Design Code: JIE431 (Ex PIE431).
Owner: Tiphook.
a JIE675 (Ex PIE675), b JIE586 (Ex PIE586).
Owner: Tiger Rail.
Tare Weight: 22.00 t(a 21.85 t).
Gross Laden Weight: 80.00 t.
Maximum Speed: 60 mph.
Length: 16040 mm (52 ft. 8 in.)
Bogie Type: Y25C.
Exchange Code: 33.
Notes: JIE675 are coded JIA. Used on various workings between the West of England and Europe (including St. Blazey to Basel) and between King's Lynn and Duxford.
Previous Number Series: 21 70 0999 000-058, except 33 87 5699 002-006 (now 001-005).

70 9382 000
70 9382 001 a
70 9382 002 a
70 9382 003 a
70 9382 004 a
70 9382 005 a
70 9382 006
70 9382 007
70 9382 008
70 9382 009
70 9382 010 b
70 9382 011
70 9382 012 a
70 9382 013
70 9382 014
70 9382 015
70 9382 016
70 9382 017 a
70 9382 018
70 9382 019 a
70 9382 020
70 9382 026
70 9382 027
70 9382 028
70 9382 029
70 9382 030
70 9382 032 a
70 9382 033 a
70 9382 034
70 9382 036
70 9382 037
70 9382 040
70 9382 041
70 9382 042
70 9382 043
70 9382 044
70 9382 045
70 9382 046
70 9382 047
70 9382 048
70 9382 049
70 9382 050
70 9382 051
70 9382 052
70 9382 053
70 9382 054
70 9382 058

70 9382 100-129 JIA
COVERED BOGIE HOPPER

Builder: Fauvet-Girel, Douai, France, 1984.
Design Code: JIE574 (Ex PIE574).
Owner: CAIB/STS.
Tare Weight: 22.60 t(a 21.85 t).
Gross Laden Weight: 80.00 t.
Maximum Speed: 75 mph.
Length: 18290 mm (60 ft. 0 in.)
Bogie Type: Y25CS2.
Exchange Code: 33.
Notes: On hire to CITA.

70 9382 100
70 9382 101
70 9382 102
70 9382 103
70 9382 104
70 9382 105
70 9382 106
70 9382 107
70 9382 108
70 9382 109
70 9382 110
70 9382 111
70 9382 112
70 9382 113
70 9382 114
70 9382 115
70 9382 116
70 9382 117
70 9382 118
70 9382 119
70 9382 120
70 9382 121
70 9382 122
70 9382 123
70 9382 124
70 9382 125
70 9382 126
70 9382 127
70 9382 128
70 9382 129

70 9385 000-029 JIB

COVERED BOGIE HOPPER

Builder: Société Nouvelle Des Ateliers, France, 1983.
Design Code: JIE518 (Ex PIE518). **Owner:** CAIB.
Tare Weight: 21.50 t. **Gross Laden Weight:** 80.00 t.
Maximum Speed: 60 mph. **Length:** 18270 mm (59 ft. 11 in.)
Bogie Type: Y25CS2. **Exchange Code:** 33.
Notes: On hire to STS. Used on various workings based at Whitemoor.

70 9385 000
70 9385 001
70 9385 002
70 9385 003
70 9385 004
70 9385 005
70 9385 006
70 9385 007
70 9385 008
70 9385 009
70 9385 010
70 9385 011
70 9385 012
70 9385 013
70 9385 014
70 9385 015
70 9385 016
70 9385 017
70 9385 018
70 9385 019
70 9385 020
70 9385 021
70 9385 022
70 9385 023
70 9385 024
70 9385 025
70 9385 026
70 9385 027
70 9385 028
70 9385 029

70 9904 003-014 FLATROL FIW

Builder: BR, Shildon, UK, 1959 (Lot No. 3258).
Design Code: FIE246. **Owner:** British Rail.
Tare Weight: 15.00 t. **Gross Laden Weight:** 36.00 t.
Maximum Speed: 60 mph. **Length:** 11531 mm (37 ft. 10 in.)
Suspension Type: Pedestal. **Exchange Code:** 21.
Notes: Used to convey ferry wagon spares to and from Europe. Will be renumbered into the BR series shortly.

70 9904 003
70 9904 007
70 9904 009
70 9904 012
70 9904 013
70 9904 014

70 9986 006-008 KYA

BOGIE NUCLEAR FLASK

Builder: BREL, Ashford, UK, 1982.
Design Code: KYE529. **Owner:** British Nuclear Fuels.
Tare Weight: 60.00 t. **Gross Laden Weight:** 144.00 t.
Maximum Speed: 60 mph. **Length:** 12460 mm (39 ft. 11 in.)
Bogie Type: Y25Cssim (Four bogies). **Exchange Code:** 33.
Notes: Used on various workings to and from Sellafield.

70 9986 006
70 9986 007
70 9986 008

71 2147 000-487 ITX

MEDIUM VAN END DOORS

Builder: Westwaggon, West Germany, 1954.
Design Code: ITE011. **Owner:** Transfesa.
Tare Weight: 13.10 t. **Gross Laden Weight:** 40.00 t.
Maximum Speed: 60 mph. **Length:** 12460 mm (39 ft. 11 in.)
Suspension Type: Double Link. **Exchange Code:** 24.
Previous Number Series: 24 71 0285 501-65/67-97/99-610/12-18/20-62/64-730/32-39/41-60/62-86/88-827/829-81/83-975/77-999.

71 2147 000
71 2147 001
71 2147 002
71 2147 003
71 2147 004
71 2147 005
71 2147 006
71 2147 007
71 2147 008
71 2147 009
71 2147 010
71 2147 011
71 2147 012
71 2147 013
71 2147 014
71 2147 015
71 2147 016
71 2147 017
71 2147 018
71 2147 019
71 2147 020
71 2147 021
71 2147 022
71 2147 023
71 2147 024
71 2147 025
71 2147 026
71 2147 027
71 2147 028
71 2147 029
71 2147 030
71 2147 031
71 2147 032
71 2147 033
71 2147 034
71 2147 035
71 2147 036
71 2147 037
71 2147 038
71 2147 039
71 2147 040
71 2147 041
71 2147 042
71 2147 043
71 2147 044
71 2147 045
71 2147 046
71 2147 047
71 2147 048
71 2147 049
71 2147 050
71 2147 051
71 2147 052
71 2147 053
71 2147 054
71 2147 055
71 2147 056
71 2147 057
71 2147 058
71 2147 059
71 2147 060
71 2147 061
71 2147 062
71 2147 063
71 2147 064
71 2147 065
71 2147 066
71 2147 067
71 2147 068
71 2147 069
71 2147 070
71 2147 071
71 2147 072
71 2147 073
71 2147 074
71 2147 075
71 2147 076
71 2147 077
71 2147 078
71 2147 079
71 2147 080
71 2147 081
71 2147 082
71 2147 083
71 2147 084
71 2147 085
71 2147 086
71 2147 087
71 2147 088
71 2147 089
71 2147 090
71 2147 091
71 2147 092
71 2147 093
71 2147 094
71 2147 095
71 2147 096
71 2147 097
71 2147 098
71 2147 099
71 2147 100
71 2147 101
71 2147 102
71 2147 103
71 2147 104
71 2147 105
71 2147 106
71 2147 107
71 2147 108
71 2147 109
71 2147 110
71 2147 111
71 2147 112
71 2147 113
71 2147 114
71 2147 115
71 2147 116
71 2147 117
71 2147 118
71 2147 119
71 2147 120
71 2147 121
71 2147 122
71 2147 123
71 2147 124
71 2147 125
71 2147 126
71 2147 127
71 2147 128
71 2147 129
71 2147 130
71 2147 131
71 2147 132
71 2147 133
71 2147 134
71 2147 135
71 2147 136
71 2147 137
71 2147 138
71 2147 139
71 2147 140
71 2147 141
71 2147 142
71 2147 143
71 2147 144
71 2147 145
71 2147 146
71 2147 147
71 2147 148
71 2147 149
71 2147 150
71 2147 151
71 2147 152
71 2147 153
71 2147 154
71 2147 155
71 2147 156
71 2147 157
71 2147 158
71 2147 159
71 2147 160
71 2147 161
71 2147 162
71 2147 163
71 2147 164
71 2147 165
71 2147 166
71 2147 167
71 2147 168
71 2147 169
71 2147 170
71 2147 171
71 2147 172
71 2147 173
71 2147 174
71 2147 175
71 2147 176
71 2147 177
71 2147 178
71 2147 179

71 2147 180
71 2147 181
71 2147 182
71 2147 183
71 2147 184
71 2147 185
71 2147 186
71 2147 187
71 2147 188
71 2147 189
71 2147 190
71 2147 191
71 2147 192
71 2147 193
71 2147 194
71 2147 195
71 2147 196
71 2147 197
71 2147 198
71 2147 199
71 2147 200
71 2147 201
71 2147 202
71 2147 203
71 2147 204
71 2147 205
71 2147 206
71 2147 207
71 2147 208
71 2147 209
71 2147 210
71 2147 211
71 2147 212
71 2147 213
71 2147 214
71 2147 215
71 2147 216
71 2147 217
71 2147 218
71 2147 219
71 2147 220
71 2147 221
71 2147 222
71 2147 223
71 2147 224
71 2147 225
71 2147 226
71 2147 227
71 2147 228
71 2147 229
71 2147 230
71 2147 231
71 2147 232
71 2147 233
71 2147 234
71 2147 235
71 2147 236
71 2147 237
71 2147 238
71 2147 239
71 2147 240
71 2147 241
71 2147 242
71 2147 243
71 2147 244
71 2147 245
71 2147 246
71 2147 247
71 2147 248
71 2147 249
71 2147 250
71 2147 251
71 2147 252
71 2147 253
71 2147 254
71 2147 255
71 2147 256
71 2147 257
71 2147 258
71 2147 259
71 2147 260
71 2147 261
71 2147 262
71 2147 263
71 2147 264
71 2147 265
71 2147 266
71 2147 267
71 2147 268
71 2147 269
71 2147 270
71 2147 271
71 2147 272
71 2147 273
71 2147 274
71 2147 275
71 2147 276
71 2147 277
71 2147 278
71 2147 279
71 2147 280
71 2147 281
71 2147 282
71 2147 283
71 2147 284
71 2147 285
71 2147 286
71 2147 287
71 2147 288
71 2147 289
71 2147 290
71 2147 291
71 2147 292
71 2147 293
71 2147 294
71 2147 295
71 2147 296
71 2147 297
71 2147 298
71 2147 299
71 2147 300
71 2147 301
71 2147 302
71 2147 303
71 2147 304
71 2147 305
71 2147 306
71 2147 307
71 2147 308
71 2147 309
71 2147 310
71 2147 311
71 2147 312
71 2147 313
71 2147 314
71 2147 315
71 2147 316
71 2147 317
71 2147 318
71 2147 319
71 2147 320
71 2147 321
71 2147 322
71 2147 323
71 2147 324
71 2147 325
71 2147 326
71 2147 327
71 2147 328
71 2147 329
71 2147 330
71 2147 331
71 2147 332
71 2147 333
71 2147 334
71 2147 335
71 2147 336
71 2147 337
71 2147 338
71 2147 339
71 2147 340
71 2147 341
71 2147 342
71 2147 343
71 2147 344
71 2147 345
71 2147 346
71 2147 347
71 2147 348
71 2147 349
71 2147 350
71 2147 351
71 2147 352
71 2147 353
71 2147 354
71 2147 355
71 2147 356
71 2147 357
71 2147 358
71 2147 359
71 2147 360
71 2147 361
71 2147 362
71 2147 363
71 2147 364
71 2147 365
71 2147 366
71 2147 367
71 2147 368
71 2147 369
71 2147 370
71 2147 371
71 2147 372
71 2147 373
71 2147 374
71 2147 375
71 2147 376
71 2147 377
71 2147 378
71 2147 379
71 2147 380
71 2147 381
71 2147 382
71 2147 383
71 2147 384
71 2147 385
71 2147 386
71 2147 387
71 2147 388
71 2147 389
71 2147 390
71 2147 391
71 2147 392
71 2147 393
71 2147 394
71 2147 395
71 2147 396
71 2147 397
71 2147 398
71 2147 399
71 2147 400
71 2147 401
71 2147 402
71 2147 403

71 2147 404
71 2147 405
71 2147 406
71 2147 407
71 2147 408
71 2147 409
71 2147 410
71 2147 411
71 2147 412
71 2147 413
71 2147 414
71 2147 415
71 2147 416
71 2147 417
71 2147 418
71 2147 419
71 2147 420
71 2147 421
71 2147 422
71 2147 423
71 2147 424
71 2147 425
71 2147 426
71 2147 427
71 2147 428
71 2147 429
71 2147 430
71 2147 431
71 2147 432
71 2147 433
71 2147 434
71 2147 435
71 2147 436
71 2147 437
71 2147 438
71 2147 439
71 2147 440
71 2147 441
71 2147 442
71 2147 443
71 2147 444
71 2147 445
71 2147 446
71 2147 447
71 2147 448
71 2147 449
71 2147 450
71 2147 451
71 2147 452
71 2147 453
71 2147 454
71 2147 455
71 2147 456
71 2147 457
71 2147 458
71 2147 459
71 2147 460
71 2147 461
71 2147 462
71 2147 463
71 2147 464
71 2147 465
71 2147 466
71 2147 467
71 2147 468
71 2147 469
71 2147 470
71 2147 471
71 2147 472
71 2147 473
71 2147 474
71 2147 475
71 2147 476
71 2147 477
71 2147 478
71 2147 479
71 2147 480
71 2147 481
71 2147 482
71 2147 483
71 2147 484
71 2147 485
71 2147 486
71 2147 487

71 2148 000-396 MEDIUM VAN ITX

Builder: Linke-Hofmann-Busch, Salzgitter, West Germany, 1954-59.
Design Code: ITE010.
Owner: Transfesa.
Tare Weight: 12.70 t.
Gross Laden Weight: 40.00 t.
Maximum Speed: 60 mph.
Length: 12460 mm (39 ft. 11 in.)
Suspension Type: Double Link.
Exchange Code: 24.
Notes: Used on various workings to and from Europe.
Previous No. Series: 24 71 0284 500-03/05-86/88-615/17-19/21-737/39-844/46-899.

71 2148 000
71 2148 001
71 2148 002
71 2148 003
71 2148 004
71 2148 005
71 2148 006
71 2148 007
71 2148 008
71 2148 009
71 2148 010
71 2148 011
71 2148 012
71 2148 013
71 2148 014
71 2148 015
71 2148 016
71 2148 017
71 2148 018
71 2148 019
71 2148 020
71 2148 021
71 2148 022
71 2148 023
71 2148 024
71 2148 025
71 2148 026
71 2148 027
71 2148 028
71 2148 029
71 2148 030
71 2148 031
71 2148 032
71 2148 033
71 2148 034
71 2148 035
71 2148 036
71 2148 037
71 2148 038
71 2148 039
71 2148 040
71 2148 041
71 2148 042
71 2148 043
71 2148 044
71 2148 045
71 2148 046
71 2148 047
71 2148 048
71 2148 049
71 2148 050
71 2148 051
71 2148 052
71 2148 053
71 2148 054
71 2148 055
71 2148 056
71 2148 057
71 2148 058
71 2148 059
71 2148 060
71 2148 061
71 2148 062
71 2148 063
71 2148 064
71 2148 065
71 2148 066
71 2148 067
71 2148 068
71 2148 069
71 2148 070
71 2148 071
71 2148 072
71 2148 073
71 2148 074
71 2148 075
71 2148 076
71 2148 077
71 2148 078
71 2148 079
71 2148 080
71 2148 081
71 2148 082
71 2148 083
71 2148 084
71 2148 085
71 2148 086
71 2148 087
71 2148 088
71 2148 089
71 2148 090
71 2148 091

71 2148 092
71 2148 093
71 2148 094
71 2148 095
71 2148 096
71 2148 097
71 2148 098
71 2148 099
71 2148 100
71 2148 101
71 2148 102
71 2148 103
71 2148 104
71 2148 105
71 2148 106
71 2148 107
71 2148 108
71 2148 109
71 2148 110
71 2148 111
71 2148 112
71 2148 113
71 2148 114
71 2148 115
71 2148 116
71 2148 117
71 2148 118
71 2148 119
71 2148 120
71 2148 121
71 2148 122
71 2148 123
71 2148 124
71 2148 125
71 2148 126
71 2148 127
71 2148 128
71 2148 129
71 2148 130
71 2148 131
71 2148 132
71 2148 133
71 2148 134
71 2148 135
71 2148 136
71 2148 137
71 2148 138
71 2148 139
71 2148 140
71 2148 141
71 2148 142
71 2148 143
71 2148 144
71 2148 145
71 2148 146
71 2148 147
71 2148 148
71 2148 149
71 2148 150
71 2148 151
71 2148 152
71 2148 153
71 2148 154
71 2148 155
71 2148 156
71 2148 157
71 2148 158
71 2148 159
71 2148 160
71 2148 161
71 2148 162
71 2148 163
71 2148 164
71 2148 165
71 2148 166
71 2148 167
71 2148 168
71 2148 169
71 2148 170
71 2148 171
71 2148 172
71 2148 173
71 2148 174
71 2148 175
71 2148 176
71 2148 177
71 2148 178
71 2148 179
71 2148 180
71 2148 181
71 2148 182
71 2148 183
71 2148 184
71 2148 185
71 2148 186
71 2148 187
71 2148 188
71 2148 189
71 2148 190
71 2148 191
71 2148 192
71 2148 193
71 2148 194
71 2148 195
71 2148 196
71 2148 197
71 2148 198
71 2148 199
71 2148 200
71 2148 201
71 2148 202
71 2148 203
71 2148 204
71 2148 205
71 2148 206
71 2148 207
71 2148 208
71 2148 209
71 2148 210
71 2148 211
71 2148 212
71 2148 213
71 2148 214
71 2148 215
71 2148 216
71 2148 217
71 2148 218
71 2148 219
71 2148 220
71 2148 221
71 2148 222
71 2148 223
71 2148 224
71 2148 225
71 2148 226
71 2148 227
71 2148 228
71 2148 229
71 2148 230
71 2148 231
71 2148 232
71 2148 233
71 2148 234
71 2148 235
71 2148 236
71 2148 237
71 2148 238
71 2148 239
71 2148 240
71 2148 241
71 2148 242
71 2148 243
71 2148 244
71 2148 245
71 2148 246
71 2148 247
71 2148 248
71 2148 249
71 2148 250
71 2148 251
71 2148 252
71 2148 253
71 2148 254
71 2148 255
71 2148 256
71 2148 257
71 2148 258
71 2148 259
71 2148 260
71 2148 261
71 2148 262
71 2148 263
71 2148 264
71 2148 265
71 2148 266
71 2148 267
71 2148 268
71 2148 269
71 2148 270
71 2148 271
71 2148 272
71 2148 273
71 2148 274
71 2148 275
71 2148 276
71 2148 277
71 2148 278
71 2148 279
71 2148 280
71 2148 281
71 2148 282
71 2148 283
71 2148 284
71 2148 285
71 2148 286
71 2148 287
71 2148 288
71 2148 289
71 2148 290
71 2148 291
71 2148 292
71 2148 293
71 2148 294
71 2148 295
71 2148 296
71 2148 297
71 2148 298
71 2148 299
71 2148 300
71 2148 301
71 2148 302
71 2148 303
71 2148 304
71 2148 305
71 2148 306
71 2148 307
71 2148 308
71 2148 309
71 2148 310
71 2148 311
71 2148 312
71 2148 313
71 2148 314
71 2148 315

71 2148 316
71 2148 317
71 2148 318
71 2148 319
71 2148 320
71 2148 321
71 2148 322
71 2148 323
71 2148 324
71 2148 325
71 2148 326
71 2148 327
71 2148 328
71 2148 329
71 2148 330
71 2148 331
71 2148 332
71 2148 333
71 2148 334
71 2148 335
71 2148 336
71 2148 337
71 2148 338
71 2148 339
71 2148 340
71 2148 341
71 2148 342
71 2148 343
71 2148 344
71 2148 345
71 2148 346
71 2148 347
71 2148 348
71 2148 349
71 2148 350
71 2148 351
71 2148 352
71 2148 353
71 2148 354
71 2148 355
71 2148 356
71 2148 357
71 2148 358
71 2148 359
71 2148 360
71 2148 361
71 2148 362
71 2148 363
71 2148 364
71 2148 365
71 2148 366
71 2148 367
71 2148 368
71 2148 369
71 2148 370
71 2148 371
71 2148 372
71 2148 373
71 2148 374
71 2148 375
71 2148 376
71 2148 377
71 2148 378
71 2148 379
71 2148 380
71 2148 381
71 2148 382
71 2148 383
71 2148 384
71 2148 385
71 2148 386
71 2148 387
71 2148 388
71 2148 389
71 2148 390
71 2148 391
71 2148 392
71 2148 393
71 2148 394
71 2148 395
71 2148 396

71 2148 397-485 MEDIUM VAN ITX

Builder: Westwaggon, West Germany, 1959.
Design Code: ITE215.
Tare Weight: 13.00 t.
Maximum Speed: 60 mph.
Suspension Type: Double Link.
Owner: Transfesa.
Gross Laden Weight: 40.00 t.
Length: 12960 mm (42 ft. 2 in.)
Exchange Code: 24.
Notes: Used on various workings to and from Europe.
Previous Number Series: 24 71 0284 900-988.

71 2148 397
71 2148 398
71 2148 399
71 2148 400
71 2148 401
71 2148 402
71 2148 403
71 2148 404
71 2148 405
71 2148 406
71 2148 407
71 2148 408
71 2148 409
71 2148 410
71 2148 411
71 2148 412
71 2148 413
71 2148 414
71 2148 415
71 2148 416
71 2148 417
71 2148 418
71 2148 419
71 2148 420
71 2148 421
71 2148 422
71 2148 423
71 2148 424
71 2148 425
71 2148 426
71 2148 427
71 2148 428
71 2148 429
71 2148 430
71 2148 431
71 2148 432
71 2148 433
71 2148 434
71 2148 435
71 2148 436
71 2148 437
71 2148 438
71 2148 439
71 2148 440
71 2148 441
71 2148 442
71 2148 443
71 2148 444
71 2148 445
71 2148 446
71 2148 447
71 2148 448
71 2148 449
71 2148 450
71 2148 451
71 2148 452
71 2148 453
71 2148 454
71 2148 455
71 2148 456
71 2148 457
71 2148 458
71 2148 459
71 2148 460
71 2148 461
71 2148 462
71 2148 463
71 2148 464
71 2148 465
71 2148 466
71 2148 467
71 2148 468
71 2148 469
71 2148 470
71 2148 471
71 2148 472
71 2148 473
71 2148 474
71 2148 475
71 2148 476
71 2148 477
71 2148 478
71 2148 479
71 2148 480
71 2148 481
71 2148 482
71 2148 483
71 2148 484
71 2148 485

Tank 23 70 7490 245 at Warrington on 1st August 1981. *(R. Wallace)*

Tank 43 70 7490 357 at Connah's Quay on 24th July 1990. *(R. Wallace)*

71 2148 486-495 MEDIUM VAN ITX

Builder:
Design Code: ITE556.
Tare Weight: 12.85 t.
Maximum Speed: 60 mph.
Suspension Type: Double Link.
Owner: Transfesa.
Gross Laden Weight: 40.00 t.
Length: 12460 mm (40 ft. 11 in.)
Exchange Code: 24.
Previous Number Series: 24 71 0284 989-997/999.

71 2148 486
71 2148 487
71 2148 488
71 2148 489
71 2148 490
71 2148 491
71 2148 492
71 2148 493
71 2148 494
71 2148 495

71 2148 496-594 MEDIUM VAN ITX

Builder: Waggonfabrik Uerdingen, Krefeld, West Germany, 1954.
Design Code: ITE555.
Tare Weight: 13.10 t.
Maximum Speed: 60 mph.
Suspension Type: Double Link.
Notes: Not currently running on British Rail.
Owner: Transfesa.
Gross Laden Weight: 40.00 t.
Length: 12960 mm (42 ft. 2 in.)
Exchange Code: 24.
Previous Number Series: 24 71 0285 001-060/062-100.

71 2148 496
71 2148 497
71 2148 498
71 2148 499
71 2148 500
71 2148 501
71 2148 502
71 2148 503
71 2148 504
71 2148 505
71 2148 506
71 2148 507
71 2148 508
71 2148 509
71 2148 510
71 2148 511
71 2148 512
71 2148 513
71 2148 514
71 2148 515
71 2148 516
71 2148 517
71 2148 518
71 2148 519
71 2148 520
71 2148 521
71 2148 522
71 2148 523
71 2148 524
71 2148 525
71 2148 526
71 2148 527
71 2148 528
71 2148 529
71 2148 530
71 2148 531
71 2148 532
71 2148 533
71 2148 534
71 2148 535
71 2148 536
71 2148 537
71 2148 538
71 2148 539
71 2148 540
71 2148 541
71 2148 542
71 2148 543
71 2148 544
71 2148 545
71 2148 546
71 2148 547
71 2148 548
71 2148 549
71 2148 550
71 2148 551
71 2148 552
71 2148 553
71 2148 554
71 2148 555
71 2148 556
71 2148 557
71 2148 558
71 2148 559
71 2148 560
71 2148 561
71 2148 562
71 2148 563
71 2148 564
71 2148 565
71 2148 566
71 2148 567
71 2148 568
71 2148 569
71 2148 570
71 2148 571
71 2148 572
71 2148 573
71 2148 574
71 2148 575
71 2148 576
71 2148 577
71 2148 578
71 2148 579
71 2148 580
71 2148 581
71 2148 582
71 2148 583
71 2148 584
71 2148 585
71 2148 586
71 2148 587
71 2148 588
71 2148 589
71 2148 590
71 2148 591
71 2148 592
71 2148 593
71 2148 594

71 2148 595-692 MEDIUM VAN ITX

Builder: Linke-Hofmann-Busch, Salzgitter, West Germany.
Design Code: ITE556.
Tare Weight: 12.85 t.
Owner: Transfesa.
Gross Laden Weight: 40.00 t.

Maximum Speed: 60 mph.
Suspension Type: Double Link.
Length: 12460 mm (40 ft. 11 in.)
Exchange Code: 24.
Notes: Not currently running on British Rail.
Previous Number Series: 24 71 0285 101-103/104-199.

71 2148 595	71 2148 620	71 2148 645	71 2148 669
71 2148 596	71 2148 621	71 2148 646	71 2148 670
71 2148 597	71 2148 622	71 2148 647	71 2148 671
71 2148 598	71 2148 623	71 2148 648	71 2148 672
71 2148 599	71 2148 624	71 2148 649	71 2148 673
71 2148 600	71 2148 625	71 2148 650	71 2148 674
71 2148 601	71 2148 626	71 2148 651	71 2148 675
71 2148 602	71 2148 627	71 2148 652	71 2148 676
71 2148 603	71 2148 628	71 2148 653	71 2148 677
71 2148 604	71 2148 629	71 2148 654	71 2148 678
71 2148 605	71 2148 630	71 2148 655	71 2148 679
71 2148 606	71 2148 631	71 2148 656	71 2148 680
71 2148 607	71 2148 632	71 2148 657	71 2148 681
71 2148 608	71 2148 633	71 2148 658	71 2148 682
71 2148 609	71 2148 634	71 2148 659	71 2148 683
71 2148 610	71 2148 635	71 2148 660	71 2148 684
71 2148 611	71 2148 636	71 2148 661	71 2148 685
71 2148 612	71 2148 637	71 2148 662	71 2148 686
71 2148 613	71 2148 638	71 2148 663	71 2148 687
71 2148 614	71 2148 639	71 2148 664	71 2148 688
71 2148 615	71 2148 640	71 2148 665	71 2148 689
71 2148 616	71 2148 641	71 2148 666	71 2148 690
71 2148 617	71 2148 642	71 2148 667	71 2148 691
71 2148 618	71 2148 643	71 2148 668	71 2148 692
71 2148 619	71 2148 644		

71 2148 693-992 MEDIUM VAN ITX

Builder: Linke-Hofmann-Busch, Salzgitter, West Germany, 1959.
Design Code: ITE010.
Owner: Transfesa.
Tare Weight: 12.70 t.
Gross Laden Weight: 40.00 t.
Maximum Speed: 60 mph.
Length: 12460 mm (40 ft. 11 in.)
Suspension Type: Double Link.
Exchange Code: 24.
Notes: Some of these wagons are not currently operating on British Rail.

71 2148 693	71 2148 708	21 2148 723	21 2148 738
71 2148 694	71 2148 709	21 2148 724	21 2148 739
71 2148 695	71 2148 710	21 2148 725	21 2148 740
71 2148 696	71 2148 711	21 2148 726	21 2148 741
71 2148 697	71 2148 712	21 2148 727	21 2148 742
71 2148 698	71 2148 713	21 2148 728	21 2148 743
71 2148 699	71 2148 714	21 2148 729	21 2148 744
71 2148 700	71 2148 715	21 2148 730	21 2148 745
71 2148 701	71 2148 716	21 2148 731	21 2148 746
71 2148 702	71 2148 717	21 2148 732	21 2148 747
71 2148 703	71 2148 718	21 2148 733	21 2148 748
71 2148 704	71 2148 719	21 2148 734	21 2148 749
71 2148 705	71 2148 720	21 2148 735	21 2148 750
71 2148 706	71 2148 721	21 2148 736	21 2148 751
71 2148 707	71 2148 722	21 2148 737	21 2148 752

71 2148 753
71 2148 754
71 2148 755
71 2148 756
71 2148 757
71 2148 758
71 2148 759
71 2148 760
71 2148 761
71 2148 762
71 2148 763
71 2148 764
71 2148 765
71 2148 766
71 2148 767
71 2148 768
71 2148 769
71 2148 770
71 2148 771
71 2148 772
71 2148 773
71 2148 774
71 2148 775
71 2148 776
71 2148 777
71 2148 778
71 2148 779
71 2148 780
71 2148 781
71 2148 782
71 2148 783
71 2148 784
71 2148 785
71 2148 786
71 2148 787
71 2148 788
71 2148 789
71 2148 790
71 2148 791
71 2148 792
71 2148 793
71 2148 794
71 2148 795
71 2148 796
71 2148 797
71 2148 798
71 2148 799
71 2148 800
71 2148 801
71 2148 802
71 2148 803
71 2148 804
71 2148 805
71 2148 806
71 2148 807
71 2148 808
71 2148 809
71 2148 810
71 2148 811
71 2148 812
71 2148 813
71 2148 814
71 2148 815
71 2148 816
71 2148 817
71 2148 818
71 2148 819
71 2148 820
71 2148 821
71 2148 822
71 2148 823
71 2148 824
71 2148 825
71 2148 826
71 2148 827
71 2148 828
71 2148 829
71 2148 830
71 2148 831
71 2148 832
71 2148 833
71 2148 834
71 2148 835
71 2148 836
71 2148 837
71 2148 838
71 2148 839
71 2148 840
71 2148 841
71 2148 842
71 2148 843
71 2148 844
71 2148 845
71 2148 846
71 2148 847
71 2148 848
71 2148 849
71 2148 850
71 2148 851
71 2148 852
71 2148 853
71 2148 854
71 2148 855
71 2148 856
71 2148 857
71 2148 858
71 2148 859
71 2148 860
71 2148 861
71 2148 862
71 2148 863
71 2148 864
21 2148 865
21 2148 866
21 2148 867
21 2148 868
21 2148 869
21 2148 870
21 2148 871
21 2148 872
21 2148 873
21 2148 874
21 2148 875
21 2148 876
21 2148 877
21 2148 878
21 2148 879
21 2148 880
21 2148 881
21 2148 882
21 2148 883
21 2148 884
21 2148 885
21 2148 886
21 2148 887
21 2148 888
21 2148 889
21 2148 890
21 2148 891
21 2148 892
21 2148 893
21 2148 894
21 2148 895
21 2148 896
21 2148 897
21 2148 898
21 2148 899
21 2148 900
21 2148 901
21 2148 902
21 2148 903
21 2148 904
21 2148 905
21 2148 906
21 2148 907
21 2148 908
21 2148 909
21 2148 910
21 2148 911
21 2148 912
21 2148 913
21 2148 914
21 2148 915
21 2148 916
21 2148 917
21 2148 918
21 2148 919
21 2148 920
21 2148 921
21 2148 922
21 2148 923
21 2148 924
21 2148 925
21 2148 926
21 2148 927
21 2148 928
21 2148 929
21 2148 930
21 2148 931
21 2148 932
21 2148 933
21 2148 934
21 2148 935
21 2148 936
21 2148 937
21 2148 938
21 2148 939
21 2148 940
21 2148 941
21 2148 942
21 2148 943
21 2148 944
21 2148 945
21 2148 946
21 2148 947
21 2148 948
21 2148 949
21 2148 950
21 2148 951
21 2148 952
21 2148 953
21 2148 954
21 2148 955
21 2148 956
21 2148 957
21 2148 958
21 2148 959
21 2148 960
21 2148 961
21 2148 962
21 2148 963
21 2148 964
21 2148 965
21 2148 966
21 2148 967
21 2148 968
21 2148 969
21 2148 970
21 2148 971
21 2148 972
21 2148 973
21 2148 974
21 2148 975
21 2148 976

21 2148 977	21 2148 981	21 2148 985	21 2148 989
21 2148 978	21 2148 982	21 2148 986	21 2148 990
21 2148 979	21 2148 983	21 2148 987	21 2148 991
21 2148 980	21 2148 984	21 2148 988	21 2148 992

71 2148 693-992 MEDIUM VAN ITX

Builder: Semat Carpeta.
Design Code: ITE407 (a ITE537).
Tare Weight: 12.70 t (a 15.50 t).
Maximum Speed: 60 mph.
Suspension Type: Double Link.
Exchange Code: 24.
Owner: Transfesa.
Gross Laden Weight: 40.00 t.
Length: 11740 mm (38 ft. 6 in.)
a 13970 mm (45 ft. 10 in.)
Notes: ITE537 is "Swap Body Flat". Not currently operating on British Rail.
Previous Number Series: 24 71 0286 105-115/117/119/122/124/125/128/129/132-134/136-144/146-151/153/154/156-158/160-164/166-180/182/184.

71 2148 993	71 2149 009	71 2149 025	71 2149 041
71 2148 994	71 2149 010	71 2149 026	71 2149 042
71 2148 995	71 2149 011	71 2149 027	71 2149 043
71 2148 996	71 2149 012	71 2149 028	71 2149 044
71 2148 997	71 2149 013	71 2149 029	71 2149 045
71 2148 998	71 2149 014	71 2149 030	71 2149 046
71 2148 999	71 2149 015	71 2149 031	71 2149 047
71 2149 000	71 2149 016	71 2149 032	71 2149 048
71 2149 001	71 2149 017	71 2149 033	71 2149 049
71 2149 002	71 2149 018	71 2149 034	71 2149 050
71 2149 003	71 2149 019	71 2149 035	71 2149 051
71 2149 004	71 2149 020 a	71 2149 036	71 2149 052
71 2149 005	71 2149 021	71 2149 037	71 2149 053
71 2149 006	71 2149 022	71 2149 038	71 2149 054
71 2149 007	71 2149 023	71 2149 039	71 2149 055
71 2149 008	71 2149 024	71 2149 040	

71 2380 000 MEDIUM VAN ITX

Builder: Direccion Gestion Commercial, Madrid, Spain.
Design Code: ITE673.
Tare Weight: 12.50 t.
Maximum Speed: 60 mph.
Suspension Type: Double Link.
Owner: Transfesa.
Gross Laden Weight: 40.00 t.
Length: 14060 mm (46 ft. 1 in.)
Exchange Code: 24.
Notes: Used on various workings to and from Europe.
Previous Number: 24 71 2148 114.

71 2380 000

71 2396 000-199 MEDIUM VAN ITX

Builder: Tafesa, Madrid, Spain, 1984.
Design Code: ITE575.
Tare Weight: 13.60 t.
Maximum Speed: 75 mph.
Suspension Type: Double Link.
Owner: Transfesa.
Gross Laden Weight: 40.00 t.
Length: 14060 mm (46 ft. 1 in.)
Exchange Code: 24.
Notes: Used on various workings to and from Europe.

71 2396 000
71 2396 001
71 2396 002
71 2396 003
71 2396 004
71 2396 005
71 2396 006
71 2396 007
71 2396 008
71 2396 009
71 2396 010
71 2396 011
71 2396 012
71 2396 013
71 2396 014
71 2396 015
71 2396 016
71 2396 017
71 2396 018
71 2396 019
71 2396 020
71 2396 021
71 2396 022
71 2396 023
71 2396 024
71 2396 025
71 2396 026
71 2396 027
71 2396 028
71 2396 029
71 2396 030
71 2396 031
71 2396 032
71 2396 033
71 2396 034
71 2396 035
71 2396 036
71 2396 037
71 2396 038
71 2396 039
71 2396 040
71 2396 041
71 2396 042
71 2396 043
71 2396 044
71 2396 045
71 2396 046
71 2396 047
71 2396 048
71 2396 049
71 2396 050
71 2396 051
71 2396 052
71 2396 053
71 2396 054
71 2396 055
71 2396 056
71 2396 057
71 2396 058
71 2396 059
71 2396 060
71 2396 061
71 2396 062
71 2396 063
71 2396 064
71 2396 065
71 2396 066
71 2396 067
71 2396 068
71 2396 069
71 2396 070
71 2396 071
71 2396 072
71 2396 073
71 2396 074
71 2396 075
71 2396 076
71 2396 077
71 2396 078
71 2396 079
71 2396 080
71 2396 081
71 2396 082
71 2396 083
71 2396 084
71 2396 085
71 2396 086
71 2396 087
71 2396 088
71 2396 089
71 2396 090
71 2396 091
71 2396 092
71 2396 093
71 2396 094
71 2396 095
71 2396 096
71 2396 097
71 2396 098
71 2396 099
71 2396 100
71 2396 101
71 2396 102
71 2396 103
71 2396 104
71 2396 105
71 2396 106
71 2396 107
71 2396 108
71 2396 109
71 2396 110
71 2396 111
71 2396 112
71 2396 113
71 2396 114
71 2396 115
71 2396 116
71 2396 117
71 2396 118
71 2396 119
71 2396 120
71 2396 121
71 2396 122
71 2396 123
71 2396 124
71 2396 125
71 2396 126
71 2396 127
71 2396 128
71 2396 129
71 2396 130
71 2396 131
71 2396 132
71 2396 133
71 2396 134
71 2396 135
71 2396 136
71 2396 137
71 2396 138
71 2396 139
71 2396 140
71 2396 141
71 2396 142
71 2396 143
71 2396 144
71 2396 145
71 2396 146
71 2396 147
71 2396 148
71 2396 149
71 2396 150
71 2396 151
71 2396 152
71 2396 153
71 2396 154
71 2396 155
71 2396 156
71 2396 157
71 2396 158
71 2396 159
71 2396 160
71 2396 161
71 2396 162
71 2396 163
71 2396 164
71 2396 165
71 2396 166
71 2396 167
71 2396 168
71 2396 169
71 2396 170
71 2396 171
71 2396 172
71 2396 173
71 2396 174
71 2396 175
71 2396 176
71 2396 177
71 2396 178
71 2396 179
71 2396 180
71 2396 181
71 2396 182
71 2396 183
71 2396 184
71 2396 185
71 2396 186
71 2396 187
71 2396 188
71 2396 189
71 2396 190
71 2396 191
71 2396 192
71 2396 193
71 2396 194
71 2396 195
71 2396 196
71 2396 197
71 2396 198
71 2396 199

71 2396 200-304 MEDIUM VAN ITX

Builder: Tafesa, Madrid, Spain, 1984.
Design Code: ITE584.

Owner: Transfesa.

Tare Weight: 13.00 t.
Gross Laden Weight: 40.00 t.
Maximum Speed: 60 mph.
Length: 14060 mm (46 ft. 1 in.)
Suspension Type: Double Link.
Exchange Code: 24.
Notes: Used on various workings to and from Europe.

71 2396 200
71 2396 201
71 2396 202
71 2396 203
71 2396 204
71 2396 205
71 2396 206
71 2396 207
71 2396 208
71 2396 209
71 2396 210
71 2396 211
71 2396 212
71 2396 213
71 2396 214
71 2396 215
71 2396 216
71 2396 217
71 2396 218
71 2396 219
71 2396 220
71 2396 221
71 2396 222
71 2396 223
71 2396 224
71 2396 225
71 2396 226
71 2396 227
71 2396 228
71 2396 229
71 2396 230
71 2396 231
71 2396 232
71 2396 233
71 2396 234
71 2396 235
71 2396 236
71 2396 237
71 2396 238
71 2396 239
71 2396 240
71 2396 241
71 2396 242
71 2396 243
71 2396 244
71 2396 245
71 2396 246
71 2396 247
71 2396 248
71 2396 249
71 2396 250
71 2396 251
71 2396 252
71 2396 253
71 2396 254
71 2396 255
71 2396 256
71 2396 257
71 2396 258
71 2396 259
71 2396 260
71 2396 261
71 2396 262
71 2396 263
71 2396 264
71 2396 265
71 2396 266
71 2396 267
71 2396 268
71 2396 279
71 2396 270
71 2396 271
71 2396 272
71 2396 273
71 2396 274
71 2396 275
71 2396 276
71 2396 277
71 2396 278
71 2396 279
71 2396 280
71 2396 281
71 2396 282
71 2396 283
71 2396 284
71 2396 285
71 2396 286
71 2396 287
71 2396 288
71 2396 289
71 2396 290
71 2396 291
71 2396 292
71 2396 293
71 2396 294
71 2396 295
71 2396 296
71 2396 297
71 2396 298
71 2396 299
71 2396 300
71 2396 301
71 2396 302
71 2396 303
71 2396 304

72 2191 000-099 MEDIUM VAN IMX

Builder: Waggonfabrik Uerdingen, Krefeld, West Germany.
Design Code: IME199.
Owner: JZ.
Tare Weight: 12.20 t.
Gross Laden Weight: 36.00 t.
Maximum Speed: 60 mph.
Length: 10580 mm (34 ft. 9 in.)
Suspension Type: Double Link.
Exchange Code: 21.
Notes: Used on various workings to and from Europe.
Previous Number Series: 21 72 2140 000-099.

72 2191 000
72 2191 001
72 2191 002
72 2191 003
72 2191 004
72 2191 005
72 2191 006
72 2191 007
72 2191 008
72 2191 009
72 2191 010
72 2191 011
72 2191 012
72 2191 013
72 2191 014
72 2191 015
72 2191 016
72 2191 017
72 2191 018
72 2191 019
72 2191 020
72 2191 021
72 2191 022
72 2191 023
72 2191 024
72 2191 025
72 2191 026
72 2191 027
72 2191 028
72 2191 029
72 2191 030
72 2191 031
72 2191 032
72 2191 033
72 2191 034
72 2191 035
72 2191 036
72 2191 037
72 2191 038
72 2191 039
72 2191 040
72 2191 041
72 2191 042
72 2191 043
72 2191 044
72 2191 045
72 2191 046
72 2191 047
72 2191 048
72 2191 049
72 2191 050
72 2191 051

72 2191 052
72 2191 053
72 2191 054
72 2191 055
72 2191 056
72 2191 057
72 2191 058
72 2191 059
72 2191 060
72 2191 061
72 2191 062
72 2191 063
72 2191 064
72 2191 065
72 2191 066
72 2191 067
72 2191 068
72 2191 069
72 2191 070
72 2191 071
72 2191 072
72 2191 073
72 2191 074
72 2191 075
72 2191 076
72 2191 077
72 2191 078
72 2191 079
72 2191 080
72 2191 081
72 2191 082
72 2191 083
72 2191 084
72 2191 085
72 2191 086
72 2191 087
72 2191 088
72 2191 089
72 2191 090
72 2191 091
72 2191 092
72 2191 093
72 2191 094
72 2191 095
72 2191 096
72 2191 097
72 2191 098
72 2191 099

72 2390 000-064 LARGE VAN ILX

Builder: Société Franco-Belge de Matériel de Chemins de Fer, Raismes, France.
Design Code: ILE415.
Owner: JZ.
Tare Weight: 14.00 t.
Gross Laden Weight: 35.00 t.
Maximum Speed: 60 mph.
Length: 14020 mm (46 ft. 0 in.)
Suspension Type: Double Link.
Exchange Code: 21.
Notes: Used on various workings to and from Europe.
Previous Number Series: 21 72 2140 200-264.

72 2390 000
72 2390 001
72 2390 002
72 2390 003
72 2390 004
72 2390 005
72 2390 006
72 2390 007
72 2390 008
72 2390 009
72 2390 010
72 2390 011
72 2390 012
72 2390 013
72 2390 014
72 2390 015
72 2390 016
72 2390 017
72 2390 018
72 2390 019
72 2390 020
72 2390 021
72 2390 022
72 2390 023
72 2390 024
72 2390 025
72 2390 026
72 2390 027
72 2390 028
72 2390 029
72 2390 030
72 2390 031
72 2390 032
72 2390 033
72 2390 034
72 2390 035
72 2390 036
72 2390 037
72 2390 038
72 2390 039
72 2390 040
72 2390 041
72 2390 042
72 2390 043
72 2390 044
72 2390 045
72 2390 046
72 2390 047
72 2390 048
72 2390 049
72 2390 050
72 2390 051
72 2390 052
72 2390 053
72 2390 054
72 2390 055
72 2390 056
72 2390 057
72 2390 058
72 2390 059
72 2390 060
72 2390 061
72 2390 062
72 2390 063
72 2390 064

74 2140 000-099 LARGE VAN ILX

Builder: AB Svenska Järnvägsverkstäderna, Falun, Sweden.
Design Code: ILE237.
Owner: SJ.
Tare Weight: 14.00 t.
Gross Laden Weight: 36.00 t.
Maximum Speed: 60 mph.
Length: 14020 mm (46 ft. 0 in.)
Suspension Type: Double Link.
Exchange Code: 21.
Notes: Used on various workings to and from Europe.

74 2140 000
74 2140 001
74 2140 002
74 2140 003
74 2140 004
74 2140 005
74 2140 006
74 2140 007
74 2140 008
74 2140 009
74 2140 010
74 2140 011
74 2140 012
74 2140 013
74 2140 014
74 2140 015
74 2140 016
74 2140 017
74 2140 018
74 2140 019

74 2140 020
74 2140 021
74 2140 022
74 2140 023
74 2140 024
74 2140 025
74 2140 026
74 2140 027
74 2140 028
74 2140 029
74 2140 030
74 2140 031
74 2140 032
74 2140 033
74 2140 034
74 2140 035
74 2140 036
74 2140 037
74 2140 038
74 2140 039
74 2140 040
74 2140 041
74 2140 042
74 2140 043
74 2140 044
74 2140 045
74 2140 046
74 2140 047
74 2140 048
74 2140 049
74 2140 050
74 2140 051
74 2140 052
74 2140 053
74 2140 054
74 2140 055
74 2140 056
74 2140 057
74 2140 058
74 2140 059
74 2140 060
74 2140 061
74 2140 062
74 2140 063
74 2140 064
74 2140 065
74 2140 066
74 2140 067
74 2140 068
74 2140 069
74 2140 070
74 2140 071
74 2140 072
74 2140 073
74 2140 074
74 2140 075
74 2140 076
74 2140 077
74 2140 078
74 2140 079
74 2140 080
74 2140 081
74 2140 082
74 2140 083
74 2140 084
74 2140 085
74 2140 086
74 2140 087
74 2140 088
74 2140 089
74 2140 090
74 2140 091
74 2140 092
74 2140 093
74 2140 094
74 2140 095
74 2140 096
74 2140 097
74 2140 098
74 2140 099

80 2140 000-149 MEDIUM VAN IMB

Builder: Gebruder Crede, West Germany, 1961.
Design Code: IME006(a IME655).
Owner: DB.
Tare Weight: 12.00 t.
Gross Laden Weight: 39.00 t.
Maximum Speed: 60 mph.
Length: 12500 mm (41 ft. 0 in.)
Suspension Type: Double Link.
Exchange Code: 21.
Notes: IME655 are coded IMX. Used on various workings to and from Europe.

80 2140 000
80 2140 001 a
80 2140 002
80 2140 003
80 2140 004 a
80 2140 005
80 2140 006 a
80 2140 007
80 2140 008 a
80 2140 009 a
80 2140 010 a
80 2140 011
80 2140 012
80 2140 013
80 2140 014
80 2140 015
80 2140 016
80 2140 017 a
80 2140 018
80 2140 019 a
80 2140 020
80 2140 021 a
80 2140 022 a
80 2140 023
80 2140 024
80 2140 025
80 2140 026
80 2140 027
80 2140 028
80 2140 029 a
80 2140 030
80 2140 031 a
80 2140 032
80 2140 033 a
80 2140 034
80 2140 035 a
80 2140 036
80 2140 037
80 2140 038 a
80 2140 039 a
80 2140 040
80 2140 041
80 2140 042
80 2140 043
80 2140 044
80 2140 045
80 2140 046
80 2140 047
80 2140 048
80 2140 049
80 2140 050
80 2140 051 a
80 2140 052
80 2140 053
80 2140 054 a
80 2140 055
80 2140 056
80 2140 057
80 2140 058
80 2140 059
80 2140 060
80 2140 061
80 2140 063
80 2140 064
80 2140 065
80 2140 066
80 2140 067
80 2140 068 a
80 2140 069
80 2140 070
80 2140 071
80 2140 072 a
80 2140 073
80 2140 074 a
80 2140 075
80 2140 076
80 2140 077
80 2140 078 a
80 2140 079
80 2140 080
80 2140 081
80 2140 082
80 2140 083
80 2140 084
80 2140 085
80 2140 086
80 2140 087
80 2140 088
80 2140 089
80 2140 090
80 2140 091 a
80 2140 092
80 2140 093 a
80 2140 094
80 2140 095 a
80 2140 096
80 2140 097
80 2140 098
80 2140 099
80 2140 100

80 2140 101
80 2140 102 a
80 2140 103
80 2140 104
80 2140 105
80 2140 106
80 2140 107
80 2140 108 a
80 2140 109 a
80 2140 110
80 2140 111
80 2140 112
80 2140 113
80 2140 114
80 2140 115
80 2140 116
80 2140 117 a
80 2140 118
80 2140 119
80 2140 120
80 2140 121
80 2140 122
80 2140 123
80 2140 124
80 2140 125
80 2140 126
80 2140 127
80 2140 128
80 2140 129
80 2140 130
80 2140 131
80 2140 132
80 2140 133
80 2140 134
80 2140 135
80 2140 136 a
80 2140 137
80 2140 138
80 2140 139
80 2140 140
80 2140 141 a
80 2140 142
80 2140 143
80 2140 144
80 2140 145 a
80 2140 146 a
80 2140 147
80 2140 148 a
80 2140 149

80 2191 000 MEDIUM VAN IMB

Builder: Gebruder Crede, West Germany, 1961.
Design Code: IME006.
Owner: DB.
Tare Weight: 12.00 t.
Gross Laden Weight: 39.00 t.
Maximum Speed: 60 mph.
Length: 12500 mm (41 ft. 0 in.)
Suspension Type: Double Link.
Exchange Code: 21.
Previous Number: 21 80 2140 062.

80 2191 000

80 2191 001-095 MEDIUM VAN IMB

Builder:
Design Code: IME637(a IME657, b IME662).
Owner: DB.
Tare Weight: 12.00 t.
Gross Laden Weight: 36.00 t.
Maximum Speed: 60 mph.
Length: 12500 mm (41 ft. 0 in.)
Suspension Type: Double Link.
Exchange Code: 21.
Notes: IME657 are coded IMX. Not currently operating on British Rail.
Previous Number Series: 21 80 2140 150-155/157-179/181/182/184-239/241-245/247-249.

80 2191 001 b
80 2191 002
80 2191 003
80 2191 004 a
80 2191 005
80 2191 006
80 2191 007
80 2191 008
80 2191 009
80 2191 010
80 2191 011
80 2191 012 a
80 2191 013
80 2191 014
80 2191 015 a
80 2191 016
80 2191 017 a
80 2191 018
80 2191 019 b
80 2191 020
80 2191 021
80 2191 022 a
80 2191 023
80 2191 024
80 2191 025
80 2191 026
80 2191 027
80 2191 028
80 2191 029
80 2191 030
80 2191 031 b
80 2191 032 a
80 2191 033
80 2191 034 a
80 2191 035
80 2191 036 a
80 2191 037
80 2191 038
80 2191 039
80 2191 040
80 2191 041 a
80 2191 042
80 2191 043
80 2191 044 a
80 2191 045
80 2191 046
80 2191 047
80 2191 048
80 2191 049 b
80 2191 050
80 2191 051
80 2191 052
80 2191 053 a
80 2191 054
80 2191 055 b
80 2191 056
80 2191 057
80 2191 058
80 2191 059
80 2191 060
80 2191 061
80 2191 062
80 2191 063
80 2191 064
80 2191 065
80 2191 066
80 2191 067
80 2191 068
80 2191 069
80 2191 070 a
80 2191 071
80 2191 072

80 2191 073 a	80 2191 079	80 2191 085 b	80 2191 091
80 2191 074	80 2191 080	80 2191 086	80 2191 092
80 2191 075	80 2191 081	80 2191 087	80 2191 093
80 2191 076	80 2191 082	80 2191 088	80 2191 094 a
80 2191 077	80 2191 083	80 2191 089	80 2191 095 b
80 2191 078	80 2191 084	80 2191 090	

80 2398 000-099 MEDIUM VAN ITX

Builder: Waggon Union, Siegen, West Germany, 1983.
Design Code: ITE552. **Owner:** Transfesa.
Tare Weight: 13.00 t. **Gross Laden Weight:** 40.00 t.
Maximum Speed: 75 mph. **Length:** 14060 mm (46 ft. 1 in.)
Suspension Type: Double Link, 2 stage.
Exchange Code: 24.
Notes: 80 2398 011/017/020/022/025/030/033/086/087 are currently used on workings to and from Europe. The remainder are not currently in use on British Rail.

80 2398 000	80 2398 025	80 2398 050	80 2398 075
80 2398 001	80 2398 026	80 2398 051	80 2398 076
80 2398 002	80 2398 027	80 2398 052	80 2398 077
80 2398 003	80 2398 028	80 2398 053	80 2398 078
80 2398 004	80 2398 029	80 2398 054	80 2398 079
80 2398 005	80 2398 030	80 2398 055	80 2398 080
80 2398 006	80 2398 031	80 2398 056	80 2398 081
80 2398 007	80 2398 032	80 2398 057	80 2398 082
80 2398 008	80 2398 033	80 2398 058	80 2398 083
80 2398 009	80 2398 034	80 2398 059	80 2398 084
80 2398 010	80 2398 035	80 2398 060	80 2398 085
80 2398 011	80 2398 036	80 2398 061	80 2398 086
80 2398 012	80 2398 037	80 2398 062	80 2398 087
80 2398 013	80 2398 038	80 2398 063	80 2398 088
80 2398 014	80 2398 039	80 2398 064	80 2398 089
80 2398 015	80 2398 040	80 2398 065	80 2398 090
80 2398 016	80 2398 041	80 2398 066	80 2398 091
80 2398 017	80 2398 042	80 2398 067	80 2398 092
80 2398 018	80 2398 043	80 2398 068	80 2398 093
80 2398 019	80 2398 044	80 2398 069	80 2398 094
80 2398 020	80 2398 045	80 2398 070	80 2398 095
80 2398 021	80 2398 046	80 2398 071	80 2398 096
80 2398 022	80 2398 047	80 2398 072	80 2398 097
80 2398 023	80 2398 048	80 2398 073	80 2398 098
80 2398 024	80 2398 049	80 2398 074	80 2398 099

80 2398 502-647 SLIDING WALL VAN IVB

Builder: Düwag, Krefeld, West Germany, 1987.
Design Code: IVE514 (Ex IPE514) **Owner:** Cargowaggon.
Tare Weight: 16.80 t. **Gross Laden Weight:** 45.00 t.
Maximum Speed: 60 mph. **Length:** 15200 mm (49 ft. 10 in.)
Suspension Type: Double Link. **Exchange Code:** 23.
Notes: On hire to Spillers (working between Deanside and Wisbech), Ford (working between Dagenham and South Wales), Volkswagen (working between Wolverton and Europe) and Evian (various workings).

80 2398 502	80 2398 539	80 2398 576	80 2398 612
80 2398 503	80 2398 540	80 2398 577	80 2398 613
80 2398 504	80 2398 541	80 2398 578	80 2398 614
80 2398 505	80 2398 542	80 2398 579	80 2398 615
80 2398 506	80 2398 543	80 2398 580	80 2398 616
80 2398 507	80 2398 544	80 2398 581	80 2398 617
80 2398 508	80 2398 545	80 2398 582	80 2398 618
80 2398 509	80 2398 546	80 2398 583	80 2398 619
80 2398 510	80 2398 547	80 2398 584	80 2398 620
80 2398 511	80 2398 548	80 2398 585	80 2398 621
80 2398 512	80 2398 549	80 2398 586	80 2398 622
80 2398 513	80 2398 550	80 2398 587	80 2398 623
80 2398 514	80 2398 551	80 2398 588	80 2398 624
80 2398 515	80 2398 552	80 2398 589	80 2398 625
80 2398 516	80 2398 553	80 2398 590	80 2398 626
80 2398 517	80 2398 554	80 2398 591	80 2398 627
80 2398 518	80 2398 555	80 2398 592	80 2398 628
80 2398 519	80 2398 556	80 2398 593	80 2398 629
80 2398 520	80 2398 557	80 2398 594	80 2398 630
80 2398 521	80 2398 558	80 2398 595	80 2398 631
80 2398 522	80 2398 559	80 2398 596	80 2398 632
80 2398 523	80 2398 560	80 2398 597	80 2398 633
80 2398 524	80 2398 561	80 2398 598	80 2398 634
80 2398 525	80 2398 562	80 2398 599	80 2398 635
80 2398 526	80 2398 563	80 2398 600	80 2398 636
80 2398 527	80 2398 564	80 2398 601	80 2398 637
80 2398 528	80 2398 565	80 2398 602	80 2398 638
80 2398 529	80 2398 566	80 2398 603	80 2398 639
80 2398 530	80 2398 567	80 2398 604	80 2398 640
80 2398 531	80 2398 568	80 2398 605	80 2398 641
80 2398 532	80 2398 569	80 2398 606	80 2398 642
80 2398 533	80 2398 570	80 2398 607	80 2398 643
80 2398 534	80 2398 571	80 2398 608	80 2398 644
80 2398 535	80 2398 572	80 2398 609	80 2398 645
80 2398 536	80 2398 573	80 2398 610	80 2398 646
80 2398 537	80 2398 574	80 2398 611	80 2398 647
80 2398 538	80 2398 575		

80 2492 000-001 LARGE VAN IVA

Builder: Düwag, Krefeld, West Germany, 1986.
Design Code: IVE663 (Ex IPE663) **Owner:** DB.
Tare Weight: 15.00 t. **Gross Laden Weight:** 45.00 t.
Maximum Speed: 60 mph. **Length:** 15200 mm (49 ft. 10 in.)
Suspension Type: Double Link. **Exchange Code:** 23.
Notes: Not currently operating on British Rail.

80 2492 000 80 2492 001

80 2493 000-001 SLIDING WALL VAN IVB

Builder: Düwag, Krefeld, West Germany, 1982.
Design Code: IVE514 (Ex IPE514) **Owner:** Cargowaggon.
Tare Weight: 16.80 t. **Gross Laden Weight:** 45.00 t.
Maximum Speed: 60 mph. **Length:** 15200 mm (49 ft. 10 in.)

Bogie Tank 33 70 7892 011 at Hoo Junction on 30th January 1985. (*R. Wallace*)

Bogie Tank 33 70 7892 040 at Immingham on 7th September 1986. (*R. Wallace*)

Suspension Type: Double Link. **Exchange Code:** 23.
Notes: On hire to Volkswagen. Work between Wolverton and Europe.

80 2493 000
80 2493 001

80 2693 000-049 LARGE VAN IWA

Builder: Linke Hofmann Busch, Salzgitter, West Germany, 1985.
Design Code: IWE593(Ex IPE593). **Owner:** VTG.
Tare Weight: 26.50 t. **Gross Laden Weight:** 90.00 t.
Maximum Speed: 60 mph. **Length:** 22200 mm (73 ft. 0 in.)
Bogie Type: **Exchange Code:** 33.
Notes: Only 037/043 are currently working on British Rail, used on various workings to and from Europe.
Previous Number Series: 83 2695 000-049.

80 2693 000
80 2693 001
80 2693 002
80 2693 003
80 2693 004
80 2693 005
80 2693 006
80 2693 007
80 2693 008
80 2693 009
80 2693 010
80 2693 011
80 2693 012
80 2693 013
80 2693 014
80 2693 015
80 2693 016
80 2693 017
80 2693 018
80 2693 019
80 2693 020
80 2693 021
80 2693 022
80 2693 023
80 2693 024
80 2693 025
80 2693 026
80 2693 027
80 2693 028
80 2693 029
80 2693 030
80 2693 031
80 2693 032
80 2693 033
80 2693 034
80 2693 035
80 2693 036
80 2693 037
80 2693 038
80 2693 039
80 2693 040
80 2693 041
80 2693 042
80 2693 043
80 2693 044
80 2693 045
80 2693 046
80 2693 047
80 2693 048
80 2693 049

80 2693 050 LARGE VAN IWA

Builder: Linke Hofmann Busch, Salzgitter, West Germany, 1977.
Design Code: IWE701(Ex IPE701). **Owner:** VTG.
Tare Weight: 27.50 t. **Gross Laden Weight:** 90.00 t.
Maximum Speed: 60 mph. **Length:** 20060 mm (65 ft. 10 in.)
Bogie Type: **Exchange Code:** 33.
Notes: Used on various workings to and from Europe.
Previous Number: 33 80 2797 032.

80 2693 050

80 2793 000-099 IZA
45 TON VAN TWIN SETS

Builder: Düwag, Krefeld, West Germany, 1986.
Design Code: IZE668(Ex IPE668). **Owner:** Cargowaggon.
Tare Weight: 27.30 t. **Gross Laden Weight:** 90.00 t.
Maximum Speed: 60 mph. **Length:** 27000 mm (97 ft. 7 in.)
Suspension Type: Double Link. **Exchange Code:** 23.
Notes: On hire to Guinness (used on various workings to and from Park Royal), Spillers (working between Deanside and Wisbech) and Rover Group (working between Swindon and Longbridge).
Previous Number Series: 23 80 2794 000-099.

80 2793 000
80 2793 001
80 2793 002
80 2793 003
80 2793 004
80 2793 005
80 2793 006
80 2793 007
80 2793 008
80 2793 009
80 2793 010
80 2793 011
80 2793 012
80 2793 013
80 2793 014
80 2793 015
80 2793 016
80 2793 017
80 2793 018
80 2793 019
80 2793 020
80 2793 021
80 2793 022
80 2793 023
80 2793 024
80 2793 025
80 2793 026
80 2793 027
80 2793 028
80 2793 029
80 2793 030
80 2793 031
80 2793 032
80 2793 033
80 2793 034
80 2793 035
80 2793 036
80 2793 037
80 2793 038
80 2793 039
80 2793 040
80 2793 041
80 2793 042
80 2793 043
80 2793 044
80 2793 045
80 2793 046
80 2793 047
80 2793 048
80 2793 049
80 2793 050
80 2793 051
80 2793 052
80 2793 053
80 2793 054
80 2793 055
80 2793 056
80 2793 057
80 2793 058
80 2793 059
80 2793 060
80 2793 061
80 2793 062
80 2793 063
80 2793 064
80 2793 065
80 2793 066
80 2793 067
80 2793 068
80 2793 069
80 2793 070
80 2793 071
80 2793 072
80 2793 073
80 2793 074
80 2793 075
80 2793 076
80 2793 077
80 2793 078
80 2793 079
80 2793 080
80 2793 081
80 2793 082
80 2793 083
80 2793 084
80 2793 085
80 2793 086
80 2793 087
80 2793 088
80 2793 089
80 2793 090
80 2793 091
80 2793 092
80 2793 093
80 2793 094
80 2793 095
80 2793 096
80 2793 097
80 2793 098
80 2793 099

80 2793 100-149 IVA

45 TON VAN TWIN SETS

Builder: Düwag, Krefeld, West Germany, 1989.
Design Code: IVE710(Ex IPE710).
Owner: Cargowaggon.
Tare Weight: 27.40 t.
Gross Laden Weight: 90.00 t.
Maximum Speed: 60 mph.
Length: 23740 mm (77 ft. 11 in.)
Suspension Type: Double Link.
Exchange Code: 23.
Notes: On hire to Evians and used on various workings to and from Europe.

80 2793 100
80 2793 101
80 2793 102
80 2793 103
80 2793 104
80 2793 105
80 2793 106
80 2793 107
80 2793 108
80 2793 109
80 2793 110
80 2793 111
80 2793 112
80 2793 113
80 2793 114
80 2793 115
80 2793 116
80 2793 117
80 2793 118
80 2793 119
80 2793 120
80 2793 121
80 2793 122
80 2793 123
80 2793 124
80 2793 125
80 2793 126
80 2793 127
80 2793 128
80 2793 129
80 2793 130
80 2793 131
80 2793 132
80 2793 133
80 2793 134
80 2793 135
80 2793 136
80 2793 137
80 2793 138
80 2793 139
80 2793 140
80 2793 141
80 2793 142
80 2793 143
80 2793 144
80 2793 145
80 2793 146
80 2793 147
80 2793 148
80 2793 149

80 2796 000-139 LARGE VAN IWB

Builder: Linke Hofmann Busch, Salzgitter, West Germany, 1977.
Design Code: IWE471 (Ex IPE471). **Owner:** VTG.
Tare Weight: 24.40 t. **Gross Laden Weight:** 80.00 t.
Maximum Speed: 60 mph. **Length:** 18900 mm (62 ft. 0 in.)
Bogie Type: LHB74. **Exchange Code:** 33.
Notes: Used on various workings to and from Europe.
Previous Number Series: 21 80 0299 000-139.

80 2796 000	80 2796 035	80 2796 070	80 2796 105
80 2796 001	80 2796 036	80 2796 071	80 2796 106
80 2796 002	80 2796 037	80 2796 072	80 2796 107
80 2796 003	80 2796 038	80 2796 073	80 2796 108
80 2796 004	80 2796 039	80 2796 074	80 2796 109
80 2796 005	80 2796 040	80 2796 075	80 2796 110
80 2796 006	80 2796 041	80 2796 076	80 2796 111
80 2796 007	80 2796 042	80 2796 077	80 2796 112
80 2796 008	80 2796 043	80 2796 078	80 2796 113
80 2796 009	80 2796 044	80 2796 079	80 2796 114
80 2796 010	80 2796 045	80 2796 080	80 2796 115
80 2796 011	80 2796 046	80 2796 081	80 2796 116
80 2796 012	80 2796 047	80 2796 082	80 2796 117
80 2796 013	80 2796 048	80 2796 083	80 2796 118
80 2796 014	80 2796 049	80 2796 084	80 2796 119
80 2796 015	80 2796 050	80 2796 085	80 2796 120
80 2796 016	80 2796 051	80 2796 086	80 2796 121
80 2796 017	80 2796 052	80 2796 087	80 2796 122
80 2796 018	80 2796 053	80 2796 088	80 2796 123
80 2796 019	80 2796 054	80 2796 089	80 2796 124
80 2796 020	80 2796 055	80 2796 090	80 2796 125
80 2796 021	80 2796 056	80 2796 091	80 2796 126
80 2796 022	80 2796 057	80 2796 092	80 2796 127
80 2796 023	80 2796 058	80 2796 093	80 2796 128
80 2796 024	80 2796 059	80 2796 094	80 2796 129
80 2796 025	80 2796 060	80 2796 095	80 2796 130
80 2796 026	80 2796 061	80 2796 096	80 2796 131
80 2796 027	80 2796 062	80 2796 097	80 2796 132
80 2796 028	80 2796 063	80 2796 098	80 2796 133
80 2796 029	80 2796 064	80 2796 099	80 2796 134
80 2796 030	80 2796 065	80 2796 100	80 2796 135
80 2796 031	80 2796 066	80 2796 101	80 2796 136
80 2796 032	80 2796 067	80 2796 102	80 2796 137
80 2796 033	80 2796 068	80 2796 103	80 2796 138
80 2796 034	80 2796 069	80 2796 104	80 2796 139

80 2797 000-211 LARGE VAN IWB

Builder: Linke Hofmann Busch, Salzgitter, West Germany, 1977-79.
Design Code: IWE481 (Ex IPE481). **Owner:** VTG.
Tare Weight: 26.00 t. **Gross Laden Weight:** 80.00 t.
Maximum Speed: 60 mph. **Length:** 20060 mm (65 ft. 10 in.)
Bogie Type: DB (Talbot). **Exchange Code:** 33 (a 83).
Notes: Some on hire to Perrier, working between Crawley and Vegele. The others are used on various workings to and from Europe.

80 2797 000
80 2797 001
80 2797 002
80 2797 003
80 2797 004
80 2797 005
80 2797 006
80 2797 007
80 2797 008
80 2797 009
80 2797 010
80 2797 011
80 2797 012
80 2797 013
80 2797 014
80 2797 015
80 2797 016
80 2797 017
80 2797 018
80 2797 019
80 2797 020
80 2797 021
80 2797 022
80 2797 023
80 2797 024
80 2797 025
80 2797 026
80 2797 027
80 2797 028
80 2797 029
80 2797 030
80 2797 031
80 2797 033
80 2797 034
80 2797 035
80 2797 036
80 2797 037
80 2797 038
80 2797 039
80 2797 040
80 2797 041
80 2797 042
80 2797 043
80 2797 044
80 2797 045
80 2797 046
80 2797 047
80 2797 048
80 2797 049
80 2797 050
80 2797 051
80 2797 052
80 2797 053
80 2797 054
80 2797 055
80 2797 056
80 2797 057
80 2797 058
80 2797 059
80 2797 060
80 2797 061
80 2797 062
80 2797 063
80 2797 064
80 2797 065
80 2797 066
80 2797 067
80 2797 068
80 2797 069
80 2797 070
80 2797 071
80 2797 072
80 2797 073
80 2797 074
80 2797 075
80 2797 076
80 2797 077
80 2797 078
80 2797 079
80 2797 080
80 2797 081
80 2797 082
80 2797 083
80 2797 084
80 2797 085
80 2797 086
80 2797 087
80 2797 088
80 2797 089
80 2797 090
80 2797 091
80 2797 092
80 2797 093
80 2797 094
80 2797 095
80 2797 096
80 2797 097
80 2797 098
80 2797 099
80 2797 100
80 2797 101
80 2797 102
80 2797 103
80 2797 104
80 2797 105
80 2797 106
80 2797 107
80 2797 108
80 2797 109
80 2797 110
80 2797 111
80 2797 112
80 2797 113
80 2797 114
80 2797 115
80 2797 116
80 2797 117
80 2797 118
80 2797 119
80 2797 120
80 2797 121
80 2797 122
80 2797 123
80 2797 124
80 2797 125
80 2797 126
80 2797 127
80 2797 128
80 2797 129
80 2797 130
80 2797 131
80 2797 132
80 2797 133
80 2797 134
80 2797 135
80 2797 136
80 2797 137
80 2797 138
80 2797 139
80 2797 140
80 2797 141
80 2797 142
80 2797 143
80 2797 144
80 2797 145
80 2797 146
80 2797 147
80 2797 148
80 2797 149
80 2797 150
80 2797 151
80 2797 152
80 2797 153
80 2797 154
80 2797 155
80 2797 156
80 2797 157
80 2797 158
80 2797 159
80 2797 160
80 2797 161 a
80 2797 162 a
80 2797 163 a
80 2797 164
80 2797 165 a
80 2797 166 a
80 2797 167 a
80 2797 168 a
80 2797 169
80 2797 170
80 2797 171
80 2797 172
80 2797 173 a
80 2797 174 a
80 2797 175 a
80 2797 176 a
80 2797 177 a
80 2797 178 a
80 2797 179
80 2797 180
80 2797 181 a
80 2797 182 a
80 2797 183 a
80 2797 184 a
80 2797 185
80 2797 186
80 2797 187 a
80 2797 188
80 2797 189
80 2797 190
80 2797 191
80 2797 192
80 2797 193 a
80 2797 194 a
80 2797 195
80 2797 196 a
80 2797 197
80 2797 198
80 2797 199
80 2797 200
80 2797 201 a
80 2797 202
80 2797 203 a
80 2797 204 a
80 2797 205
80 2797 206 a
80 2797 207 a
80 2797 208
80 2797 209 a
80 2797 210
80 2797 211

80 2797 500-579 LARGE VAN IWB

Builder: Waggonfabrik Uerdingen, Krefeld, West Germany, 1977.
Design Code: IWE476(Ex IPE476). **Owner:** Cargowaggon.
Tare Weight: 26.23 t. **Gross Laden Weight:** 80.00 t.
Maximum Speed: 60 mph. **Length:** 21700 mm (71 ft. 5 in.)
Bogie Type: DB (Talbot). **Exchange Code:** 33.
Notes: Used on various workings to and from Europe.
Previous Number Series: 21 80 0298 000-079.

80 2797 500
80 2797 501
80 2797 502
80 2797 503
80 2797 504
80 2797 505
80 2797 506
80 2797 507
80 2797 508
80 2797 509
80 2797 510
80 2797 511
80 2797 512
80 2797 513
80 2797 514
80 2797 515
80 2797 516
80 2797 517
80 2797 518
80 2797 519
80 2797 520
80 2797 521
80 2797 522
80 2797 523
80 2797 524
80 2797 525
80 2797 526
80 2797 527
80 2797 528
80 2797 529
80 2797 530
80 2797 531
80 2797 532
80 2797 533
80 2797 534
80 2797 535
80 2797 536
80 2797 537
80 2797 538
80 2797 539
80 2797 540
80 2797 541
80 2797 542
80 2797 543
80 2797 544
80 2797 545
80 2797 546
80 2797 547
80 2797 548
80 2797 549
80 2797 550
80 2797 551
80 2797 552
80 2797 553
80 2797 554
80 2797 555
80 2797 556
80 2797 557
80 2797 558
80 2797 559
80 2797 560
80 2797 561
80 2797 562
80 2797 563
80 2797 564
80 2797 565
80 2797 566
80 2797 567
80 2797 568
80 2797 569
80 2797 570
80 2797 571
80 2797 572
80 2797 573
80 2797 574
80 2797 575
80 2797 576
80 2797 577
80 2797 578
80 2797 579

80 2797 580-699 LARGE VAN IWB

Builder: Waggonfabrik Uerdingen, Krefeld, West Germany, 1979-80.
Design Code: IWE512(Ex IPE512). **Owner:** Cargowaggon.
Tare Weight: 27.00 t. **Gross Laden Weight:** 80.00 t.
Maximum Speed: 60 mph. **Length:** 21700 mm (71 ft. 5 in.)
Bogie Type: DB (Talbot). **Exchange Code:** 33.
Notes: Some on hire to Rover Group and used on workings to and from Longbridge. The others are used on various workings to and from Europe.
Previous Number Series: 83 80 2797 580-699.

80 2797 580
80 2797 581
80 2797 582
80 2797 583
80 2797 584
80 2797 585
80 2797 586
80 2797 587
80 2797 588
80 2797 589
80 2797 590
80 2797 591
80 2797 592
80 2797 593
80 2797 594
80 2797 595
80 2797 596
80 2797 597
80 2797 598
80 2797 599
80 2797 600
80 2797 601
80 2797 602
80 2797 603
80 2797 604
80 2797 605
80 2797 606
80 2797 607
80 2797 608
80 2797 609
80 2797 610
80 2797 611
80 2797 612
80 2797 613
80 2797 614
80 2797 615
80 2797 616
80 2797 617
80 2797 618
80 2797 619
80 2797 620
80 2797 621
80 2797 622
80 2797 623
80 2797 624
80 2797 625
80 2797 626
80 2797 627
80 2797 628
80 2797 629
80 2797 630
80 2797 631

80 2797 632	80 2797 649	80 2797 666	80 2797 683
80 2797 633	80 2797 650	80 2797 667	80 2797 684
80 2797 634	80 2797 651	80 2797 668	80 2797 685
80 2797 635	80 2797 652	80 2797 669	80 2797 686
80 2797 636	80 2797 653	80 2797 670	80 2797 687
80 2797 637	80 2797 654	80 2797 671	80 2797 688
80 2797 638	80 2797 655	80 2797 672	80 2797 689
80 2797 639	80 2797 656	80 2797 673	80 2797 690
80 2797 640	80 2797 657	80 2797 674	80 2797 691
80 2797 641	80 2797 658	80 2797 675	80 2797 692
80 2797 642	80 2797 659	80 2797 676	80 2797 693
80 2797 643	80 2797 660	80 2797 677	80 2797 694
80 2797 644	80 2797 661	80 2797 678	80 2797 695
80 2797 645	80 2797 662	80 2797 679	80 2797 696
80 2797 646	80 2797 663	80 2797 680	80 2797 697
80 2797 647	80 2797 664	80 2797 681	80 2797 698
80 2797 648	80 2797 665	80 2797 682	80 2797 699

80 2797 700-734 LARGE VAN IWA

Builder: Waggon Union, Siegen, West Germany, 1983.
Design Code: IWE551(Ex IPE551). **Owner:** Cargowaggon.
Tare Weight: 27.00 t. **Gross Laden Weight:** 80.00 t.
Maximum Speed: 60 mph. **Length:** 21700 mm (71 ft. 5 in.)
Bogie Type: DB (Talbot). **Exchange Code:** 33.
Notes: Some on hire to Rover Group and used on workings to and from Longbridge. The others are used on various workings to and from Europe.
Previous Number Series: 83 80 2797 700-734.

80 2797 700	80 2797 709	80 2797 718	80 2797 727
80 2797 701	80 2797 710	80 2797 719	80 2797 728
80 2797 702	80 2797 711	80 2797 720	80 2797 729
80 2797 703	80 2797 712	80 2797 721	80 2797 730
80 2797 704	80 2797 713	80 2797 722	80 2797 731
80 2797 705	80 2797 714	80 2797 723	80 2797 732
80 2797 706	80 2797 715	80 2797 724	80 2797 733
80 2797 707	80 2797 716	80 2797 725	80 2797 734
80 2797 708	80 2797 717	80 2797 726	

80 2798 000-014 LARGE VAN IWA

Builder: Waggon Union, Siegen, West Germany, 1983.
Design Code: IWE551(Ex IPE551). **Owner:** Cargowaggon.
Tare Weight: 27.00 t. **Gross Laden Weight:** 80.00 t.
Maximum Speed: 60 mph. **Length:** 21700 mm (71 ft. 5 in.)
Bogie Type: DB (Talbot). **Exchange Code:** 33.
Notes: Used on variaus workings to and from Europe.
Previous Number Series: 83 80 2798 000-014.

80 2798 000	80 2798 004	80 2798 008	80 2798 012
80 2798 001	80 2798 005	80 2798 009	80 2798 013
80 2798 002	80 2798 006	80 2798 010	80 2798 014
80 2798 003	80 2798 007	80 2798 011	

80 4141 000-002 CONTAINER FLAT IEB

Builder: Siegener, Siegen, West Germany, 1982.
Design Code: IEE222(Ex IPE222). **Owner:** Degussa.
Tare Weight: 9.95 t. **Gross Laden Weight:** 30.00 t.
Maximum Speed: 60 mph. **Length:** 11000 mm (36 ft. 1 in.)
Suspension Type: Double Link. **Exchange Code:** 23.
Notes: Not currently operating on British Rail.
Previous Number Series: 21 80 0486 503-505.

80 4141 000 | 80 4141 001 | 80 4141 002

80 4141 500-502 CONTAINER FLAT IEB

Builder: Franz Kaminski, Hameln, West Germany, 1979.
Design Code: IEE501(Ex IPE501). **Owner:** Schering.
Tare Weight: 11.50 t. **Gross Laden Weight:** 40.00 t.
Maximum Speed: 60 mph. **Length:** 11240 mm (36 ft. 11 in.)
Suspension Type: Double Link. **Exchange Code:** 23.
Notes: Not currently operating on British Rail.

80 4141 500 | 80 4141 501 | 80 4141 502

80 4142 000-024 LOWSIDE OPEN IFB

Builder: ???, 1984.
Design Code: IFE568. **Owner:** DB.
Tare Weight: 12.00 t. **Gross Laden Weight:** 40.00 t.
Maximum Speed: 60 mph. **Length:** 12500 mm (41 ft. 0 in.)
Suspension Type: Double Link. **Exchange Code:** 21.
Notes: Used on various workings to and from Europe.
Previous Number Series: 21 80 4140 000-024.

80 4142 000	80 4142 007	80 4142 013	80 4142 019
80 4142 001	80 4142 008	80 4142 014	80 4142 020
80 4142 002	80 4142 009	80 4142 015	80 4142 021
80 4142 003	80 4142 010	80 4142 016	80 4142 022
80 4142 004	80 4142 011	80 4142 017	80 4142 023
80 4142 006	80 4142 012	80 4142 018	80 4142 024

80 4142 025-154 LOWSIDE OPEN IFX

Builder: Linke Hofmann Busch, Salzgitter, West Germany, 1963.
Design Code: IFE259. **Owner:** DB.
Tare Weight: 12.30 t. **Gross Laden Weight:** 40.00 t.
Maximum Speed: 60 mph. **Length:** 12500 mm (41 ft. 0 in.)
Suspension Type: Double Link. **Exchange Code:** 21.
Notes: Used on various workings to and from Europe.
Previous Number Series: 21 80 4140 025-145.

80 4142 025
80 4142 026
80 4142 027
80 4142 028
80 4142 029
80 4142 030
80 4142 031
80 4142 032
80 4142 033
80 4142 034
80 4142 035
80 4142 036
80 4142 037
80 4142 038
80 4142 039
80 4142 040
80 4142 041
80 4142 042
80 4142 043
80 4142 044
80 4142 045
80 4142 046
80 4142 047
80 4142 048
80 4142 049
80 4142 050
80 4142 051
80 4142 052
80 4142 053
80 4142 054
80 4142 055
80 4142 056
80 4142 057
80 4142 058
80 4142 059
80 4142 060
80 4142 061
80 4142 062
80 4142 063
80 4142 064
80 4142 065
80 4142 066
80 4142 067
80 4142 068
80 4142 069
80 4142 070
80 4142 071
80 4142 072
80 4142 073
80 4142 074
80 4142 076
80 4142 077
80 4142 078
80 4142 079
80 4142 080
80 4142 081
80 4142 082
80 4142 083
80 4142 084
80 4142 085
80 4142 086
80 4142 087
80 4142 088
80 4142 089
80 4142 090
80 4142 091
80 4142 092
80 4142 093
80 4142 094
80 4142 095
80 4142 096
80 4142 097
80 4142 098
80 4142 099
80 4142 100
80 4142 101
80 4142 102
80 4142 103
80 4142 104
80 4142 105
80 4142 106
80 4142 107
80 4142 108
80 4142 109
80 4142 110
80 4142 111
80 4142 112
80 4142 113
80 4142 114
80 4142 115
80 4142 116
80 4142 117
80 4142 118
80 4142 119
80 4142 120
80 4142 121
80 4142 122
80 4142 123
80 4142 124
80 4142 125
80 4142 126
80 4142 127
80 4142 128
80 4142 129
80 4142 130
80 4142 131
80 4142 132
80 4142 133
80 4142 134
80 4142 135
80 4142 136
80 4142 137
80 4142 138
80 4142 139
80 4142 140
80 4142 141
80 4142 142
80 4142 143
80 4142 144
80 4142 145
80 4142 146
80 4142 147
80 4142 148
80 4142 149
80 4142 150
80 4142 151
80 4142 152
80 4142 153
80 4142 154

80 4647 000-049 FLAT IGA

Builder: Waggon Union, Siegen, West Germany, 1983.
Design Code: IGE557(Ex IPE557).
Owner: Cargowaggon.
Tare Weight: 23.94 t.
Gross Laden Weight: 90.00 t.
Maximum Speed: 75 mph.
Length: 21700 mm (71 ft. 2 in.)
Bogie Type: DB 665/WU 83.
Exchange Code: 33.
Notes: Used on various workings to and from Europe.
Previous Number Series: 33 80 4747 000-049.

80 4647 000
80 4647 001
80 4647 002
80 4647 003
80 4647 004
80 4647 005
80 4647 006
80 4647 007
80 4647 008
80 4647 009
80 4647 010
80 4647 011
80 4647 012
80 4647 013
80 4647 014
80 4647 015
80 4647 016
80 4647 017
80 4647 018
80 4647 019
80 4647 020
80 4647 021
80 4647 022
80 4647 023
80 4647 024
80 4647 025
80 4647 026
80 4647 027
80 4647 028
80 4647 029
80 4647 030
80 4647 031
80 4647 032
80 4647 033
80 4647 034
80 4647 035
80 4647 036
80 4647 037
80 4647 038
80 4647 039
80 4647 040
80 4647 041
80 4647 042
80 4647 043

80 4647 044	80 4647 046	80 4647 048	80 4647 049
80 4647 045	80 4647 047		

80 4667 000-049 STEEL HOOD IHA

Builder: Linke Hofmann Busch, Salzgitter, West Germany, 1985.
Design Code: IHE587(Ex IPE587). **Owner:** VTG.
Tare Weight: 24.50 t. **Gross Laden Weight:** 90.00 t.
Maximum Speed: 60 mph. **Length:** 14540 mm (47 ft. 9 in.)
Bogie Type: LHB78. **Exchange Code:** 33.
Notes: Only 001 is currently operating on British Rail, and is used on various workings to and from Europe.
Previous Number Series: 33 80 4746 000-049.

80 4667 000	80 4667 013	80 4667 026	80 4667 038
80 4667 001	80 4667 014	80 4667 027	80 4667 039
80 4667 002	80 4667 015	80 4667 028	80 4667 040
80 4667 003	80 4667 016	80 4667 029	80 4667 041
80 4667 004	80 4667 017	80 4667 030	80 4667 042
80 4667 005	80 4667 018	80 4667 031	80 4667 043
80 4667 006	80 4667 019	80 4667 032	80 4667 044
80 4667 007	80 4667 020	80 4667 033	80 4667 045
80 4667 008	80 4667 021	80 4667 034	80 4667 046
80 4667 009	80 4667 022	80 4667 035	80 4667 047
80 4667 010	80 4667 023	80 4667 036	80 4667 048
80 4667 011	80 4667 024	80 4667 037	80 4667 049
80 4667 012	80 4667 025		

80 4736 000-049 FLAT IGA

Builder: Waggon Union, Siegen, West Germany, 1986.
Design Code: IGE670(Ex IPE670). **Owner:** Cargowaggon.
Tare Weight: 25.00 t. **Gross Laden Weight:** 90.00 t.
Maximum Speed: 60 mph. **Length:** 21700 mm (71 ft. 2 in.)
Bogie Type: DB WU03/m. **Exchange Code:** 33.
Notes: Used on various workings to and from Europe.
Previous Number Series: 33 80 4737 000-049.

80 4736 000	80 4736 013	80 4736 026	80 4736 038
80 4736 001	80 4736 014	80 4736 027	80 4736 039
80 4736 002	80 4736 015	80 4736 028	80 4736 040
80 4736 003	80 4736 016	80 4736 029	80 4736 041
80 4736 004	80 4736 017	80 4736 030	80 4736 042
80 4736 005	80 4736 018	80 4736 031	80 4736 043
80 4736 006	80 4736 019	80 4736 032	80 4736 044
80 4736 007	80 4736 020	80 4736 033	80 4736 045
80 4736 008	80 4736 021	80 4736 034	80 4736 046
80 4736 009	80 4736 022	80 4736 035	80 4736 047
80 4736 010	80 4736 023	80 4736 036	80 4736 048
80 4736 011	80 4736 024	80 4736 037	80 4736 049
80 4736 012	80 4736 025		

80 4736 100-149 FLAT IGA

Builder: Waggon Union, Siegen, West Germany, 1990.
Design Code: IGE726. **Owner:** Cargowaggon.
Tare Weight: 26.00 t. **Gross Laden Weight:** 90.00 t.
Maximum Speed: 60 mph. **Length:** 23740 mm (77 ft. 11 in.)
Bogie Type: **Exchange Code:** 83.
Notes: Used on various workings to and from Europe.

80 4736 100	80 4736 113	80 4736 126	80 4736 138
80 4736 101	80 4736 114	80 4736 127	80 4736 139
80 4736 102	80 4736 115	80 4736 128	80 4736 140
80 4736 103	80 4736 116	80 4736 129	80 4736 141
80 4736 104	80 4736 117	80 4736 130	80 4736 142
80 4736 105	80 4736 118	80 4736 131	80 4736 143
80 4736 106	80 4736 119	80 4736 132	80 4736 144
80 4736 107	80 4736 120	80 4736 133	80 4736 145
80 4736 108	80 4736 121	80 4736 134	80 4736 146
80 4736 109	80 4736 122	80 4736 135	80 4736 147
80 4736 110	80 4736 123	80 4736 136	80 4736 148
80 4736 111	80 4736 124	80 4736 137	80 4736 149
80 4736 112	80 4736 125		

80 4741 000 SLIDING WALL VAN IWA

Builder: Waggon Union, Siegen, West Germany, 1984.
Design Code: IWE576 (Ex IPE576). **Owner:** Cargowaggon.
Tare Weight: 28.50 t. **Gross Laden Weight:** 80.00 t.
Maximum Speed: 60 mph. **Length:** 21700 mm (71 ft. 2 in.)
Bogie Type: DB WU83.1. **Exchange Code:** 33.
Notes: Used on various workings to and from Europe.

80 4741 000

80 4741 001-160 HOLDALL VAN IWA

Builder: Waggon Union, Siegen, West Germany, 1987.
Design Code: ILE690 (Ex IPE690). **Owner:** Cargowaggon.
Tare Weight: 26.00 t. **Gross Laden Weight:** 90.00 t.
Maximum Speed: 60 mph. **Length:** 20760 mm (68 ft. 2 in.)
Bogie Type: DB 642. **Exchange Code:** 83.
Notes: On hire to Kemira Fertilisers (used on various workings to and from Ince & Elton) and Norsk Hydro (used on various workings to and from Immingham).

80 4741 001	80 4741 011	80 4741 021	80 4741 031
80 4741 002	80 4741 012	80 4741 022	80 4741 032
80 4741 003	80 4741 013	80 4741 023	80 4741 033
80 4741 004	80 4741 014	80 4741 024	80 4741 034
80 4741 005	80 4741 015	80 4741 025	80 4741 035
80 4741 006	80 4741 016	80 4741 026	80 4741 036
80 4741 007	80 4741 017	80 4741 027	80 4741 037
80 4741 008	80 4741 018	80 4741 028	80 4741 038
80 4741 009	80 4741 019	80 4741 029	80 4741 039
80 4741 010	80 4741 020	80 4741 030	80 4741 040

80 4741 041
80 4741 042
80 4741 043
80 4741 044
80 4741 045
80 4741 046
80 4741 047
80 4741 048
80 4741 049
80 4741 040
80 4741 051
80 4741 052
80 4741 053
80 4741 054
80 4741 055
80 4741 056
80 4741 057
80 4741 058
80 4741 059
80 4741 060
80 4741 061
80 4741 062
80 4741 063
80 4741 064
80 4741 065
80 4741 066
80 4741 067
80 4741 068
80 4741 069
80 4741 070
80 4741 071
80 4741 072
80 4741 073
80 4741 074
80 4741 075
80 4741 076
80 4741 077
80 4741 078
80 4741 079
80 4741 080
80 4741 081
80 4741 082
80 4741 083
80 4741 084
80 4741 085
80 4741 086
80 4741 087
80 4741 088
80 4741 089
80 4741 090
80 4741 091
80 4741 092
80 4741 093
80 4741 094
80 4741 095
80 4741 096
80 4741 097
80 4741 098
80 4741 099
80 4741 100
80 4741 101
80 4741 102
80 4741 103
80 4741 104
80 4741 105
80 4741 106
80 4741 107
80 4741 108
80 4741 109
80 4741 110
80 4741 111
80 4741 112
80 4741 113
80 4741 114
80 4741 115
80 4741 116
80 4741 117
80 4741 118
80 4741 119
80 4741 120
80 4741 121
80 4741 122
80 4741 123
80 4741 124
80 4741 125
80 4741 126
80 4741 127
80 4741 128
80 4741 129
80 4741 130
80 4741 131
80 4741 132
80 4741 133
80 4741 134
80 4741 135
80 4741 136
80 4741 137
80 4741 138
80 4741 139
80 4741 140
80 4741 141
80 4741 142
80 4741 143
80 4741 144
80 4741 145
80 4741 146
80 4741 147
80 4741 148
80 4741 149
80 4741 150
80 4741 151
80 4741 152
80 4741 153
80 4741 154
80 4741 155
80 4741 156
80 4741 157
80 4741 158
80 4741 159
80 4741 160

80 4742 000-049 FLAT IGB

Builder: Waggon Union, Siegen, West Germany, 1979.
Design Code: IGE502(Ex IPE502).
Owner: Eva.
Tare Weight: 23.00 t.
Gross Laden Weight: 80.00 t.
Maximum Speed: 60 mph.
Length: 21700 mm (71 ft. 2 in.)
Bogie Type: DB (Talbot).
Exchange Code: 33.
Notes: On hire to Caberboard (work between Inverurie and Irvine) and ASW (used on various workings to and from Cardiff). Others are used on various workings to and from Europe.

80 4742 000
80 4742 001
80 4742 002
80 4742 003
80 4742 004
80 4742 005
80 4742 006
80 4742 007
80 4742 008
80 4742 009
80 4742 010
80 4742 011
80 4742 012
80 4742 013
80 4742 014
80 4742 015
80 4742 016
80 4742 017
80 4742 018
80 4742 019
80 4742 020
80 4742 021
80 4742 022
80 4742 023
80 4742 024
80 4742 025
80 4742 026
80 4742 027
80 4742 028
80 4742 029
80 4742 030
80 4742 031
80 4742 032
80 4742 033
80 4742 034
80 4742 035
80 4742 036
80 4742 037
80 4742 038
80 4742 039
80 4742 040
80 4742 041
80 4742 042
80 4742 043
80 4742 044
80 4742 045
80 4742 046
80 4742 047
80 4742 048
80 4742 049

Covered Bogie Hopper 33 70 9280 066 at Whitemoor Yard on 13th August 1988. *(Wallace)*

Medium Van 24 71 2148 421 at Hoo Junction on 12th April 1985. *(R. Wallace)*

80 4743 000 LARGE VAN IWB

Builder: Waggon Union, Siegen, West Germany, 1981.
Design Code: IWE521 (Ex IPE521). **Owner:** Eva.
Tare Weight: 27.00 t. **Gross Laden Weight:** 80.00 t.
Maximum Speed: 60 mph. **Length:** 21700 mm (71 ft. 2 in.)
Bogie Type: Talbot. **Exchange Code:** 83.
Notes: Used on various workings to and from Europe.

80 4743 000

80 5795 000 SLIDING ROOF VAN IMX

Builder: Gebruder Crede, West Germany, 1965.
Design Code: IME277. **Owner:** DB.
Tare Weight: 13.50 t. **Gross Laden Weight:** 40.00 t.
Maximum Speed: 60 mph. **Length:** 12500 mm (41 ft. 0 in.)
Suspension Type: Double Link. **Exchange Code:** 21.
Notes: Used on various workings to and from Europe.
Previous Number: 21 80 5729 000.

80 5795 000

80 5798 000-002 SLIDING ROOF VAN IVB

Builder: Waggon Union, Siegen, West Germany.
Design Code: IVE443(Ex IPE443). **Owner:** Degussa.
Tare Weight: 14.00 t. **Gross Laden Weight:** 40.00 t.
Maximum Speed: 60 mph. **Length:** 12300 mm (40 ft. 4 in.)
Suspension Type: Double Link. **Exchange Code:** 23.
Notes: Used on various workings to and from Europe.
Previous Number Series: 21 80 0585 000-003.

80 5798 000 80 5798 002 80 5798 003

80 7088 000-002 TANK IBB

Builder: British Rail, Shildon, UK.
Design Code: IBE278 (Ex ICE278)[a IBE639 (Ex ICE639)].
Owner: BASF.
Tare Weight: 14.00 t. **Gross Laden Weight:** 40.00 t.
Maximum Speed: 50 mph. **Length:** 8740 mm (28 ft. 8 in.)
Suspension Type: Double Link. **Exchange Code:** 23.
Notes: Used on various workings to and from Europe.
Previous Number Series: 21 80 0080 422-424.

80 7088 000 80 7088 001 80 7088 002 a

80 7088 501-517 TANK IBB

Builder:
Design Code: IBE626(Ex ICE626). **Owner:** VTG.

Tare Weight: 12.60 t.
Gross Laden Weight: 40.00 t.
Maximum Speed: 60 mph.
Length: 8839 mm (29 ft. 0 in.)
Suspension Type:
Exchange Code: 23.
Notes: Not currently operating on British Rail.
Previous Number Series: 21 80 0780 331/332/347.

80 7088 501 | 80 7088 502 | 80 7088 517

80 7187 000 TANK IBB

Builder: Linke Hofmann Busch, Salzgitter, West Germany.
Design Code: IBE376(Ex ICE376).
Owner: VTG.
Tare Weight: 13.40 t.
Gross Laden Weight: 36.00 t.
Maximum Speed: 50 mph.
Length: 8800 mm (28 ft. 10 in.)
Suspension Type: Single Link.
Exchange Code: 23.
Notes: Not currently operating on British Rail.
Previous Number Series: 21 80 0780 401.

80 7187 000

80 7190 004-015 TANK IBB

Builder: VTG, Hamburg, West Germany.
Design Code: IBE154(Ex ICE154).
Owner: VTG.
Tare Weight: 12.50 t.
Gross Laden Weight: 31.00 t.
Maximum Speed: 50 mph.
Length: 8800 mm (28 ft. 10 in.)
Suspension Type: Single Link.
Exchange Code: 23.
Notes: Not currently operating on British Rail.
Previous Number Series: 21 80 0780 229/273/296/301/394.

80 7190 004 | 80 7190 008 | 80 7190 009 | 80 7190 015
80 7190 006

80 7190 400-404 TANK IBB

Builder:
Design Code: IBE240 (Ex ICE240).
Owner: BASF.
Tare Weight: 12.36 t.
Gross Laden Weight: 36.00 t.
Maximum Speed: 60 mph.
Length: 8800 mm (28 ft. 10 in.)
Suspension Type: Double Link.
Exchange Code: 23.
Notes: Used on various workings to and from Europe.
Previous Number Series: 21 80 0080 400-404.

80 7190 400 | 80 7190 402 | 80 7190 403 | 80 7190 404
80 7190 401

80 7191 000 TANK IBB

Builder:
Design Code: IBE062(Ex ICE062).
Owner: VTG.
Tare Weight: 10.00 t.
Gross Laden Weight: 33.00 t.
Maximum Speed: 60 mph.
Length: 8800 mm (28 ft. 10 in.)
Suspension Type:
Exchange Code: 23.

Notes: Not currently operating on British Rail.
Previous Number: 21 80 0780 324.

80 7191 000

80 7191 004-008 TANK IBB

Builder:
Design Code: IBE613 (Ex ICE613).
Owner: VTG.
Tare Weight: 9.50 t.
Gross Laden Weight: 31.50 t.
Maximum Speed: 60 mph.
Length: 8839 mm (29 ft. 0 in.)
Suspension Type:
Exchange Code: 23.
Notes: Not currently operating on British Rail.
Previous Number Series: 21 80 0780 372/378.

80 7191 004 80 7191 008

80 7191 400 TANK IBB

Builder: Eva.
Design Code: IBE352(Ex ICE352).
Owner: Eva.
Tare Weight: 11.00 t.
Gross Laden Weight: 40.00 t.
Maximum Speed: 50 mph.
Length: 8800 mm (28 ft. 10 in.)
Suspension Type: Single Link.
Exchange Code: 23.
Notes: Used on various workings to and from Europe.
Previous Number: 21 80 0782 999.

80 7191 400

80 7191 700-702 TANK IBB

Builder: BASF, Ludwigshafen, West Germany.
Design Code: IBE282(Ex ICE282) [a IBE141 (Ex ICE141)].
Owner: BASF.
Tare Weight: 11.50 t (a 10.50 t).
Gross Laden Weight: 36.00 t (a 33.00 t).
Maximum Speed: 50 mph.
Length: 8800 mm (28 ft. 10 in.) [a 8740 mm (28 ft 8 in)].
Suspension Type: Single Link (a Double).
Exchange Code: 23.
Notes: Used on various workings to and from Europe.
Previous Number Series: 21 80 0080 427/430/431.

80 7191 700 80 7191 701 a 80 7191 702 a

80 7192 000-006 TANK IBB

Builder: VTG, Hamburg, West Germany.
Design Code: IBE154(Ex ICE154).
Owner: VTG.
Tare Weight: 12.50 t.
Gross Laden Weight: 31.00 t.
Maximum Speed: 50 mph.
Length: 8800 mm (28 ft. 10 in.)
Suspension Type: Single Link.
Exchange Code: 23.
Notes: Not currently operating on British Rail.
Previous Number Series: 21 80 0780 217/228/269/312.

80 7192 000 80 7192 002 80 7192 005 80 7192 006

80 7193 000-009 TANK IBB

Builder:
Design Code: IBE617 (Ex ICE617)[a IBE158 (Ex ICE158), b IBE234 (Ex ICE234), c IBE650 (Ex ICE650)]. **Owner:** VTG.
Tare Weight: ?? t (a 14.00 t, c 10.46 t). **Gross Laden Weight:** ?? t (a & c 32.00 t).
Maximum Speed: 50 mph. **Length:** ?? mm (a 8800 mm (28 ft 10 in).
Suspension Type: Single Link. **Exchange Code:** 23.
Notes: IBE073 and IBE234 are coded IBX. Not currently operating on British Rail.
Previous Number Series: 21 80 0780 117/123/129/130/132/351/352/355.

80 7193 000	80 7193 003 a	80 7193 005	80 7193 008 b
80 7193 001	80 7193 004 a	80 7193 007 c	80 7193 009 c

80 7197 001-017 TANK IBB

Builder:
Design Code: IBE073(Ex ICE073)[a IBE626(Ex ICE626)].
Owner:
Tare Weight: **Gross Laden Weight:**
Maximum Speed: 60 mph. **Length:**
Suspension Type: **Exchange Code:** 23.
Notes: Not currently operating on British Rail.
Previous Number Series: 21 80 0780 330/333-335/340/342/343/345/346/348.

80 7197 001	80 7197 006	80 7197 012	80 7197 015 a
80 7197 004 a	80 7197 010	80 7197 014 a	80 7197 017 a
80 7197 005	80 7197 011		

80 7197 029 TANK IBB

Builder: VTG, Hamburg, West Germany.
Design Code: IBE356(Ex ICE365). **Owner:** VTG.
Tare Weight: 12.70 t. **Gross Laden Weight:** 40.00 t.
Maximum Speed: 60 mph. **Length:** 8800 mm (28 ft. 10 in.)
Suspension Type: Single Link. **Exchange Code:** 23.
Notes: Not currently operating on British Rail.
Previous Number: 21 80 0780 400.

80 7197 029

80 7197 400-405 TANK IBB

Builder:
Design Code: IBE001 (Ex ICE001)[a IBE072 (Ex ICE072), b IBE160 (Ex ICE160), c IBE609 (Ex ICE609)]. **Owner:** BASF.
Tare Weight: 11.20 t (a 10.00 t, b 12.75 t, c ??.?? t).
Gross Laden Weight: 32.00 t (a 40.00 t, b 30.00 t, c ??.?? t).
Maximum Speed: 50 mph. **Exchange Code:** 23.
Length: 8800 mm (28 ft. 10 in.)[b 9800 mm (32 ft 2 in).
Suspension Type: Double Link (a & b Single Link).
Notes: Used on variuos workings to and from Europe.
Previous Number Series: 21 80 0080 406-409/411.

80 7197 400 b
80 7197 401
80 7197 402 a
80 7197 403 a
80 7197 405 c

80 7199 017 TANK IBB

Builder: VTG, Hamburg, West Germany.
Design Code: IBE154(Ex ICE154).
Owner: VTG.
Tare Weight: 12.50 t.
Gross Laden Weight: 31.00 t.
Maximum Speed: 50 mph.
Length: 8800 mm (28 ft. 10 in.)
Suspension Type: Single Link.
Exchange Code: 23.
Notes: Not currently operating on British Rail.
Previous Number: 21 80 0780 289.

80 7199 017

80 7277 010-015 TANK IBB

Builder:
Owner: VTG.
Design Code: IBE647(Ex ICE647)[a IBE617 (Ex ICE617)].
Tare Weight: 14.00 t.
Gross Laden Weight: 32.00 t.
Maximum Speed: 50 mph.
Length: 8839 mm (29 ft. 0 in.)
Suspension Type:
Exchange Code: 23.
Notes: Not currently operating on British Rail.
Previous Number Series: 21 80 0780 110/113/115.

80 7277 010
80 7277 013
80 7277 015 a

80 7287 000-005 TANK IBB

Builder: VTG, Hamburg, West Germany.
Design Code: IBE154 (Ex ICE154)[a IBE613 (Ex ICE613)].
Owner: VTG.
Tare Weight: 12.50 t(a 9.50 t)
Gross Laden Weight: 31.00 t (a 31.50 t).
Maximum Speed: 50 mph.
Length: 8800 mm (28 ft. 10 in.)[a 8839 mm (29 ft 0 in)].
Suspension Type: Single Link.
Exchange Code: 23.
Notes: Not currently operating on British Rail.
Previous Number Series: 21 80 0780 230/374.

80 7287 000
80 7207 005 a

80 7287 400-414 TANK IBX

Builder:
Design Code: IBE629(Ex ICE629).
Owner: Fva.
Tare Weight: 16.50 t.
Gross Laden Weight: 40.00 t.
Maximum Speed: 60 mph.
Length: 8863 mm (29 ft. 1 in.)
Suspension Type:
Exchange Code: 23.
Notes: Used on various workings to and from Europe.
Previous Number Series: 21 80 0080 351-354/356-366.

80 7287 400
80 7287 401
80 7287 402
80 7287 403
80 7287 404
80 7287 405
80 7287 406
80 7287 407
80 7287 408
80 7287 409
80 7287 410
80 7287 411
80 7287 412
80 7287 413
80 7287 414

80 7288 000 TANK IBA

Builder: BASF, Ludwigshafen, West Germany.
Design Code: IBE064(Ex ICE064). **Owner:** BASF.
Tare Weight: 15.42 t. **Gross Laden Weight:** 32.00 t.
Maximum Speed: 50 mph. **Length:** 9500 mm (31 ft. 2 in.)
Suspension Type: Single Link. **Exchange Code:** 23.
Notes: Used on various workings to and from Europe.
Previous Number: 21 80 0080 432.

80 7288 000

80 7289 000-004 TANK IBB

Builder: VTG, Hamburg, West Germany.
Design Code: IBE154(Ex ICE154). **Owner:** VTG.
Tare Weight: 12.50 t. **Gross Laden Weight:** 31.00 t.
Maximum Speed: 50 mph. **Length:** 8800 mm (28 ft. 10 in.)
Suspension Type: Single Link. **Exchange Code:** 23.
Notes: Not currently operating on British Rail.
Previous Number Series: 21 80 0780 258/287/293.

80 7289 000 80 7289 003 80 7289 004

80 7289 008-009 TANK IBX

Builder:
Design Code: IBE073(Ex ICE073). **Owner:** VTG.
Tare Weight: **Gross Laden Weight:**
Maximum Speed: 60 mph. **Length:**
Suspension Type: **Exchange Code:** 23.
Notes: Not currently operating on British Rail.
Previous Number Series: 21 80 0780 337/341.

80 7289 008 80 7289 009

80 7390 400-404 TANK IBX

Builder: Waggonfabrik Uerdingen, Krefeld, West Germany.
Design Code: IBE091(Ex ICE091). **Owner:** Danzas.
Tare Weight: 12.20 t. **Gross Laden Weight:** 40.00 t.
Maximum Speed: 60 mph. **Length:** 10740 mm (35 ft. 3 in.)
Suspension Type: Double Link. **Exchange Code:** 24.
Notes: Used on various workings to and from Europe.
Previous Number Series: 24 80 0085 500-504.

80 7390 400 80 7390 402 80 7390 403 80 7390 404
80 7390 401

80 7390 405 TANK IBX

Builder: Heinrich Wilhelm, West Germany.
Design Code: IBE289(Ex ICE289).
Tare Weight: 14.00 t.
Maximum Speed: 60 mph.
Suspension Type: Double Link.
Owner: Hibernia.
Gross Laden Weight: 40.00 t.
Length: 9040 mm (29 ft. 8 in.)
Exchange Code: 23.
Notes: Used on various workings to and from Europe.
Previous Number: 21 80 0085 153.

80 7390 405

80 7390 406-407 TANK IBB

Builder: Franz Kaminski, Hameln, West Germany.
Design Code: IBE323(Ex ICE323).
Tare Weight: 11.00 t.
Maximum Speed: 60 mph.
Suspension Type: Double Link.
Owner: Elektro.
Gross Laden Weight: 40.00 t.
Length: 8740 mm (28 ft. 8 in.)
Exchange Code: 23.
Notes: Used on various workings to and from Europe.
Previous Number Series: 21 80 0085 700-701.

80 7390 406
80 7390 407

80 7390 408-416 TANK IBB

Builder: Franz Kaminski, Hameln, West Germany, 1970.
Design Code: IBE340(Ex ICE340).
Tare Weight: 10.00 t.
Maximum Speed: 60 mph.
Suspension Type:
Owner: Elektro.
Gross Laden Weight: 40.00 t.
Length: 8740 mm (28 ft. 8 in.)
Exchange Code: 23.
Notes: Used on various workings to and from Europe.
Previous Number Series: 21 80 0085 702-710.

80 7390 408
80 7390 409
80 7390 410
80 7390 411
80 7390 412
80 7390 413
80 7390 414
80 7390 415
80 7390 416

80 7391 000-004 TANK IBB

Builder: VTG, Hamburg, West Germany.
Design Code: IBE273(Ex ICE273).
Tare Weight: 14.80 t.
Maximum Speed: 60 mph.
Suspension Type: Double Link.
Owner: VTG.
Gross Laden Weight: 40.00 t.
Length: 12300 mm (40 ft. 4 in.)
Exchange Code: 23.
Notes: Used on various workings to and from Europe.
Previous Number Series: 21 80 0785 100/101/107-109.

80 7391 000
80 7391 001
80 7391 002
80 7391 003
80 7391 004

80 7391 005-011 TANK IBB

Builder:
Design Code: IBE630(Ex ICE630)[a IBE731].
Owner: VTG.
Tare Weight: 14.80 t. **Gross Laden Weight:** 40.00 t.
Maximum Speed: 60 mph. **Length:** 12400 mm (40 ft. 8 in.)
Suspension Type: **Exchange Code:** 23.
Notes: Used on various workings to and from Europe.
Previous Number Series: 21 80 0785 112/114-118.

80 7391 005 80 7391 008 80 7391 010 80 7391 011
80 7391 007 80 7391 009

80 7391 012-013 TANK IBB

Builder:
Design Code: IBE321(Ex ICE321). **Owner:** Hauser.
Tare Weight: 11.40 t. **Gross Laden Weight:** 40.00 t.
Maximum Speed: 60 mph. **Length:** 8800 mm (28 ft. 10 in.)
Suspension Type: Double Link. **Exchange Code:** 23.
Notes: Not currently operating on British Rail.
Previous Number Series: 21 80 0785 119-120.

80 7391 012 80 7391 013

80 7391 014-016 TANK IBB

Builder:
Design Code: IBE641(Ex ICE641)[a IBE302 (Ex ICE302)].
Owner: VTG. **Tare Weight:** 13.50 t(a 11.00 t).
Gross Laden Weight: 40.00 t. **Maximum Speed:** 60 mph.
Length: 10800 mm (35 ft. 5 in.) a 8800 mm (28 ft. 10 in.)
Suspension Type: Double Link. **Exchange Code:** 23.
Notes: Used on various workings to and from Europe.
Previous Number Series: 21 80 0785 136/145.

80 7391 014 80 7391 016 a

80 7391 017-023 TANK IBB

Builder: Graaff Kommanditgesellschaft, Elze, West Germany.
Design Code: IBE355(Ex ICE355). **Owner:** VTG.
Tare Weight: 14.80 t. **Gross Laden Weight:** 40.00 t.
Maximum Speed: 50 mph. **Length:** 8800 mm (28 ft. 10 in.)
Suspension Type: Double Link. **Exchange Code:** 23.
Notes: On hire to Associated Octel. Used on various workings to and from Ellesmere Port.
Previous Number Series: 21 80 0785 166-172.

80 7391 017 80 7391 019 80 7391 021 80 7391 023
80 7391 018 80 7391 020 80 7391 022

80 7391 024-025 TANK IBB

Builder:
Design Code: IBE356(Ex ICE356).
Owner: VTG.
Tare Weight: 12.70 t.
Gross Laden Weight: 40.00 t.
Maximum Speed: 60 mph.
Length: 8800 mm (28 ft. 10 in.)
Suspension Type: Single Link.
Exchange Code: 23.
Notes: Not currently operating on British Rail.
Previous Number Series: 21 80 0785 173-174.

80 7391 024 80 7391 025

80 7391 026-034 TANK IBB

Builder: Graaff Kommanditgesellschaft, Elze, West Germany.
Design Code: IBE372(Ex ICE372).
Owner: VTG.
Tare Weight: 12.52 t.
Gross Laden Weight: 40.00 t.
Maximum Speed: 60 mph.
Length: 10400 mm (34 ft. 2 in.)
Suspension Type: Single Link.
Exchange Code: 23.
Notes: Used on various workings to and from Europe.
Previous Number Series: 21 80 0785 175-183.

80 7391 026
80 7391 027
80 7391 028
80 7391 029
80 7391 030
80 7391 031
80 7391 032
80 7391 033
80 7391 034

80 7391 035-045 TANK IBB

Builder:
Design Code: IBE374(Ex ICE374).
Owner: VTG.
Tare Weight: 13.00 t.
Gross Laden Weight: 39.00 t.
Maximum Speed: 60 mph.
Length: 10400 mm (34 ft. 1 in.)
Suspension Type:
Exchange Code: 23.
Notes: Used on various workings to and from Europe.
Previous Number Series: 21 80 0785 184-193.

80 7391 035
80 7391 036
80 7391 037
80 7391 038
80 7391 039
80 7391 040
80 7391 041
80 7391 042
80 7391 044
80 7391 045

80 7391 046 TANK IBA

Builder: Graaff Kommanditgesellschaft, Elze, West Germany.
Design Code: IBE378(Ex ICE378).
Owner: VTG.
Tare Weight: 14.00 t.
Gross Laden Weight: 40.00 t.
Maximum Speed: 60 mph.
Length: 11600 mm (38 ft. 1 in.)
Suspension Type: Single Link.
Exchange Code: 23.
Notes: Used on various workings to and from Europe.
Previous Number: 21 80 0785 194.

80 7391 046

80 7391 047-048 TANK IBB

Builder: Franz Kaminski, Hameln, West Germany.
Design Code: IBE447(Ex ICE447). **Owner:** VTG.
Tare Weight: 11.10 t. **Gross Laden Weight:** 40.00 t.
Maximum Speed: 60 mph. **Length:** 8800 mm (28 ft. 10 in.)
Suspension Type: Double Link. **Exchange Code:** 23.
Notes: Not currently operating on British Rail.
Previous Number Series: 21 80 0785 201-202.

80 7391 047 80 7391 048

80 7391 049-050 TANK IBB

Builder: Graaff Kommanditgesellschaft, Elze, West Germany, 1968-69.
Design Code: IBE355(Ex ICE355). **Owner:** VTG.
Tare Weight: 14.80 t. **Gross Laden Weight:** 40.00 t.
Maximum Speed: 50 mph. **Length:** 8800 mm (28 ft. 10 in.)
Suspension Type: Double Link. **Exchange Code:** 23.
Notes: On hire to Associated Octel. Used on various workings to and from Ellesmere Port.
Previous Number Series: 21 80 0785 146-148.

80 7391 049 80 7391 050 80 7391 051

80 7391 053-056 TANK IBB

Builder: Graaff Kommanditgesellschaft, Elze, West Germany, 1977.
Design Code: IBE469(Ex ICE469). **Owner:**
Tare Weight: 11.50 t. **Gross Laden Weight:** 40.00 t.
Maximum Speed: 60 mph. **Length:** 9800 mm (32 ft. 2 in.)
Suspension Type: Double Link. **Exchange Code:** 23.
Notes: Not currently operating on British Rail.

80 7391 053 80 7391 054 80 7391 055 80 7391 056

80 7391 057 TANK IBB

Builder: Linke Hofmann Busch. Salzgitter, West Germany, 1978.
Design Code: IBE489(Ex ICE489). **Owner:** VTG.
Tare Weight: 10.70 t. **Gross Laden Weight:** 40.00 t.
Maximum Speed: 60 mph. **Length:** 8800 mm (28 ft. 10 in.)
Suspension Type: Single Link. **Exchange Code:** 23.
Notes: Used on various workings to and from Europe.
Previous Number: 21 80 0785 228.

80 7391 057

80 7391 058-059 TANK IBA

Builder: Franz Kaminski, Hameln, West Germany, 1983.
Design Code: IBE563(Ex ICE563). **Owner:** VTG.
Tare Weight: 14.00 t. **Gross Laden Weight:** 40.00 t.

Maximum Speed: 60 mph. **Length:** 8800 mm (28 ft. 10 in.)
Suspension Type: Double Link. **Exchange Code:** 23.
Notes: Used on various workings to and from Europe.

80 7391 058 80 7391 059

80 7391 070 TANK IBA

Builder: VTG, Hamburg, West Germany, 1985.
Design Code: IBE588(Ex ICE588). **Owner:** VTG.
Tare Weight: 14.40 t. **Gross Laden Weight:** 40.00 t.
Maximum Speed: 60 mph. **Length:** 8740 mm (28 ft. 8 in.)
Suspension Type: Double Link. **Exchange Code:** 23.
Notes: Not currently operating on British Rail.

80 7391 070

80 7391 400-402 TANK IBX

Builder: Franz Kaminski, Hameln, West Germany.
Design Code: IBE274(Ex ICE274). **Owner:** Eva.
Tare Weight: 14.80 t. **Gross Laden Weight:** 40.00 t.
Maximum Speed: 60 mph. **Length:** 8740 mm (28 ft. 8 in.)
Suspension Type: Double Link. **Exchange Code:** 23.
Notes: Used on various workings to and from Europe.
Previous Number Series: 21 80 0785 997-999.

80 7391 400 80 7391 401 80 7391 402

80 7391 700-702 TANK IBA

Builder: **Owner:** Huls Chemicals.
Design Code: IBE109(Ex ICE109)[a IBE110 (Ex ICE110), b IBE111 (Ex ICE111)].
Tare Weight: 11.30 t(a 10.65 t, b 13.60 t). **Gross Laden Weight:** 40.00 t.
Maximum Speed: 60 mph. **Length:** 8740 mm (28 ft. 8 in.)
Suspension Type: Double Link. **Exchange Code:** 23.
Notes: ICE111 is coded IBB. Used on various workings to and from Europe.
Previous Number Series: 21 80 0085 154/155/157.

80 7391 700 80 7391 701 a 80 7391 702 b

80 7391 703-707 TANK IBB

Builder: Graaff Kommanditgesellschaft, Elze, West Germany.
Design Code: IBE336(Ex ICE336). **Owner:** Kon Oil.
Tare Weight: 12.40 t. **Gross Laden Weight:** 40.00 t.
Maximum Speed: 60 mph. **Length:** 9940 mm (32 ft. 7 in.)
Suspension Type: **Exchange Code:** 23.
Notes: Used on various workings to and from Europe.
Previous Number Series: 21 80 0785 885-889.

80 7391 703
80 7391 704
80 7391 705 80 7391 706 80 7391 707

Medium Van 43 80 2396 065 at Hoo Junction on 16th September 1984. *(R. Wallace)*

Flat 83 80 4736 107 at Warrington on 21st April 1990. *(R. Wallace)*

80 7391 708-717 TANK IBB

Builder: Graaff Kommanditgesellschaft, Elze, West Germany.
Design Code: IBE317(Ex ICE317). **Owner:** Continental Oil.
Tare Weight: 12.40 t. **Gross Laden Weight:** 40.00 t.
Maximum Speed: 60 mph. **Length:** 10000 mm (32 ft. 10 in.)
Suspension Type: Double Link. **Exchange Code:** 23.
Notes: Used on various workings to and from Europe.
Previous Number Series: 21 80 0785 890-897/899.

80 7391 708
80 7391 709
80 7391 710
80 7391 711
80 7391 712
80 7391 713
80 7391 714
80 7391 715
80 7391 717

80 7391 718-720 TANK IBB

Builder: BASF, Ludwigshafen, West Germany.
Design Code: IBE141(Ex ICE141). **Owner:** BASF.
Tare Weight: 10.50 t. **Gross Laden Weight:** 33.00 t.
Maximum Speed: 50 mph. **Length:** 8740 mm (28 ft. 8 in.)
Suspension Type: Double Link. **Exchange Code:** 23.
Notes: Used on various workings to and from Europe.
Previous Number Series: 21 80 0085 400-402.

80 7391 718
80 7391 719
80 7391 720

80 7391 721 TANK IBB

Builder: BASF, Ludwigshafen, West Germany.
Design Code: IBE038(Ex ICE038). **Owner:** BASF.
Tare Weight: 13.50 t. **Gross Laden Weight:** 40.00 t.
Maximum Speed: 60 mph. **Length:** 8740 mm (28 ft. 8 in.)
Suspension Type: Single link. **Exchange Code:** 23.
Notes: Used on various workings to and from Europe.
Previous Number: 21 80 0085 406.

80 7391 721

80 7393 000-009 TANK IBA

Builder: Graaff Kommanditgesellschaft, Elze, West Germany, 1984.
Design Code: IBE571(Ex ICE571). **Owner:** VTG.
Tare Weight: 12.50 t. **Gross Laden Weight:** 40.00 t.
Maximum Speed: 75 mph. **Length:** 9300 mm (30 ft. 6 in.)
Suspension Type: Double Link. **Exchange Code:** 24.
Notes: Not currently operating on British Rail.

80 7393 000
80 7393 001
80 7393 002
80 7393 003
80 7393 004
80 7393 005
80 7393 006
80 7393 007
80 7393 008
80 7393 009

80 7394 000-001 TANK IBB

Builder: VTG, Hamburg, West Germany.
Design Code: IBE307(Ex ICE307). **Owner:** VTG.
Tare Weight: 14.00 t. **Gross Laden Weight:** 40.00 t.
Maximum Speed: 60 mph. **Length:** 9500 mm (31 ft. 2 in.)
Suspension Type: Double Link. **Exchange Code:** 23.
Notes: Not currently operating on British Rail.
Previous Number Series: 21 80 0785 050-051.

80 7394 000 80 7394 001

80 7394 002-009 TANK IBB

Builder: Graaff Kommanditgesellschaft, Elze, West Germany, 1965.
Design Code: IBE633 (Ex ICE633). **Owner:** VTG.
Tare Weight: **Gross Laden Weight:**
Maximum Speed: 60 mph. **Length:**
Suspension Type: **Exchange Code:** 23.
Notes: On hire to ICI Mond and used on various workings between Runcorn and Europe.

80 7394 002	80 7394 004	80 7394 006	80 7394 008
80 7394 003	80 7394 005	80 7394 007	80 7394 009

80 7394 010-019 TANK IBB

Builder: Linke Hoffman Busch, Salzgitter, West Germany, 1979.
Design Code: IBE509(Ex ICE509). **Owner:** VTG.
Tare Weight: 12.30 t. **Gross Laden Weight:** 40.00 t.
Maximum Speed: 60 mph. **Length:** 8800 mm (28 ft 8 in).
Suspension Type: Double Link. **Exchange Code:** 23.
Notes: Not currently operating on British Rail.
Previous Number Series: 21 80 0785 064-073.

80 7394 010	80 7394 013	80 7394 016	80 7394 018
80 7394 011	80 7394 014	80 7394 017	80 7394 019
80 7394 012	80 7394 015		

80 7394 400 TANK IBX

Builder: Waggonfabrik Uerdingen, Krefeld, West Germany, 1979.
Design Code: IBE200(Ex ICE200). **Owner:** Eva.
Tare Weight: 14.00 t. **Gross Laden Weight:** 31.00 t.
Maximum Speed: 60 mph. **Length:** 9660 mm (31 ft 9 in).
Suspension Type: Double Link. **Exchange Code:** 23.
Notes: Used on various workings to and from Europe.
Previous Number: 21 80 0785 991.

80 7394 400

80 7395 000-001 TANK IBB

Builder:
Design Code: IBE224(Ex ICE200).
Owner: Huls Chemicals.
Tare Weight: 14.00 t.
Gross Laden Weight: 37.00 t.
Maximum Speed: 50 mph.
Length: 8740 mm (28 ft 8 in).
Suspension Type: Double Link.
Exchange Code: 23.
Notes: Used on various workings to and from Europe.
Previous Number Series: 21 80 0085 150-151.

80 7395 000 80 7395 001

80 7395 002-005 TANK IBA

Builder: Waggonfabrik Uerdingen, Krefeld, West Germany.
Design Code: IBE217(Ex ICE200).
Owner: ICI.
Tare Weight: 15.50 t.
Gross Laden Weight: 26.00 t.
Maximum Speed: 60 mph.
Length: 8740 mm (28 ft 8 in).
Suspension Type: Double Link.
Exchange Code: 23.
Notes: Used on various workings to and from Europe.
Previous Number Series: 21 80 0085 152/158-160.

80 7395 002 80 7395 003 80 7395 004 80 7395 005

80 7395 400-405 TANK IBA

Builder: Waggonfabrik Uerdingen, Krefeld, West Germany, 1986.
Design Code: IBE594(Ex ICE594).
Owner: ICI.
Tare Weight: 13.50 t.
Gross Laden Weight: 40.00 t.
Maximum Speed: 60 mph.
Length: 9660 mm (31 ft 9 in).
Suspension Type: Double Link.
Exchange Code: 23.
Notes: Used on various workings to and from Europe.

80 7395 400 80 7395 402 80 7395 404 80 7395 405
80 7395 401 80 7395 403

80 7397 000 TANK IBB

Builder: Graaff Kommanditgesellschaft, Elze, West Germany.
Design Code: IBE357(Ex ICE357).
Owner: Eva.
Tare Weight: 12.50 t.
Gross Laden Weight: 40.00 t.
Maximum Speed: 60 mph.
Length: 8800 mm (28 ft. 10 in.)
Suspension Type:
Exchange Code: 23.
Notes: Used on various workings to and from Europe.
Previous Number: 21 80 0785 879.

80 7397 000

80 7397 001-005 TANK IBB

Builder: Graaff Kommanditgesellschaft, Elze, West Germany.
Design Code: IBE335(Ex ICE335).
Owner: Eva.

Tare Weight: 12.50 t.
Gross Laden Weight: 40.00 t.
Maximum Speed: 60 mph.
Length: 8800 mm (28 ft. 10 in.)
Suspension Type: Double Link.
Exchange Code: 23.
Notes: Used on various workings to and from Europe.
Previous Number Series: 21 80 0785 880-884.

80 7397 001
80 7397 002
80 7397 003
80 7397 004
80 7397 005

80 7397 400-402 TANK IBB

Builder:
Design Code: IBE638(Ex ICE638)[a IBE444(exICE444), b IBE283(ICE283)].
Owner: Eva.
Tare Weight: 11.20 t(a 11.00 t, b 14.80 t).
Gross Laden Weight: 40.00 t.
Maximum Speed: 60 mph.
Length: 10800 mm (35 ft. 5 in.)[a 9800 mm (32 ft 2 in), b 8800 mm (28 ft 11 in.)].
Suspension Type: Double Link.
Exchange Code: 23.
Notes: Used on various workings to and from Europe.
Previous Number Series: 21 80 0085 403/405/407.

80 7397 400
80 7397 401 a
80 7397 402 b

80 7398 000 TANK IBB

Builder: VTG, Hamburg, West Germany.
Design Code: IBE351(Ex ICE351).
Owner: VTG.
Tare Weight: 13.40 t.
Gross Laden Weight: 40.00 t.
Maximum Speed: 60 mph.
Length: 10800 mm (35 ft. 5 in.)
Suspension Type: Double Link.
Exchange Code: 23.
Notes: Not currently operating on British Rail.
Previous Number: 21 80 0785 061.

80 7398 000

80 7398 001-005 TANK IBB

Builder: VTG, Hamburg, West Germany.
Design Code: IBE273(Ex ICE273).
Owner: VTG.
Tare Weight: 14.80 t.
Gross Laden Weight: 40.00 t.
Maximum Speed: 60 mph.
Length: 12300 mm (40 ft. 4 in.)
Suspension Type: Double Link.
Exchange Code: 23.
Notes: Used on various workings to and from Europe.
Previous Number Series: 21 80 0785 102-106.

80 7398 001
80 7398 002
80 7398 003
80 7398 004
80 7398 005

80 7398 006-007 TANK IBB

Builder: VTG, Hamburg, West Germany.
Design Code: IBE281(Ex ICE281).
Owner: VTG.
Tare Weight: 12.50 t.
Gross Laden Weight: 40.00 t.
Maximum Speed: 60 mph.
Length: 10800 mm (35 ft. 5 in.)

Suspension Type: Double Link. **Exchange Code:** 23.
Notes: Not currently operating on British Rail.
Previous Number Series: 21 80 0785 110-111.

80 7398 006 80 7398 007

80 7398 016-024 TANK IBB

Builder:
Design Code: IBE641(Ex ICE641). **Owner:** VTG.
Tare Weight: 13.50 t. **Gross Laden Weight:** 40.00 t.
Maximum Speed: 60 mph. **Length:** 10800 mm (35 ft. 5 in.)
Suspension Type: Double Link. **Exchange Code:** 23.
Notes: 020 is the only vehicle currently operating on British Rail.
Previous Number Series: 21 80 0785 131/133-140

80 7398 016 80 7398 019 80 7398 021 80 7398 023
80 7398 018 80 7398 020 80 7398 022 80 7398 024

80 7398 027-036 TANK IBB

Builder: Linke Hoffman Busch, Salzgitter, West Germany, 1974.
Design Code: IBE451(Ex ICE451). **Owner:** VTG.
Tare Weight: 13.40 t. **Gross Laden Weight:** 40.00 t.
Maximum Speed: 60 mph. **Length:** 11300 mm (37 ft. 1 in.)
Suspension Type: Double Link. **Exchange Code:** 23.
Notes: 030/034/035 are on hire to Dow Chemicals.
Previous Number Series: 21 80 0785 203-212.

80 7398 027 80 7398 030 80 7398 033 80 7398 035
80 7398 028 80 7398 031 80 7398 034 80 7398 036
80 7398 029 80 7398 032

80 7398 037-046 TANK IBB

Builder: Graaff Kommanditgesellschaft, Elze, West Germany.
Design Code: IBE463(Ex ICE463). **Owner:** VTG.
Tare Weight: 12.00 t. **Gross Laden Weight:** 40.00 t.
Maximum Speed: 60 mph. **Length:** 9800 mm (32 ft. 2 in.)
Suspension Type: Double Link. **Exchange Code:** 23.
Notes: Not currently operating on British Rail.
Previous Number Series: 21 80 0785 213-222.

80 7398 037 80 7398 040 80 7398 043 80 7398 045
80 7398 038 80 7398 041 80 7398 044 80 7398 046
80 7398 039 80 7398 042

80 7398 047 TANK IBB

Builder: Graaff Kommanditgesellschaft, Elze, West Germany, 1976.
Design Code: IBE469(Ex ICE469). **Owner:** VTG.
Tare Weight: 11.50 t. **Gross Laden Weight:** 40.00 t.
Maximum Speed: 60 mph. **Length:** 9740 mm (31 ft. 11 in.)

Suspension Type: Single Link. **Exchange Code:** 23.
Notes: Not currently operating on British Rail.
Previous Number: 21 80 0785 223.

80 7398 047

80 7398 053-062 TANK IBB

Builder: Graaff Kommanditgesellschaft, Elze, West Germany, 1979.
Design Code: IBE500(Ex ICE500). **Owner:** VTG.
Tare Weight: 13.00 t. **Gross Laden Weight:** 40.00 t.
Maximum Speed: 60 mph. **Length:** 11100 mm (36 ft. 5 in.)
Suspension Type: Double Link. **Exchange Code:** 23.
Notes: Not currently operating on British Rail.
Previous Number Series: 21 80 0785 229-238.

80 7398 053	80 7398 056	80 7398 059	80 7398 061
80 7398 054	80 7398 057	80 7398 060	80 7398 062
80 7398 055	80 7398 058		

80 7398 066-077 TANK IBA

Builder: Linke Hoffman Busch, Salzgitter, West Germany, 1984.
Design Code: IBE547(Ex ICE547)[a IBE572(Ex ICE572)].
Owner: VTG. **Tare Weight:** 14.00 t. (a 13.00 t).
Gross Laden Weight: 40.00 t. **Maximum Speed:** 60 mph.
Length: 8800 mm (28 ft. 11 in.)
Suspension Type: Double Link (a Single Link).
Exchange Code: 23.
Notes: Used on various workings to and from Europe.

80 7398 066 80 7398 077 a

80 7398 400 TANK IBB

Builder: Deutsche Bundesbahn, Minden, West Germany.
Design Code: IBE371(Ex ICE371). **Owner:** Eva.
Tare Weight: 12.50 t. **Gross Laden Weight:** 40.00 t.
Maximum Speed: 60 mph. **Length:** 9700 mm (31 ft. 10 in.)
Suspension Type: Single Link. **Exchange Code:** 23.
Notes: Used on various workings to and from Europe.
Previous Number: 21 80 0785 873.

80 7398 400

80 7398 401-405 TANK IBB

Builder: Graaff Kommanditgesellschaft, Elze, West Germany.
Design Code: IBE336(Ex ICE336). **Owner:** Continental Oil.
Tare Weight: 12.40 t. **Gross Laden Weight:** 40.00 t.
Maximum Speed: 60 mph. **Length:** 10000 mm (32 ft. 10 in.)
Suspension Type: Double Link. **Exchange Code:** 23.
Notes: Used on various workings to and from Europe.
Previous Number Series: 21 80 0785 874-878.

80 7398 401 80 7398 403 80 7398 404 80 7398 405
80 7398 402

80 7398 600 TANK IBB

Builder: Huls Chemicals, Recklinghausen, West Germany.
Design Code: IBE112(Ex ICE112). **Owner:** Huls Chemicals.
Tare Weight: 13.30 t. **Gross Laden Weight:** 40.00 t.
Maximum Speed: 60 mph. **Length:** 8740 mm (28 ft. 8 in.)
Suspension Type: Double Link. **Exchange Code:** 23.
Notes: Used on various workings to and from Europe.
Previous Number: 21 80 0085 156.

80 7398 600

80 7398 601-602 TANK IBA

Builder:
Design Code: IBE002(Ex ICE002) [a IBE227(Ex ICE227)].
Owner: BASF. **Tare Weight:** 14.00 t (a 12.30 t).
Gross Laden Weight: 32.00 t (a 40.00 t). **Maximum Speed:** 50 mph (a 60 mph).
Length: 9500 mm (31 ft. 2 in.)[a 8800 mm (28 ft 11 in).
Suspension Type: Single Link. **Exchange Code:** 23.
Notes: Used on various workings to and from Europe.
Previous Number Series: 21 80 0085 404/408.

80 7398 601 80 7398 602 a

80 7398 603 TANK IBB

Builder: Graaff Kommanditgesellschaft, Elze, West Germany.
Design Code: IBE319(Ex ICE319). **Owner:** Continental Oil.
Tare Weight: 11.80 t. **Gross Laden Weight:** 40.00 t.
Maximum Speed: 60 mph. **Length:** 9500 mm (31 ft. 2 in.)
Suspension Type: Double Link. **Exchange Code:** 23.
Notes: Used on various workings to and from Europe.

80 7398 603

80 7490 000-002 TANK IBB

Builder: Huls Chemicals, Recklinghausen, West Germany.
Design Code: IBE008(Ex ICE008)[a IBE600(Ex ICE600)].
Owner: Huls Chemicals. **Tare Weight:** 10.60 t.
Gross Laden Weight: 33.00 t. **Maximum Speed:** 60 mph.
Length: 8800 mm (28 ft. 10 in.) **Suspension Type:** Single Link.
Exchange Code: 23.
Notes: IBE600 is coded IBA. Used on various workings to and from Europe.
Previous Number Series: 21 80 0085 163-165.

80 7490 000 80 7490 001 80 7490 002 a

80 7491 000-012 TANK IBB

Builder: VTG, Hamburg, West Germany, 1968.
Design Code: IBE355(Ex ICE355). **Owner:** VTG.
Tare Weight: 14.80 t. **Gross Laden Weight:** 40.00 t.
Maximum Speed: 50 mph. **Length:** 8800 mm (28 ft. 10 in.)
Suspension Type: Double Link. **Exchange Code:** 23.
Notes: Used on various workings between Ellesmere Port and Europe.
Previous Number Series: 21 80 0785 153-165.

80 7491 000	80 7491 004	80 7491 007	80 7491 010
80 7491 001	80 7491 005	80 7491 008	80 7491 011
80 7491 002	80 7491 006	80 7491 009	80 7491 012
80 7491 003			

80 7491 013-017 TANK IBA

Builder: Franz Kaminski, Hameln, West Germany, 1984.
Design Code: IBE577(Ex ICE577). **Owner:** VTG.
Tare Weight: 15.70 t. **Gross Laden Weight:** 40.00 t.
Maximum Speed: 60 mph. **Length:** 8800 mm (28 ft. 10 in.)
Suspension Type: Double Link. **Exchange Code:** 23.
Notes: Not currently operating on British Rail.

80 7491 013	80 7491 015	80 7491 016	80 7491 017
80 7491 014			

80 7490 400-401 TANK IBX

Builder: Huls Chemicals, Recklinghausen, West Germany.
Design Code: IBE243(Ex ICE243). **Owner:** Huls Chemicals.
Tare Weight: 10.80 t. **Gross Laden Weight:** 33.00 t.
Maximum Speed: 60 mph. **Length:** 8800 mm (28 ft. 10 in.)
Suspension Type: Single Link. **Exchange Code:** 23.
Notes: Used on various workings to and from Europe.
Previous Number Series: 21 80 0085 161/2.

80 7491 400	80 7490 401

80 7492 000-002 TANK IBB

Builder: VTG, Hamburg, West Germany.
Design Code: IBE350(Ex ICE350). **Owner:** VTG.
Tare Weight: 14.00 t. **Gross Laden Weight:** 39.00 t.
Maximum Speed: 60 mph. **Length:** 9500 mm (31 ft. 2 in.)
Suspension Type: Double Link. **Exchange Code:** 23.
Notes: Not currently operating on British Rail.
Previous Number Series: 21 80 0785 060/062/063.

80 7492 000	80 7492 001	80 7492 002

80 7495 000-009 TANK IBA

Builder: Graaff Kommanditgesellschaft, Elze, West Germany, 1983.
Design Code: IBE564(Ex ICE564).
Owner: VTG.
Tare Weight: 12.00 t.
Gross Laden Weight: 40.00 t.
Maximum Speed: 75 mph.
Length: 9300 mm (30 ft. 6 in.)
Suspension Type: Double Link.
Exchange Code: 24.
Notes: Not currently operating on British Rail.

80 7495 000	80 7495 003	80 7495 006	80 7495 008
80 7495 001	80 7495 004	80 7495 007	80 7495 009
80 7495 002	80 7495 005		

80 7495 010-019 TANK IBA

Builder: Graaff Kommanditgesellschaft, Elze, West Germany, 1984.
Design Code: IBE580(Ex ICE580).
Owner: VTG.
Tare Weight: 11.30 t.
Gross Laden Weight: 40.00 t.
Maximum Speed: 75 mph.
Length: 9300 mm (30 ft. 6 in.)
Suspension Type: Double Link.
Exchange Code: 23.
Notes: Not currently operating on British Rail.

80 7495 010	80 7495 013	80 7495 016	80 7495 018
80 7495 011	80 7495 014	80 7495 017	80 7495 019
80 7495 012	80 7495 015		

80 7495 020-022 TANK IBA

Builder: Franz Kaminski, Hameln, West Germany, 1987.
Design Code: IBE687(Ex ICE687).
Owner: VTG.
Tare Weight: 15.00 t.
Gross Laden Weight: 45.00 t.
Maximum Speed: 60 mph.
Length: 9800 mm (32 ft. 2 in.)
Suspension Type: Double Link.
Exchange Code: 23.
Notes: Used on various workings to and from Europe.

80 7495 020	80 7495 021	80 7495 022

80 7497 000-009 TANK IBA

Builder: Graaff Kommanditgesellschaft, Elze, West Germany, 1983.
Design Code: IBE558(Ex ICE558).
Owner: VTG.
Tare Weight: 13.00 t.
Gross Laden Weight: 40.00 t.
Maximum Speed: 75 mph.
Length: 9300 mm (30 ft. 6 in.)
Suspension Type: Double Link.
Exchange Code: 23.
Notes: Not currently operating on British Rail.
Previous Number Series: 24 80 7398 067-076.

80 7497 000	80 7497 003	80 7497 006	80 7497 008
80 7497 001	80 7497 004	80 7497 007	80 7497 009
80 7497 002	80 7497 005		

80 7498 000-003 TANK IBB

Builder:
Design Code: IBE634(Ex ICE634). **Owner:** VTG.
Tare Weight: 15.50 t. **Gross Laden Weight:** 40.00 t.
Maximum Speed: 60 mph. **Length:** 12300 mm (40 ft. 4 in.)
Suspension Type: Double Link. **Exchange Code:** 23.
Notes: Not currently operating on British Rail.
Previous Number Series: 21 80 0785 149-152.

80 7498 000 80 7498 001 80 7498 002 80 7498 003

80 7793 000-019 TANK ICA

Builder: Linke Hofmann Busch, Salzgitter, West Germany, 1986-87.
Design Code: ICE674. **Owner:** VTG.
Tare Weight: 25.60 t. **Gross Laden Weight:** 90.00 t.
Maximum Speed: 60 mph. **Length:** 15800 mm (51 ft. 11 in.)
Bogie Type: DB WU80. **Exchange Code:** 33.
Notes: Not currently operating on British Rail.

80 7793 000	80 7793 005	80 7793 010	80 7793 015
80 7793 001	80 7793 006	80 7793 011	80 7793 016
80 7793 002	80 7793 007	80 7793 012	80 7793 017
80 7793 003	80 7793 008	80 7793 013	80 7793 018
80 7793 004	80 7793 009	80 7793 014	80 7793 019

80 7794 000-004 TANK ICB

Builder: Waggon Union, Siegen, West Germany, 1984.
Design Code: ICE534. **Owner:** VTG.
Tare Weight: 25.50 t. **Gross Laden Weight:** 80.00 t.
Maximum Speed: 60 mph. **Length:** 14900 mm (48 ft. 10 in.)
Bogie Type: Waggon Union. **Exchange Code:** 33.
Notes: Used on workings between Barry and Europe.
Previous number Series: 33 80 7891 200-204.

80 7794 000 80 7794 002 80 7794 003 80 7794 004
80 7794 001

80 7794 015-016 TANK ICA

Builder: Linke Hofmann Busch, Salzgitter, West Germany, 1987.
Design Code: ICE681. **Owner:** VTG.
Tare Weight: 25.00 t. **Gross Laden Weight:** 80.00 t.
Maximum Speed: 60 mph. **Length:** 14800 mm (48 ft. 7 in.)
Bogie Type: DB standard. **Exchange Code:** 33.
Notes: Used on workings between Barry and Europe.

80 7794 015 80 7794 016

80 7794 027-036 TANK ICA

Builder: Linke Hofmann Busch, Salzgitter, West Germany, 1987.
Design Code: ICE679. **Owner:** VTG.
Tare Weight: 32.50 t. **Gross Laden Weight:** 90.00 t.
Maximum Speed: 60 mph. **Length:** 19650 mm (64 ft. 6 in.)
Bogie Type: LHB 82. **Exchange Code:** 33.
Notes: On hire to ICIA, used on workings between Haverton Hill and Europe.

80 7794 027
80 7794 028
80 7794 029
80 7794 030
80 7794 035
80 7794 036

80 7891 002-003 TANK ICB

Builder: Waggon Union, Siegen, West Germany, 1981.
Design Code: ICE527. **Owner:** VTG.
Tare Weight: 27.30 t. **Gross Laden Weight:** 80.00 t.
Maximum Speed: 60 mph. **Length:** 15600 mm (51 ft. 2 in.)
Bogie Type: DB BA661.1. **Exchange Code:** 33.
Notes: Used on various workings to and from Europe.

80 7891 002
80 7891 003

80 7891 205-207 TANK ICA

Builder: Waggon Union, Siegen, West Germany, 1981.
Design Code: ICE730. **Owner:** VTG.
Tare Weight: 30.20 t. **Gross Laden Weight:** 80.00 t.
Maximum Speed: 60 mph. **Length:** 18900 mm (62 ft. 0 in.)
Bogie Type: DB BA661.1. **Exchange Code:** 33.
Notes: On hire to ICIA, used on workings between Haverton Hill and Europe.

80 7891 002
80 7891 003

80 7892 000-036 TANK ICB

Builder: Waggon Union, Siegen, West Germany.
Design Code: ICE467. **Owner:** VTG.
Tare Weight: 30.20 t. **Gross Laden Weight:** 80.00 t.
Maximum Speed: 60 mph. **Length:** 18000 mm (62 ft. 0 in.)
Bogie Type: **Exchange Code:** 33.
Notes: Used on workings between Barry and Europe and also between King's Lynn and Terneuzen.
Previous Number Series: 21 80 0798 000-010/013 & 33 80 7895 000.

80 7892 000
80 7892 001
80 7892 002
80 7892 003
80 7892 004
80 7892 005
80 7892 006
80 7892 007
80 7892 008
80 7892 009
80 7892 010
80 7892 013
80 7892 036

Sliding Roof Van 21 80 5795 000 at Hoo Junction on 14th February 1988. *(R. Wallace)*

Tank 23 80 7391 053 at Dewsbury on 26th January 1986. *(R. Wallace)*

80 7894 011-019 TANK ICB

Builder: Waggon Union, Siegen, West Germany.
Design Code: ICE467.
Owner: VTG.
Tare Weight: 30.20 t.
Gross Laden Weight: 80.00 t.
Maximum Speed: 60 mph.
Length: 18900 mm (62 ft. 0 in.)
Bogie Type:
Exchange Code: 33.
Notes: 011 is on hire to Associated Octel, working between Ellesmere Port and Biebesheim. 019 is used on various workings to and from Europe.
Previous Number Series: 33 80 7892 027/035.

80 7894 011 80 7894 019

80 7895 010-012 TANK ICB

Builder: Linke Hofmann Busch, Salzgitter, West Germany, 1979.
Design Code: ICE508.
Owner: VTG.
Tare Weight: 27.50 t.
Gross Laden Weight: 80.00 t.
Maximum Speed: 60 mph.
Length: 14400 mm (47 ft. 3 in.)
Bogie Type: LHB77.
Exchange Code: 33.
Notes: Used on various workings to and from Europe.
Previous Number Series: 21 80 0798 053-055.

80 7895 010 80 7895 011 80 7895 012

80 7895 400-401 TANK ICB

Builder: Stalwerke Brunighaus, West Germany, 1980.
Design Code: ICE517.
Owner: Eva.
Tare Weight: 26.80 t.
Gross Laden Weight: 80.00 t.
Maximum Speed: 60 mph.
Length: 15600 mm (51 ft. 2 in.)
Bogie Type: DB BA661.1.
Exchange Code: 33.
Notes: Used on various workings to and from Europe.

80 7895 400 80 7895 401

80 7897 000-019 TANK ICA

Builder: Linke Hofmann Busch, Salzgitter, West Germany, 1984.
Design Code: ICE579.
Owner: VTG.
Tare Weight: 22.20 t.
Gross Laden Weight: 90.00 t.
Maximum Speed: 75 mph.
Length: 14400 mm (47 ft. 3 in.)
Bogie Type: LHB78.
Exchange Code: 34.
Notes: Not currently operating on British Rail.

80 7897 000
80 7897 001
80 7897 002
80 7897 003
80 7897 004
80 7897 005
80 7897 006
80 7897 007
80 7897 008
80 7897 009
80 7897 010
80 7897 011
80 7897 012
80 7897 013
80 7897 014
80 7897 015
80 7897 016
80 7897 017
80 7897 018
80 7897 019

80 7899 000-009 TANK ICA

Builder: Franz Kaminski, Hameln, West Germany.
Design Code: ICE676.
Tare Weight: 23.30 t.
Maximum Speed: 60 mph.
Bogie Type: LHB82.
Owner: VTG.
Gross Laden Weight: 80.00 t.
Length: 17900 mm (58 ft. 9 in.)
Exchange Code: 34.
Notes: Used on various workings to and from Europe.

80 7899 000
80 7899 001
80 7899 002
80 7899 003
80 7899 004
80 7899 005
80 7899 006
80 7899 007
80 7899 008
80 7899 009

80 7934 000-002 TANK ICA

Builder:
Design Code: ICE713.
Tare Weight: 24.70 t.
Maximum Speed: 50 mph.
Bogie Type:
Owner: VTG.
Gross Laden Weight: 80.00 t.
Length: 14300 mm (46 ft. 11 in.)
Exchange Code: 33.
Notes: Used on workings between Roosendaal and Langley Green.

80 7934 000
80 7934 001
80 7934 002

80 7934 003 TANK ICA

Builder:
Design Code: ICE709.
Tare Weight: 24.70 t.
Maximum Speed: 50 mph.
Bogie Type:
Owner: VTG.
Gross Laden Weight: 80.00 t.
Length: 14300 mm (46 ft. 11 in.)
Exchange Code: 33.
Notes: Used on workings between Roosendaal and Langley Green.

80 7934 003

80 7934 006 TANK ICA

Builder:
Design Code: ICE711.
Tare Weight: 24.30 t.
Maximum Speed: 60 mph.
Bogie Type:
Owner: VTG.
Gross Laden Weight: 80.00 t.
Length: 14400 mm (47 ft. 3 in.)
Exchange Code: 33.
Notes: Used on workings between Roosendaal and Langley Green.

80 7934 006

80 7934 007 TANK ICA

Builder:
Design Code: ICE717.
Tare Weight: 24.30 t.
Maximum Speed: 60 mph.
Owner: VTG.
Gross Laden Weight: 80.00 t.
Length: 14400 mm (47 ft. 3 in.)

Bogie Type: **Exchange Code:** 33.
Notes: Used on workings between Roosendaal and Langley Green.

80 7934 007

80 7934 400-404 TANK ICA

Builder:
Design Code: ICE712(a ICE714, b ICE716).
Owner: VTG.
Tare Weight: 23.90 t.
Gross Laden Weight: 80.00 t.
Maximum Speed: 60 mph.
Length: 14400 mm (47 ft. 3 in.)
Bogie Type:
Exchange Code: 33.
Notes: Used on workings between Roosendaal and Langley Green.

80 7934 400	80 7934 402	80 7934 403	80 7934 404 b
80 7934 401 a			

80 7995 000-002 TANK ICB

Builder: Linke Hofmann Busch, Salzgitter, West Germany.
Design Code: ICE472.
Owner: VTG.
Tare Weight: 24.60 t.
Gross Laden Weight: 80.00 t.
Maximum Speed: 60 mph.
Length: 14400 mm (47 ft. 3 in.)
Bogie Type: DB standard.
Exchange Code: 33.
Notes: Used on workings between Roosendaal and Langley Green.
Previous Number Series: 21 80 0798 050-052.

80 7995 000	80 7995 001	80 7995 002

80 7995 003-012 TANK ICA

Builder: Linke Hofmann Busch, Salzgitter, West Germany, 1979.
Design Code: ICE511.
Owner: VTG.
Tare Weight: 23.70 t.
Gross Laden Weight: 80.00 t.
Maximum Speed: 60 mph.
Length: 17900 mm (58 ft. 9 in.)
Bogie Type: LHB77.
Exchange Code: 33.
Notes: 80 7995 003-007/009, are on hire to Kelvin and are used on workings between Fawley and Terneuzen, others are used on various workings to and from Europe.

80 7995 003	80 7995 006	80 7995 009	80 7995 011
80 7995 004	80 7995 007	80 7995 010	80 7995 012
80 7995 005	80 7995 008		

80 7995 500-515 TANK ICB

Builder: C.F.M.F, 1981.
Design Code: ICE524.
Owner: VTG.
Tare Weight: 22.10 t.
Gross Laden Weight: 80.00 t.
Maximum Speed: 60 mph.
Length: 15680 mm (51 ft. 5 in.)
Bogie Type: Talbot.
Exchange Code: 33.
Notes: Used on various workings to and from Europe.

80 7995 500	80 7995 504	80 7995 508	80 7995 512
80 7995 501	80 7995 505	80 7995 509	80 7995 513
80 7995 502	80 7995 506	80 7995 510	80 7995 514
80 7995 503	80 7995 507	80 7995 511	80 7995 515

80 7996 000 TANK ICA

Builder: Linke Hofmann Busch, Salzgitter, West Germany, 1984.
Design Code: ICE565. **Owner:** VTG.
Tare Weight: 24.20 t. **Gross Laden Weight:** 80.00 t.
Maximum Speed: 75 mph. **Length:** 14100 mm (46 ft. 3 in.)
Bogie Type: DB standard. **Exchange Code:** 33.
Notes: Used on various workings to and from Europe.

80 7996 000

80 7996 001-010 TANK ICA

Builder: Graaff Kommanditgesellschaft, Elze, West Germany, 1989.
Design Code: ICE718. **Owner:** CAIB.
Tare Weight: 25.00 t. **Gross Laden Weight:** 80.00 t.
Maximum Speed: 60 mph. **Length:** 14460 mm (47 ft. 5 in.)
Bogie Type: **Exchange Code:** 33.
Notes: Used on workings between Roosendaal and Langley Green.

80 7996 001	80 7996 004	80 7996 007	80 7996 009
80 7996 002	80 7996 005	80 7996 008	80 7996 010
80 7996 003	80 7996 006		

80 7998 000-004 TANK ICB

Builder: Waggon Union, Siegen, West Germany, 1980.
Design Code: ICE519. **Owner:** VTG.
Tare Weight: 31.50 t. **Gross Laden Weight:** 80.00 t.
Maximum Speed: 60 mph. **Length:** 15200 mm (49 ft. 10 in.)
Bogie Type: DB standard. **Exchange Code:** 33.
Notes: Used on various workings to and from Europe.

80 7998 000	80 7998 002	80 7998 003	80 7998 004
80 7998 001			

80 7998 900-904 TANK ICA

Builder: Waggon Union, Siegen, West Germany, 1982.
Design Code: ICE548. **Owner:** VTG.
Tare Weight: 31.50 t. **Gross Laden Weight:** 80.00 t.
Maximum Speed: 60 mph. **Length:** 15200 mm (49 ft. 10 in.)
Bogie Type: BA661.1. **Exchange Code:** 33.
Notes: Used on various workings to and from Europe.

80 7998 900	80 7998 902	80 7998 903	80 7998 904
80 7998 901			

80 9185 000-006 TANK IBB

Builder: Waggon Fabrik Uerdingen, Krefeld, West Germany.
Design Code: IBE314 (Ex ICE314). **Owner:** Eva.
Tare Weight: 15.20 t. **Gross Laden Weight:** 40.00 t.
Maximum Speed: 60 mph. **Length:** 12640 mm (41 ft. 5 in.)
Suspension Type: Double Link. **Exchange Code:** 23.
Notes: Used on workings between Rivesaltes and Crewe.
Previous Number Series: 21 80 0985 000-006.

80 9185 000
80 9185 001
80 9185 002
80 9185 003
80 9185 004
80 9185 005
80 9185 006

80 9185 008-009 TANK IBB

Builder: Waggon Fabrik Uerdingen, Krefeld, West Germany.
Design Code: IBE333 (Ex ICE333). **Owner:** Eva.
Tare Weight: 15.50 t. **Gross Laden Weight:** 40.00 t.
Maximum Speed: 60 mph. **Length:** 10600 mm (34 ft. 9 in.)
Suspension Type: Double Link. **Exchange Code:** 23.
Notes: Used on workings between Rivesaltes and Crewe.
Previous Number Series: 21 80 0985 008-009.

80 9185 008
80 9185 009

80 9195 000-001 CONTAINER FLAT IEX

Builder: Linke Hofmann Busch, Salzgitter, West Germany, 1984.
Design Code: IEE566 (Ex IPE566). **Owner:** Schering.
Tare Weight: 11.00 t. **Gross Laden Weight:** 39.00 t.
Maximum Speed: 60 mph. **Length:** 12960 mm (42 ft. 2 in.)
Suspension Type: Double Link. **Exchange Code:** 24.
Notes: Not currently operating on British Rail.

80 9195 000
80 9195 001

80 9985 000-001 NUCLEAR FLASK CARRIER IQA

Builder:
Design Code: IQE697 (Ex IPE697). **Owner:** Nuclear Transport.
Tare Weight: 37.50 t. **Gross Laden Weight:** 128.00 t.
Maximum Speed: 45 mph. **Length:** 18980 mm (62 ft. 3 in.)
Bogie Type: **Exchange Code:** 33.
Notes: Used on workings between Braunkohl and Sellafield.

80 9985 000
80 9985 001

81 2141 010-015 MEDIUM VAN IMX

Builder:
Design Code: IME604. **Owner:** ÖBB.
Tare Weight: **Gross Laden Weight:**

Maximum Speed: 60 mph.
Length:
Suspension Type:
Exchange Code: 21.
Notes: Not currently operating on British Rail.

81 2141 010	81 2141 012	81 2141 013	81 2141 015
81 2141 011			

81 7204 050-057 TANK IBB

Builder:
Design Code: IBE368 (Ex ICE368).
Owner: ÖBB.
Tare Weight: 12.00 t.
Gross Laden Weight: 36.00 t.
Maximum Speed: 50 mph.
Length: 8800 mm (28 ft. 11 in.)
Suspension Type: Single Link.
Exchange Code: 23.
Notes: Used on various workings to and from Europe.
Previous Number Series: 21 81 0708 801/816.

81 7204 050	81 7204 057

81 7391 000-001 TANK IBA

Builder: Simmering-Graz-Pauker, 1987.
Design Code: IBE669 (Ex ICE669).
Owner: ÖBB.
Tare Weight: 11.50 t.
Gross Laden Weight: 40.00 t.
Maximum Speed: 60 mph.
Length: 11840 mm (38 ft. 10 in.)
Suspension Type: Double Link.
Exchange Code: 23.
Notes: Not currently operating on British Rail.

81 7391 000	81 7391 001

83 2382 000-299 LARGE VAN ILB

Builder:
Design Code: ILE651.
Owner: FS.
Tare Weight: 14.00 t.
Gross Laden Weight: 39.50 t.
Maximum Speed: 60 mph.
Length: 14021 mm (46 ft. 0 in.)
Suspension Type: Double Link.
Exchange Code: 21.
Notes: Used on various workings to and from Europe.
Previous Number Series: 21 83 2148 000-299.

83 2382 000	83 2382 014	83 2382 028	83 2382 042
83 2382 001	83 2382 015	83 2382 029	83 2382 043
83 2382 002	83 2382 016	83 2382 030	83 2382 044
83 2382 003	83 2382 017	83 2382 031	83 2382 045
83 2382 004	83 2382 018	83 2382 032	83 2382 046
83 2382 005	83 2382 019	83 2382 033	83 2382 047
83 2382 006	83 2382 020	83 2382 034	83 2382 048
83 2382 007	83 2382 021	83 2382 035	83 2382 049
83 2382 008	83 2382 022	83 2382 036	83 2382 050
83 2382 009	83 2382 023	83 2382 037	83 2382 051
83 2382 010	83 2382 024	83 2382 038	83 2382 052
83 2382 011	83 2382 025	83 2382 039	83 2382 053
83 2382 012	83 2382 026	83 2382 040	83 2382 054
83 2382 013	83 2382 027	83 2382 041	83 2382 055

83 2382 056
83 2382 057
83 2382 058
83 2382 059
83 2382 060
83 2382 061
83 2382 062
83 2382 063
83 2382 064
83 2382 065
83 2382 066
83 2382 067
83 2382 068
83 2382 069
83 2382 070
83 2382 071
83 2382 072
83 2382 073
83 2382 074
83 2382 075
83 2382 076
83 2382 077
83 2382 078
83 2382 079
83 2382 080
83 2382 081
83 2382 082
83 2382 083
83 2382 084
83 2382 085
83 2382 086
83 2382 087
83 2382 088
83 2382 089
83 2382 090
83 2382 091
83 2382 092
83 2382 093
83 2382 094
83 2382 095
83 2382 096
83 2382 097
83 2382 098
83 2382 099
83 2382 100
83 2382 101
83 2382 102
83 2382 103
83 2382 104
83 2382 105
83 2382 106
83 2382 107
83 2382 108
83 2382 109
83 2382 110
83 2382 111
83 2382 112
83 2382 113
83 2382 114
83 2382 115
83 2382 116
83 2382 117
83 2382 118
83 2382 119
83 2382 120
83 2382 121
83 2382 122
83 2382 123
83 2382 124
83 2382 125
83 2382 126
83 2382 127
83 2382 128
83 2382 129
83 2382 130
83 2382 131
83 2382 132
83 2382 133
83 2382 134
83 2382 135
83 2382 136
83 2382 137
83 2382 138
83 2382 139
83 2382 140
83 2382 141
83 2382 142
83 2382 143
83 2382 144
83 2382 145
83 2382 146
83 2382 147
83 2382 148
83 2382 149
83 2382 150
83 2382 151
83 2382 152
83 2382 153
83 2382 154
83 2382 155
83 2382 156
83 2382 157
83 2382 158
83 2382 159
83 2382 160
83 2382 161
83 2382 162
83 2382 163
83 2382 164
83 2382 165
83 2382 166
83 2382 167
83 2382 168
83 2382 169
83 2382 170
83 2382 171
83 2382 172
83 2382 173
83 2382 174
83 2382 175
83 2382 176
83 2382 177
83 2382 178
83 2382 179
83 2382 180
83 2382 181
83 2382 182
83 2382 183
83 2382 184
83 2382 185
83 2382 186
83 2382 187
83 2382 188
83 2382 189
83 2382 190
83 2382 191
83 2382 192
83 2382 193
83 2382 194
83 2382 195
83 2382 196
83 2382 197
83 2382 198
83 2382 199
83 2382 200
83 2382 201
83 2382 202
83 2382 203
83 2382 204
83 2382 205
83 2382 206
83 2382 207
83 2382 208
83 2382 209
83 2382 210
83 2382 211
83 2382 212
83 2382 213
83 2382 214
83 2382 215
83 2382 216
83 2382 217
83 2382 218
83 2382 219
83 2382 220
83 2382 221
83 2382 222
83 2382 223
83 2382 224
83 2382 225
83 2382 226
83 2382 227
83 2382 228
83 2382 229
83 2382 230
83 2382 231
83 2382 232
83 2382 233
83 2382 234
83 2382 235
83 2382 236
83 2382 237
83 2382 238
83 2382 239
83 2382 240
83 2382 241
83 2382 242
83 2382 243
83 2382 244
83 2382 245
83 2382 246
83 2382 247
83 2382 248
83 2382 249
83 2382 250
83 2382 251
83 2382 252
83 2382 253
83 2382 254
83 2382 255
83 2382 256
83 2382 257
83 2382 258
83 2382 259
83 2382 260
83 2382 261
83 2382 262
83 2382 263
83 2382 264
83 2382 265
83 2382 266
83 2382 267
83 2382 268
83 2382 269
83 2382 270
83 2382 271
83 2382 272
83 2382 273
83 2382 274
83 2382 275
83 2382 276
83 2382 277
83 2382 278
83 2382 279

83 2382 280	83 2382 285	83 2382 290	83 2382 295
83 2382 281	83 2382 286	83 2382 291	83 2382 296
83 2382 282	83 2382 287	83 2382 292	83 2382 297
83 2382 283	83 2382 288	83 2382 293	83 2382 298
83 2382 284	83 2382 289	83 2382 294	83 2382 299

83 2382 300-699 ILB

LARGE VAN END DOOR

Builder: Officine Flore, Italy, 1969-70.
Design Code: ILE652(a ILE345). **Owner:** FS.
Tare Weight: 14.00 t. **Gross Laden Weight:** 40.00 t.
Maximum Speed: 60 mph. **Length:** 14020 mm (46 ft. 0 in.)
Suspension Type: Double Link. **Exchange Code:** 21.
Notes: Used on various workings to and from Europe.
Previous Number Series: 21 83 2147 000-399.

83 2382 300	83 2382 339	83 2382 378	83 2382 417
83 2382 301	83 2382 340	83 2382 379	83 2382 418
83 2382 302	83 2382 341	83 2382 380	83 2382 419
83 2382 303	83 2382 342	83 2382 381	83 2382 420
83 2382 304	83 2382 343	83 2382 382	83 2382 421
83 2382 305	83 2382 344	83 2382 383	83 2382 422
83 2382 306	83 2382 345	83 2382 384	83 2382 423
83 2382 307	83 2382 346	83 2382 385	83 2382 424
83 2382 308	83 2382 347	83 2382 386	83 2382 425
83 2382 309	83 2382 348	83 2382 387	83 2382 426
83 2382 310	83 2382 349	83 2382 388	83 2382 427
83 2382 311	83 2382 350	83 2382 389	83 2382 428
83 2382 312	83 2382 351	83 2382 390	83 2382 429
83 2382 313	83 2382 352	83 2382 391	83 2382 430
83 2382 314	83 2382 353	83 2382 392	83 2382 431
83 2382 315	83 2382 354	83 2382 393	83 2382 432
83 2382 316	83 2382 355	83 2382 394	83 2382 433
83 2382 317	83 2382 356	83 2382 395	83 2382 434
83 2382 318	83 2382 357	83 2382 396	83 2382 435
83 2382 319	83 2382 358	83 2382 397	83 2382 436
83 2382 320	83 2382 359	83 2382 398	83 2382 437
83 2382 321	83 2382 360	83 2382 399	83 2382 438
83 2382 322	83 2382 361	83 2382 400	83 2382 439
83 2382 323	83 2382 362	83 2382 401	83 2382 440
83 2382 324	83 2382 363	83 2382 402	83 2382 441
83 2382 325	83 2382 364	83 2382 403	83 2382 442
83 2382 326	83 2382 365	83 2382 404	83 2382 443
83 2382 327	83 2382 366	83 2382 405	83 2382 444
83 2382 328	83 2382 367	83 2382 406	83 2382 445
83 2382 329	83 2382 368	83 2382 407	83 2382 446
83 2382 330	83 2382 369	83 2382 408	83 2382 447
83 2382 331	83 2382 370	83 2382 409	83 2382 448
83 2382 332	83 2382 371	83 2382 410	83 2382 449
83 2382 333	83 2382 372	83 2382 411	83 2382 450
83 2382 334	83 2382 373	83 2382 412	83 2382 451
83 2382 335	83 2382 374	83 2382 413	83 2382 452
83 2382 336	83 2382 375	83 2382 414	83 2382 453
83 2382 337	83 2382 376	83 2382 415	83 2382 454
83 2382 338	83 2382 377	83 2382 416	83 2382 455

83 2382 456
83 2382 457
83 2382 458
83 2382 459
83 2382 460
83 2382 461
83 2382 462
83 2382 463
83 2382 464
83 2382 465
83 2382 466
83 2382 467
83 2382 468
83 2382 469
83 2382 470
83 2382 471
83 2382 472
83 2382 473
83 2382 474
83 2382 475
83 2382 476
83 2382 477
83 2382 478
83 2382 479
83 2382 480
83 2382 481
83 2382 482
83 2382 483
83 2382 484
83 2382 485
83 2382 486
83 2382 487
83 2382 488
83 2382 489
83 2382 490
83 2382 491
83 2382 492
83 2382 493
83 2382 494
83 2382 495
83 2382 496
83 2382 497
83 2382 498
83 2382 499
83 2382 500
83 2382 501
83 2382 502
83 2382 503
83 2382 504
83 2382 505
83 2382 506
83 2382 507
83 2382 508
83 2382 509
83 2382 510
83 2382 511
83 2382 512
83 2382 513
83 2382 514
83 2382 515
83 2382 516
83 2382 517
83 2382 518
83 2382 519
83 2382 520
83 2382 521
83 2382 522
83 2382 523
83 2382 524
83 2382 525
83 2382 526
83 2382 527
83 2382 528
83 2382 529
83 2382 530
83 2382 531
83 2382 532
83 2382 533
83 2382 534
83 2382 535
83 2382 536
83 2382 537
83 2382 538
83 2382 539
83 2382 540
83 2382 541
83 2382 542
83 2382 543
83 2382 544
83 2382 545
83 2382 546
83 2382 547
83 2382 548
83 2382 549
83 2382 550
83 2382 551
83 2382 552
83 2382 553
83 2382 554
83 2382 555
83 2382 556
83 2382 557
83 2382 558
83 2382 559
83 2382 560
83 2382 561
83 2382 562
83 2382 563
83 2382 564
83 2382 565
83 2382 566
83 2382 567
83 2382 568
83 2382 569
83 2382 570
83 2382 571
83 2382 572
83 2382 573
83 2382 574
83 2382 575
83 2382 576
83 2382 577
83 2382 578
83 2382 579
83 2382 580
83 2382 581
83 2382 582
83 2382 583
83 2382 584
83 2382 585
83 2382 586
83 2382 587
83 2382 588
83 2382 589
83 2382 590
83 2382 591
83 2382 592
83 2382 593
83 2382 594
83 2382 595
83 2382 596
83 2382 597
83 2382 598
83 2382 599
83 2382 600
83 2382 601
83 2382 602
83 2382 603
83 2382 604
83 2382 605
83 2382 606
83 2382 607
83 2382 608
83 2382 609
83 2382 610
83 2382 611
83 2382 612
83 2382 613
83 2382 614
83 2382 615 a
83 2382 616
83 2382 617
83 2382 618
83 2382 619
83 2382 620
83 2382 621
83 2382 622
83 2382 623
83 2382 624
83 2382 625
83 2382 626
83 2382 627
83 2382 628
83 2382 629
83 2382 630
83 2382 631
83 2382 632
83 2382 633
83 2382 634
83 2382 635
83 2382 636
83 2382 637
83 2382 638
83 2382 639
83 2382 640
83 2382 641
83 2382 642
83 2382 643
83 2382 644
83 2382 645
83 2382 646
83 2382 647
83 2382 648
83 2382 649
83 2382 650
83 2382 651
83 2382 652
83 2382 653
83 2382 654
83 2382 655
83 2382 656
83 2382 657
83 2382 658
83 2382 659
83 2382 660
83 2382 661
83 2382 662 a
83 2382 663
83 2382 664
83 2382 665
83 2382 666
83 2382 667
83 2382 668
83 2382 669
83 2382 670
83 2382 671
83 2382 672
83 2382 673
83 2382 674
83 2382 675
83 2382 676
83 2382 677
83 2382 678
83 2382 679

83 2382 680	83 2382 685	83 2382 690	83 2382 695
83 2382 681	83 2382 686	83 2382 691	83 2382 696
83 2382 682	83 2382 687	83 2382 692	83 2382 697
83 2382 683	83 2382 688	83 2382 693	83 2382 698
83 2382 684	83 2382 689	83 2382 694	83 2382 699

83 2382 700-749 LARGE VAN ILB

Builder:
Design Code: ILE654. **Owner:** FS.
Tare Weight: 14.50 t. **Gross Laden Weight:** 40.00 t.
Maximum Speed: 60 mph. **Length:** 14630 mm (48 ft. 0 in.)
Suspension Type: Double Link. **Exchange Code:** 21.
Notes: Used on various workings to and from Europe.
Previous Number series: 21 83 2148 450-499.

83 2382 700	83 2382 713	83 2382 726	83 2382 738
83 2382 701	83 2382 714	83 2382 727	83 2382 739
83 2382 702	83 2382 715	83 2382 728	83 2382 740
83 2382 703	83 2382 716	83 2382 729	83 2382 741
83 2382 704	83 2382 717	83 2382 730	83 2382 742
83 2382 705	83 2382 718	83 2382 731	83 2382 743
83 2382 706	83 2382 719	83 2382 732	83 2382 744
83 2382 707	83 2382 720	83 2382 733	83 2382 745
83 2382 708	83 2382 721	83 2382 734	83 2382 746
83 2382 709	83 2382 722	83 2382 735	83 2382 747
83 2382 710	83 2382 723	83 2382 736	83 2382 748
83 2382 711	83 2382 724	83 2382 737	83 2382 749
83 2382 712	83 2382 725		

83 2388 000-049 LARGE VAN IWB

Builder: FS.
Design Code: IWE653 (Ex ILE653). **Owner:** FS.
Tare Weight: 14.00 t. **Gross Laden Weight:** 40.00 t.
Maximum Speed: 60 mph. **Length:** 14020 mm (46 ft. 0 in.)
Suspension Type: Double Link. **Exchange Code:** 21.
Notes: Used on various workings to and from Europe.
Previous Number Series: 21 83 2147 900-949.

83 2388 000	83 2388 013	83 2388 026	83 2388 038
83 2388 001	83 2388 014	83 2388 027	83 2388 039
83 2388 002	83 2388 015	83 2388 028	83 2388 040
83 2388 003	83 2388 016	83 2388 029	83 2388 041
83 2388 004	83 2388 017	83 2388 030	83 2388 042
83 2388 005	83 2388 018	83 2388 031	83 2388 043
83 2388 006	83 2388 019	83 2388 032	83 2388 044
83 2388 007	83 2388 020	83 2388 033	83 2388 045
83 2388 008	83 2388 021	83 2388 034	83 2388 046
83 2388 009	83 2388 022	83 2388 035	83 2388 047
83 2388 010	83 2388 023	83 2388 036	83 2388 048
83 2388 011	83 2388 024	83 2388 037	83 2388 049
83 2388 012	83 2388 025		

83 2795 000-200 BOGIE LARGE VAN IMA

Builder: Ferrosud, Matera, Italy, 1982.
Design Code: IME553 (Ex ILE553). **Owner:** FS.
Tare Weight: 26.00 t. **Gross Laden Weight:** 80.00 t.
Maximum Speed: 60 mph. **Length:** 20060 mm (65 ft. 11 in.)
Bogie Type: Y25CS2. **Exchange Code:** 31.
Notes: Used on various workings to and from Europe.

83 2795 000
83 2795 001
83 2795 002
83 2795 003
83 2795 004
83 2795 005
83 2795 006
83 2795 007
83 2795 008
83 2795 009
83 2795 010
83 2795 011
83 2795 012
83 2795 013
83 2795 014
83 2795 015
83 2795 016
83 2795 017
83 2795 018
83 2795 019
83 2795 020
83 2795 021
83 2795 022
83 2795 023
83 2795 024
83 2795 025
83 2795 026
83 2795 027
83 2795 028
83 2795 029
83 2795 030
83 2795 031
83 2795 032
83 2795 033
83 2795 034
83 2795 035
83 2795 036
83 2795 037
83 2795 038
83 2795 039
83 2795 040
83 2795 041
83 2795 042
83 2795 043
83 2795 044
83 2795 045
83 2795 046
83 2795 047
83 2795 048
83 2795 049
83 2795 050
83 2795 051
83 2795 052
83 2795 053
83 2795 054
83 2795 055
83 2795 056
83 2795 057
83 2795 058
83 2795 059
83 2795 060
83 2795 061
83 2795 062
83 2795 063
83 2795 064
83 2795 065
83 2795 066
83 2795 067
83 2795 068
83 2795 069
83 2795 070
83 2795 071
83 2795 072
83 2795 073
83 2795 074
83 2795 075
83 2795 076
83 2795 077
83 2795 078
83 2795 079
83 2795 080
83 2795 081
83 2795 082
83 2795 083
83 2795 084
83 2795 085
83 2795 086
83 2795 087
83 2795 088
83 2795 089
83 2795 090
83 2795 091
83 2795 092
83 2795 093
83 2795 094
83 2795 095
83 2795 096
83 2795 097
83 2795 098
83 2795 099
83 2795 100
83 2795 101
83 2795 102
83 2795 103
83 2795 104
83 2795 105
83 2795 106
83 2795 107
83 2795 108
83 2795 109
83 2795 110
83 2795 111
83 2795 112
83 2795 113
83 2795 114
83 2795 115
83 2795 116
83 2795 117
83 2795 118
83 2795 119
83 2795 120
83 2795 121
83 2795 122
83 2795 123
83 2795 124
83 2795 125
83 2795 126
83 2795 127
83 2795 128
83 2795 129
83 2795 130
83 2795 131
83 2795 132
83 2795 133
83 2795 134
83 2795 135
83 2795 136
83 2795 137
83 2795 138
83 2795 139
83 2795 140
83 2795 141
83 2795 142
83 2795 143
83 2795 144
83 2795 145
83 2795 146
83 2795 147
83 2795 148
83 2795 149
83 2795 150
83 2795 151
83 2795 152
83 2795 153
83 2795 154
83 2795 155
83 2795 156
83 2795 157
83 2795 158
83 2795 159
83 2795 160
83 2795 161
83 2795 162
83 2795 163
83 2795 164
83 2795 165
83 2795 166
83 2795 167
83 2795 168
83 2795 169
83 2795 170
83 2795 171
83 2795 172
83 2795 173
83 2795 174
83 2795 175
83 2795 176
83 2795 177
83 2795 178
83 2795 179
83 2795 180
83 2795 181
83 2795 182
83 2795 183

Tank 33 80 7998 000 at Dover Yard on 31st August 1990. *(R. Wallace)*

31 83 2797 088 at Dover Yard on 27th September 1987. *(R. Wallace)*

83 2795 184	83 2795 189	83 2795 193	83 2795 197
83 2795 185	83 2795 190	83 2795 194	83 2795 198
83 2795 186	83 2795 191	83 2795 195	83 2795 199
83 2795 187	83 2795 192	83 2795 196	83 2795 200
83 2795 188			

83 7190 000 TANK IBX

Builder: Montecatini, Italy.
Design Code: IBE220 (Ex ICE220).
Owner: Sicedison.
Tare Weight: 11.00 t.
Gross Laden Weight: 35.70 t.
Maximum Speed: 50 mph.
Length: 9000 mm (29 ft. 6 in.)
Suspension Type: Single Link.
Exchange Code: 23.
Notes: Used on various workings to and from Europe.
Previous Number Series: 21 83 0780 019.

83 7190 000

83 7190 001-002 TANK IBX

Builder: A. Gallinari, Reggio Emilia, Italy.
Design Code: IBE221 (Ex ICE221).
Owner: Sicedison.
Tare Weight: 10.60 t.
Gross Laden Weight: 36.00 t.
Maximum Speed: 50 mph.
Length: 9000 mm (29 ft. 6 in.)
Suspension Type: Single Link.
Exchange Code: 23.
Notes: Used on various workings to and from Europe.
Previous Number Series: 21 83 0780 021/024.

83 7190 001	83 7190 002

83 7190 003-007 TANK IBX

Builder: Marchetti, Milan, Italy.
Design Code: IBE177 (Ex ICE177).
Owner: Montedison.
Tare Weight: 13.95 t.
Gross Laden Weight: 36.00 t.
Maximum Speed: 50 mph.
Length: 10390 mm (34 ft. 1 in.)
Suspension Type: Single Link.
Exchange Code: 23.
Notes: Used on various workings to and from Europe.
Previous Number Series: 21 83 0781 001/002/004-006.

83 7190 003	83 7190 005	83 7190 006	83 7190 007
83 7190 004			

83 7190 008-031 TANK IBB

Builder: Ateliers de Joigny, France, 1977.
Design Code: IBE470 (Ex ICE470).
Owner: Etra.
Tare Weight: 10.10 t.
Gross Laden Weight: 40.00 t.
Maximum Speed: 45 mph.
Length: 8800 mm (28 ft. 11 in.)
Suspension Type: Single Link.
Exchange Code: 23.
Notes: Used on various workings to and from Europe.
Previous Number Series: 21 83 0780 049-072.

83 7190 008	83 7190 014	83 7190 020	83 7190 026
83 7190 009	83 7190 015	83 7190 021	83 7190 027
83 7190 010	83 7190 016	83 7190 022	83 7190 028
83 7190 011	83 7190 017	83 7190 023	83 7190 029
83 7190 012	83 7190 018	83 7190 024	83 7190 030
83 7190 013	83 7190 019	83 7190 025	83 7190 031

83 7197 000-007 TANK IBB

Builder: Edison, Milan, Italy.
Design Code: IBE263 (Ex ICE263). **Owner:** Montedison.
Tare Weight: 11.90 t. **Gross Laden Weight:** 40.00 t.
Maximum Speed: 50 mph. **Length:** 10390 mm (34 ft. 1 in.)
Suspension Type: Single Link. **Exchange Code:** 23.
Notes: Used on various workings to and from Europe.
Previous Number Series: 21 83 0780 000-007.

83 7197 000	83 7197 002	83 7197 004	83 7197 006
83 7197 001	83 7197 003	83 7197 005	83 7197 007

83 7197 008-015 TANK IBB

Builder: Siai Lerici, Italy.
Design Code: IBE170 (Ex ICE170). **Owner:** Montedison.
Tare Weight: 11.20 t. **Gross Laden Weight:** 35.00 t.
Maximum Speed: 50 mph. **Length:** 9740 mm (32 ft. 0 in.)
Suspension Type: Single Link. **Exchange Code:** 23.
Notes: Used on various workings to and from Europe.
Previous Number Series: 21 83 0780 008-015.

83 7197 008	83 7197 010	83 7197 012	83 7197 014
83 7197 009	83 7197 011	83 7197 013	83 7197 015

83 7197 016-017 TANK IBB

Builder: A.L.P., Piedimulera, Italy.
Design Code: IBE142(Ex ICE142). **Owner:** Montedison.
Tare Weight: 10.50 t. **Gross Laden Weight:** 36.00 t.
Maximum Speed: 50 mph. **Length:** 9740 mm (32 ft. 0 in.)
Suspension Type: Single Link. **Exchange Code:** 23.
Notes: Used on various workings to and from Europe.
Previous Number Series: 21 83 0780 016-017.

83 7197 016	83 7197 017

83 7197 018-019 TANK IBX

Builder: Montecantini, Italy.
Design Code: IBE220(Ex ICE220). **Owner:** Sicedison.
Tare Weight: 11.00 t. **Gross Laden Weight:** 35.70 t.
Maximum Speed: 50 mph. **Length:** 9000 mm (29 ft. 6 in.)
Suspension Type: Single Link. **Exchange Code:** 23.
Notes: Used on various workings to and from Europe.

Previous Number Series: 21 83 0780 018/020.

83 7197 018 83 7197 019

83 7197 020-021 TANK IBX

Builder: A. Gallinari, Reggio Emilia, Italy.
Design Code: IBE221(Ex ICE221).
Owner: Sicedison.
Tare Weight: 10.60 t.
Gross Laden Weight: 36.00 t.
Maximum Speed: 50 mph.
Length: 9000 mm (29 ft. 6 in.)
Suspension Type: Single Link.
Exchange Code: 23.
Notes: Used on various workings to and from Europe.
Previous Number Series: 21 83 0780 022-023.

83 7197 020 83 7197 021

83 7197 022-023 TANK IBB

Builder: Siai Lerici, Italy.
Design Code: IBE225(Ex ICE225).
Owner: Sicedison.
Tare Weight: 11.80 t.
Gross Laden Weight: 40.00 t.
Maximum Speed: 50 mph.
Length: 9000 mm (29 ft. 6 in.)
Suspension Type: Single Link.
Exchange Code: 23.
Notes: Used on various workings to and from Europe.
Previous Number Series: 21 83 0780 025-026.

83 7197 022 83 7197 023

83 7197 024-029 TANK IBX

Builder: Carro Cisterna, Italy.
Design Code: IBE623(Ex ICE623).
Owner: Sicedison.
Tare Weight: 11.80 t.
Gross Laden Weight: 40.00 t.
Maximum Speed: 50 mph.
Length: 9000 mm (29 ft. 6 in.)
Suspension Type: Single Link.
Exchange Code: 23.
Notes: Used on various workings to and from Europe.
Previous Number Series: 21 83 0780 027-032.

83 7197 024 83 7197 025 83 7197 026 83 7197 027 83 7197 028 83 7197 029

83 7197 030-041 TANK IBB

Builder: Siai Lerici, Italy.
Design Code: IBE261(Ex ICE261)[a IBE230(Ex ICE230), b IBE244(Ex ICE244)].
Owner: Montedison.
Tare Weight: 11.74 t (a 12.20 t, b 11.50 t).
Gross Laden Weight: 36.00 t (a 40.00 t).
Maximum Speed: 50 mph.
Length: 9000 mm (29 ft. 6 in.)[a 10740 mm (35ft 3 in).
Suspension Type: Single Link (a Double Link).
Exchange Code: 23.
Notes: Used on various workings to and from Europe.
Previous Number Series: 21 83 0780 033-039/042-045/047.

83 7197 030	83 7197 033	83 7197 036	83 7197 039 b
83 7197 031	83 7197 034	83 7197 037 a	83 7197 040 b
83 7197 032	83 7197 035	83 7197 038 a	83 7197 041

83 7288 000-001 TANK IBB

Builder:
Design Code: IBE079(Ex ICE079)[a IBE177(Ex ICE177)].
Owner: Sicedison. **Tare Weight:** 13.50 t (a 13.95 t).
Gross Laden Weight: 32.00 t (a 36.00 t). **Maximum Speed:** 50 mph.
Length: 8330 mm (27 ft. 4 in.)[a 10390 mm (34 ft. 1 in)].
Suspension Type: Single Link. **Exchange Code:** 23.
Notes: Used on various workings to and from Europe.
Previous Number Series: 21 83 0780 000/003.

83 7288 000 83 7288 001 a

83 7397 900 TANK IBA

Builder: Costamasnaga, Como, Italy, 1986.
Design Code: IBE595(Ex ICE595). **Owner:** Montedison.
Tare Weight: 12.10 t. **Gross Laden Weight:** 46.00 t.
Maximum Speed: 60 mph. **Length:** 9000 mm (29 ft. 6 in.)
Suspension Type: Single Link. **Exchange Code:** 23.
Notes: Used on various workings to and from Europe.

83 7397 900

83 8083 000-004 REFRIGERATED VAN IIX

Builder:
Design Code: IIE430. **Owner:** Interfrigo.
Tare Weight: 13.50 t. **Gross Laden Weight:** 39.70 t.
Maximum Speed: 60 mph. **Length:** 14020 mm (46 ft. 0 in.)
Suspension Type: Double Link. **Exchange Code:** 04.
Notes: Not currently operating on British Rail.
Previous Number Series: 14 83 0891 500-504.

83 8083 000	83 8083 002	83 8083 003	83 8083 004
83 8083 001			

83 8083 700-740 REFRIGERATED VAN IIX

Builder: Snia Viscosa, Italy, 1972.
Design Code: IIE418. **Owner:** Transfesa.
Tare Weight: 13.30 t. **Gross Laden Weight:** 40.00 t.
Maximum Speed: 45 mph. **Length:** 14020 mm (46 ft. 0 in.)
Suspension Type: Double Link. **Exchange Code:** 06.
Notes: Used on various workings to and from Europe.
Previous Number Series: 14 83 0891 700-740.

83 8083 700
83 8083 701
83 8083 702
83 8083 703
83 8083 704
83 8083 705
83 8083 706
83 8083 707
83 8083 708
83 8083 709
83 8083 710
83 8083 711
83 8083 712
83 8083 713
83 8083 714
83 8083 715
83 8083 716
83 8083 717
83 8083 718
83 8083 719
83 8083 720
83 8083 721
83 8083 722
83 8083 723
83 8083 724
83 8083 725
83 8083 726
83 8083 727
83 8083 728
83 8083 729
83 8083 730
83 8083 731
83 8083 732
83 8083 733
83 8083 734
83 8083 735
83 8083 736
83 8083 737
83 8083 738
83 8083 739
83 8083 740

83 8083 741-750 REFRIGERATED VAN IIX

Builder:
Design Code: IIE417.
Owner: Transfesa.
Tare Weight: 13.00 t.
Gross Laden Weight: 40.00 t.
Maximum Speed: 45 mph.
Length: 14020 mm (46 ft. 0 in.)
Suspension Type: Single Link.
Exchange Code: 06.
Notes: Used on various workings to and from Europe.
Previous Number Series: 14 83 0891 741-750.

83 8083 741
83 8083 742
83 8083 743
83 8083 744
83 8083 745
83 8083 746
83 8083 747
83 8083 748
83 8083 749
83 8083 750

83 8087 000-029 REFRIGERATED VAN IIB

Builder: Brugeoise et Nivelles, Brussles, Belgium, 1972.
Design Code: IIE591.
Owner: Interfrigo.
Tare Weight: 13.90 t.
Gross Laden Weight: 40.00 t.
Maximum Speed: 60 mph.
Length: 14020 mm (46 ft. 0 in.)
Suspension Type: Double Link.
Exchange Code: 03.
Notes: Used on various workings to and from Europe.
Previous Number Series: Renumbered at random from number series 03 83 8089 002-194.

83 8087 000
83 8087 001
83 8087 002
83 8087 003
83 8087 004
83 8087 005
83 8087 006
83 8087 007
83 8087 008
83 8087 009
83 8087 010
83 8087 011
83 8087 012
83 8087 013
83 8087 014
83 8087 015
83 8087 016
83 8087 017
83 8087 018
83 8087 019
83 8087 020
83 8087 021
83 8087 022
83 8087 023
83 8087 024
83 8087 025
83 8087 026
83 8087 027
83 8087 028
83 8087 029

83 8088 000-049 REFRIGERATED VAN IIB

Builder: Brugeoise et Nivelles, Brussels, Belgium.
Design Code: IIE590.
Owner: Interfrigo.
Tare Weight: 16.80 t.
Gross Laden Weight: 40.00 t.
Maximum Speed: 60 mph.
Length: 14020 mm (46 ft. 0 in.)
Suspension Type: Double Link.
Exchange Code: 04.
Notes: Used on various workings to and from Europe.

Previous Number Series: 14 83 0888 430-454, 04 83 8092 200-418 series.

83 8088 000
83 8088 001
83 8088 002
83 8088 003
83 8088 004
83 8088 005
83 8088 006
83 8088 007
83 8088 008
83 8088 009
83 8088 010
83 8088 011
83 8088 012
83 8088 013
83 8088 014
83 8088 015
83 8088 016
83 8088 017
83 8088 018
83 8088 019
83 8088 020
83 8088 021
83 8088 022
83 8088 023
83 8088 024
83 8088 025
83 8088 026
83 8088 027
83 8088 028
83 8088 029
83 8088 030
83 8088 031
83 8088 032
83 8088 033
83 8088 034
83 8088 035
83 8088 036
83 8088 037
83 8088 038
83 8088 039
83 8088 040
83 8088 041
83 8088 042
83 8088 043
83 8088 044
83 8088 045
83 8088 046
83 8088 047
83 8088 048
83 8088 049

83 8089 000-979 REFRIGERATED VAN IIB

Builder: Snia Viscosa, Italy, 1972-74.
Design Code: IIE375.
Tare Weight: 14.20 t.
Maximum Speed: 60 mph.
Suspension Type: Double Link.
Owner: Interfrigo.
Gross Laden Weight: 40.00 t.
Length: 14020 mm (46 ft. 0 in.)
Exchange Code: 03.
Notes: Used on various workings to and from Europe.

83 8089 000
83 8089 001
83 8089 003
83 8089 004
83 8089 005
83 8089 006
83 8089 007
83 8089 008
83 8089 009
83 8089 011
83 8089 012
83 8089 013
83 8089 015
83 8089 017
83 8089 018
83 8089 019
83 8089 021
83 8089 022
83 8089 023
83 8089 024
83 8089 025
83 8089 026
83 8089 027
83 8089 028
83 8089 029
83 8089 030
83 8089 031
83 8089 032
83 8089 033
83 8089 034
83 8089 035
83 8089 036
83 8089 037
83 8089 038
83 8089 039
83 8089 040
83 8089 041
83 8089 042
83 8089 043
83 8089 044
83 8089 045
83 8089 046
83 8089 047
83 8089 048
83 8089 049
83 8089 050
83 8089 051
83 8089 052
83 8089 053
83 8089 054
83 8089 056
83 8089 057
83 8089 058
83 8089 059
83 8089 060
83 8089 061
83 8089 062
83 8089 063
83 8089 064
83 8089 065
83 8089 066
83 8089 067
83 8089 068
83 8089 069
83 8089 070
83 8089 071
83 8089 072
83 8089 074
83 8089 075
83 8089 076
83 8089 077
83 8089 078
83 8089 079
83 8089 080
83 8089 081
83 8089 082
83 8089 083
83 8089 085
83 8089 086
83 8089 088
83 8089 089
83 8089 091
83 8089 092
83 8089 093
83 8089 094
83 8089 095
83 8089 096
83 8089 097
83 8089 098
83 8089 099
83 8089 100
83 8089 101
83 8089 102
83 8089 103
83 8089 104
83 8089 105
83 8089 106
83 8089 107
83 8089 108
83 8089 110
83 8089 114
83 8089 115
83 8089 116
83 8089 117
83 8089 118
83 8089 119
83 8089 120
83 8089 121
83 8089 122
83 8089 123
83 8089 124
83 8089 127
83 8089 128
83 8089 129
83 8089 130
83 8089 131

83 8089 132
83 8089 133
83 8089 134
83 8089 135
83 8089 136
83 8089 137
83 8089 138
83 8089 141
83 8089 144
83 8089 145
83 8089 146
83 8089 147
83 8089 148
83 8089 149
83 8089 150
83 8089 151
83 8089 153
83 8089 154
83 8089 155
83 8089 156
83 8089 158
83 8089 160
83 8089 161
83 8089 162
83 8089 163
83 8089 165
83 8089 167
83 8089 169
83 8089 170
83 8089 171
83 8089 172
83 8089 173
83 8089 175
83 8089 176
83 8089 178
83 8089 179
83 8089 180
83 8089 181
83 8089 182
83 8089 183
83 8089 184
83 8089 185
83 8089 186
83 8089 188
83 8089 189
83 8089 190
83 8089 191
83 8089 192
83 8089 193
83 8089 195
83 8089 196
83 8089 197
83 8089 198
83 8089 199
83 8089 200
83 8089 201
83 8089 202
83 8089 203
83 8089 204
83 8089 205
83 8089 206
83 8089 207
83 8089 208
83 8089 209
83 8089 210
83 8089 211
83 8089 212
83 8089 213
83 8089 214
83 8089 215
83 8089 216
83 8089 217
83 8089 218
83 8089 219
83 8089 220
83 8089 221
83 8089 222
83 8089 223
83 8089 224
83 8089 225
83 8089 226
83 8089 227
83 8089 228
83 8089 229
83 8089 230
83 8089 231
83 8089 232
83 8089 233
83 8089 234
83 8089 235
83 8089 236
83 8089 237
83 8089 238
83 8089 239
83 8089 240
83 8089 241
83 8089 242
83 8089 243
83 8089 244
83 8089 245
83 8089 246
83 8089 247
83 8089 248
83 8089 249
83 8089 250
83 8089 251
83 8089 252
83 8089 253
83 8089 254
83 8089 255
83 8089 256
83 8089 257
83 8089 258
83 8089 259
83 8089 260
83 8089 261
83 8089 262
83 8089 263
83 8089 264
83 8089 265
83 8089 266
83 8089 267
83 8089 268
83 8089 269
83 8089 270
83 8089 271
83 8089 272
83 8089 273
83 8089 274
83 8089 275
83 8089 276
83 8089 277
83 8089 278
83 8089 279
83 8089 280
83 8089 281
83 8089 282
83 8089 283
83 8089 284
83 8089 285
83 8089 286
83 8089 287
83 8089 288
83 8089 289
83 8089 290
83 8089 291
83 8089 292
83 8089 293
83 8089 294
83 8089 295
83 8089 296
83 8089 297
83 8089 298
83 8089 299
83 8089 300
83 8089 301
83 8089 302
83 8089 303
83 8089 304
83 8089 305
83 8089 306
83 8089 307
83 8089 308
83 8089 309
83 8089 310
83 8089 311
83 8089 312
83 8089 313
83 8089 314
83 8089 315
83 8089 316
83 8089 317
83 8089 318
83 8089 319
83 8089 320
83 8089 321
83 8089 322
83 8089 323
83 8089 324
83 8089 325
83 8089 326
83 8089 327
83 8089 328
83 8089 329
83 8089 330
83 8089 331
83 8089 332
83 8089 333
83 8089 334
83 8089 335
83 8089 336
83 8089 337
83 8089 338
83 8089 339
83 8089 340
83 8089 341
83 8089 342
83 8089 343
83 8089 344
83 8089 345
83 8089 346
83 8089 347
83 8089 348
83 8089 349
83 8089 350
83 8089 351
83 8089 352
83 8089 353
83 8089 354
83 8089 355
83 8089 356
83 8089 357
83 8089 358
83 8089 359
83 8089 360
83 8089 361
83 8089 362
83 8089 363
83 8089 364
83 8089 365
83 8089 366
83 8089 367
83 8089 368
83 8089 369

83 8089 370
83 8089 371
83 8089 372
83 8089 373
83 8089 374
83 8089 375
83 8089 376
83 8089 377
83 8089 378
83 8089 379
83 8089 380
83 8089 381
83 8089 382
83 8089 383
83 8089 384
83 8089 385
83 8089 386
83 8089 387
83 8089 388
83 8089 389
83 8089 390
83 8089 391
83 8089 392
83 8089 393
83 8089 394
83 8089 395
83 8089 396
83 8089 397
83 8089 398
83 8089 399
83 8089 400
83 8089 401
83 8089 402
83 8089 403
83 8089 404
83 8089 405
83 8089 406
83 8089 407
83 8089 408
83 8089 409
83 8089 410
83 8089 411
83 8089 412
83 8089 413
83 8089 414
83 8089 415
83 8089 416
83 8089 417
83 8089 418
83 8089 419
83 8089 420
83 8089 421
83 8089 422
83 8089 423
83 8089 424
83 8089 425
83 8089 426
83 8089 427
83 8089 428
83 8089 429
83 8089 430
83 8089 431
83 8089 432
83 8089 433
83 8089 434
83 8089 435
83 8089 436
83 8089 437
83 8089 438
83 8089 439
83 8089 440
83 8089 441
83 8089 442
83 8089 443
83 8089 444
83 8089 445
83 8089 446
83 8089 447
83 8089 448
83 8089 449
83 8089 450
83 8089 451
83 8089 452
83 8089 453
83 8089 454
83 8089 455
83 8089 456
83 8089 457
83 8089 458
83 8089 459
83 8089 460
83 8089 461
83 8089 462
83 8089 463
83 8089 464
83 8089 465
83 8089 466
83 8089 467
83 8089 468
83 8089 469
83 8089 470
83 8089 471
83 8089 472
83 8089 473
83 8089 474
83 8089 475
83 8089 476
83 8089 477
83 8089 478
83 8089 479
83 8089 480
83 8089 481
83 8089 482
83 8089 483
83 8089 484
83 8089 485
83 8089 486
83 8089 487
83 8089 488
83 8089 489
83 8089 490
83 8089 491
83 8089 492
83 8089 493
83 8089 494
83 8089 495
83 8089 496
83 8089 497
83 8089 498
83 8089 499
83 8089 500
83 8089 501
83 8089 502
83 8089 503
83 8089 504
83 8089 505
83 8089 506
83 8089 507
83 8089 508
83 8089 509
83 8089 510
83 8089 511
83 8089 512
83 8089 513
83 8089 514
83 8089 515
83 8089 516
83 8089 517
83 8089 518
83 8089 519
83 8089 520
83 8089 521
83 8089 522
83 8089 523
83 8089 524
83 8089 525
83 8089 526
83 8089 527
83 8089 528
83 8089 529
83 8089 530
83 8089 531
83 8089 532
83 8089 533
83 8089 534
83 8089 535
83 8089 536
83 8089 537
83 8089 538
83 8089 539
83 8089 540
83 8089 541
83 8089 542
83 8089 543
83 8089 544
83 8089 545
83 8089 546
83 8089 547
83 8089 548
83 8089 549
83 8089 550
83 8089 551
83 8089 552
83 8089 553
83 8089 554
83 8089 555
83 8089 556
83 8089 557
83 8089 558
83 8089 559
83 8089 560
83 8089 561
83 8089 562
83 8089 563
83 8089 564
83 8089 565
83 8089 566
83 8089 567
83 8089 568
83 8089 569
83 8089 570
83 8089 571
83 8089 572
83 8089 573
83 8089 574
83 8089 575
83 8089 576
83 8089 577
83 8089 578
83 8089 579
83 8089 580
83 8089 581
83 8089 582
83 8089 583
83 8089 584
83 8089 585
83 8089 586
83 8089 587
83 8089 588
83 8089 589
83 8089 590
83 8089 591
83 8089 592
83 8089 593

83 8089 594
83 8089 595
83 8089 596
83 8089 597
83 8089 598
83 8089 599
83 8089 600
83 8089 601
83 8089 602
83 8089 603
83 8089 604
83 8089 605
83 8089 606
83 8089 607
83 8089 608
83 8089 609
83 8089 610
83 8089 611
83 8089 612
83 8089 613
83 8089 614
83 8089 615
83 8089 616
83 8089 617
83 8089 618
83 8089 619
83 8089 620
83 8089 621
83 8089 622
83 8089 623
83 8089 624
83 8089 625
83 8089 626
83 8089 627
83 8089 628
83 8089 629
83 8089 630
83 8089 631
83 8089 632
83 8089 633
83 8089 634
83 8089 635
83 8089 636
83 8089 637
83 8089 638
83 8089 639
83 8089 640
83 8089 641
83 8089 642
83 8089 643
83 8089 644
83 8089 645
83 8089 646
83 8089 647
83 8089 648
83 8089 649
83 8089 650
83 8089 651
83 8089 652
83 8089 653
83 8089 654
83 8089 655
83 8089 656
83 8089 657
83 8089 658
83 8089 659
83 8089 660
83 8089 661
83 8089 662
83 8089 663
83 8089 664
83 8089 665
83 8089 666
83 8089 667
83 8089 668
83 8089 669
83 8089 670
83 8089 671
83 8089 672
83 8089 673
83 8089 674
83 8089 675
83 8089 676
83 8089 677
83 8089 678
83 8089 679
83 8089 680
83 8089 681
83 8089 682
83 8089 683
83 8089 684
83 8089 685
83 8089 686
83 8089 687
83 8089 688
83 8089 689
83 8089 690
83 8089 691
83 8089 692
83 8089 693
83 8089 694
83 8089 695
83 8089 696
83 8089 697
83 8089 698
83 8089 699
83 8089 700
83 8089 701
83 8089 702
83 8089 703
83 8089 704
83 8089 705
83 8089 706
83 8089 707
83 8089 708
83 8089 709
83 8089 710
83 8089 711
83 8089 712
83 8089 713
83 8089 714
83 8089 715
83 8089 716
83 8089 717
83 8089 718
83 8089 719
83 8089 720
83 8089 721
83 8089 722
83 8089 723
83 8089 724
83 8089 725
83 8089 726
83 8089 727
83 8089 728
83 8089 729
83 8089 730
83 8089 731
83 8089 732
83 8089 733
83 8089 734
83 8089 735
83 8089 736
83 8089 737
83 8089 738
83 8089 739
83 8089 740
83 8089 741
83 8089 742
83 8089 743
83 8089 744
83 8089 745
83 8089 746
83 8089 747
83 8089 748
83 8089 749
83 8089 750
83 8089 751
83 8089 752
83 8089 753
83 8089 754
83 8089 755
83 8089 756
83 8089 757
83 8089 758
83 8089 759
83 8089 760
83 8089 761
83 8089 762
83 8089 763
83 8089 764
83 8089 765
83 8089 766
83 8089 767
83 8089 768
83 8089 769
83 8089 770
83 8089 771
83 8089 772
83 8089 773
83 8089 774
83 8089 775
83 8089 776
83 8089 777
83 8089 778
83 8089 779
83 8089 780
83 8089 781
83 8089 782
83 8089 783
83 8089 784
83 8089 785
83 8089 786
83 8089 787
83 8089 788
83 8089 789
83 8089 790
83 8089 791
83 8089 792
83 8089 793
83 8089 794
83 8089 795
83 8089 796
83 8089 797
83 8089 798
83 8089 799
83 8089 800
83 8089 801
83 8089 802
83 8089 803
83 8089 804
83 8089 805
83 8089 806
83 8089 807
83 8089 808
83 8089 809
83 8089 810
83 8089 811
83 8089 812
83 8089 813
83 8089 814
83 8089 815
83 8089 816
83 8089 817

83 8089 818
83 8089 819
83 8089 820
83 8089 821
83 8089 822
83 8089 823
83 8089 824
83 8089 825
83 8089 826
83 8089 827
83 8089 828
83 8089 829
83 8089 830
83 8089 831
83 8089 832
83 8089 833
83 8089 834
83 8089 835
83 8089 836
83 8089 837
83 8089 838
83 8089 839
83 8089 840
83 8089 841
83 8089 842
83 8089 843
83 8089 844
83 8089 845
83 8089 846
83 8089 847
83 8089 848
83 8089 849
83 8089 850
83 8089 851
83 8089 852
83 8089 853
83 8089 854
83 8089 855
83 8089 856
83 8089 857
83 8089 858
83 8089 859
83 8089 860
83 8089 861
83 8089 862
83 8089 863
83 8089 864
83 8089 865
83 8089 866
83 8089 867
83 8089 868
83 8089 869
83 8089 870
83 8089 871
83 8089 872
83 8089 873
83 8089 874
83 8089 875
83 8089 876
83 8089 877
83 8089 878
83 8089 879
83 8089 880
83 8089 881
83 8089 882
83 8089 883
83 8089 884
83 8089 885
83 8089 886
83 8089 887
83 8089 888
83 8089 889
83 8089 890
83 8089 891
83 8089 892
83 8089 893
83 8089 894
83 8089 895
83 8089 896
83 8089 897
83 8089 898
83 8089 899
83 8089 900
83 8089 901
83 8089 902
83 8089 903
83 8089 904
83 8089 905
83 8089 906
83 8089 907
83 8089 908
83 8089 909
83 8089 910
83 8089 911
83 8089 912
83 8089 913
83 8089 914
83 8089 915
83 8089 916
83 8089 917
83 8089 918
83 8089 919
83 8089 920
83 8089 921
83 8089 922
83 8089 923
83 8089 924
83 8089 925
83 8089 926
83 8089 927
83 8089 928
83 8089 929
83 8089 930
83 8089 931
83 8089 932
83 8089 933
83 8089 934
83 8089 935
83 8089 936
83 8089 937
83 8089 938
83 8089 939
83 8089 940
83 8089 941
83 8089 942
83 8089 943
83 8089 944
83 8089 945
83 8089 946
83 8089 947
83 8089 948
83 8089 949
83 8089 950
83 8089 951
83 8089 952
83 8089 953
83 8089 954
83 8089 955
83 8089 956
83 8089 957
83 8089 958
83 8089 959
83 8089 960
83 8089 961
83 8089 962
83 8089 963
83 8089 964
83 8089 965
83 8089 966
83 8089 967
83 8089 968
83 8089 969
83 8089 970
83 8089 971
83 8089 972
83 8089 973
83 8089 974
83 8089 975
83 8089 976
83 8089 977
83 8089 978
83 8089 979

83 8090 000-049 REFRIGERATED VAN IIB

Builder: Servizio Materiale e Traziane, Italy.
Design Code: IIE332.
Owner: Interfrigo.
Tare Weight: 18.65 t.
Gross Laden Weight: 36.00 t.
Maximum Speed: 60 mph.
Length: 14100 mm (46 ft. 3 in.)
Suspension Type: Double Link.
Exchange Code: 01.
Notes: Used on various workings to and from Europe.
Previous Number Series: 11 83 8193 000-049.

83 8090 000
83 8090 001
83 8090 002
83 8090 003
83 8090 004
83 8090 005
83 8090 006
83 8090 007
83 8090 008
83 8090 009
83 8090 010
83 8090 011
83 8090 012
83 8090 013
83 8090 014
83 8090 015
83 8090 016
83 8090 017
83 8090 018
83 8090 019
83 8090 020
83 8090 021
83 8090 022
83 8090 023
83 8090 024
83 8090 025
83 8090 026
83 8090 027
83 8090 028
83 8090 029
83 8090 030
83 8090 031
83 8090 032
83 8090 033
83 8090 034
83 8090 035
83 8090 036
83 8090 037
83 8090 038
83 8090 039
83 8090 040
83 8090 041
83 8090 042
83 8090 043
83 8090 044
83 8090 045
83 8090 046
83 8090 047
83 8090 048
83 8090 049

83 8091 000 REFRIGERATED VAN IIX

Builder: Snia Viscosa, Italy.
Design Code: IIE452.
Owner: Interfrigo.
Tare Weight: 16.00 t.
Gross Laden Weight: 36.00 t.
Maximum Speed: 60 mph.
Length: 14020 mm (46 ft. 0 in.)
Suspension Type: Double Link.
Exchange Code: 04.
Notes: Not currently operating on British Rail.
Previous Number: 14 83 0891 998.

83 8091 000

83 8092 201-484 REFRIGERATED VAN IIB

Builder: Brugeoise et Nivelles, Bruges, Belgium.
Design Code: IIE348.
Owner: Interfrigo.
Tare Weight: 17.40 t.
Gross Laden Weight: 40.00 t.
Maximum Speed: 60 mph.
Length: 14020 mm (46 ft. 0 in.)
Suspension Type: Double Link.
Exchange Code: 04.
Notes: Used on various workings to and from Europe.
Previous Number Series: 14 83 0888 201-429/455-509.

83 8092 201
83 8092 202
83 8092 203
83 8092 205
83 8092 206
83 8092 207
83 8092 208
83 8092 209
83 8092 210
83 8092 212
83 8092 213
83 8092 214
83 8092 215
83 8092 216
83 8092 218
83 8092 219
83 8092 220
83 8092 221
83 8092 222
83 8092 223
83 8092 224
83 8092 225
83 8092 227
83 8092 229
83 8092 230
83 8092 231
83 8092 232
83 8092 233
83 8092 235
83 8092 236
83 8092 237
83 8092 238
83 8092 239
83 8092 240
83 8092 242
83 8092 243
83 8092 244
83 8092 245
83 8092 246
83 8092 247
83 8092 248
83 8092 249
83 8092 250
83 8092 251
83 8092 253
83 8092 254
83 8092 256
83 8092 257
83 8092 258
83 8092 259
83 8092 260
83 8092 261
83 8092 262
83 8092 263
83 8092 265
83 8092 266
83 8092 267
83 8092 268
83 8092 269
83 8092 270
83 8092 271
83 8092 272
83 8092 273
83 8092 274

Refigerated Van 01 83 8090 008 at Rochester on 26th December 1982. *(R. Wallace)*

40 ft FLAT 21 87 4145 221 at Tees Yard on 20th September 1987. *(R. Wallace)*

83 8092 275
83 8092 276
83 8092 277
83 8092 279
83 8092 280
83 8092 281
83 8092 283
83 8092 284
83 8092 285
83 8092 286
83 8092 287
83 8092 288
83 8092 289
83 8092 290
83 8092 291
83 8092 292
83 8092 293
83 8092 294
83 8092 295
83 8092 296
83 8092 297
83 8092 298
83 8092 299
83 8092 300
83 8092 301
83 8092 302
83 8092 303
83 8092 304
83 8092 305
83 8092 306
83 8092 307
83 8092 309
83 8092 310
83 8092 312
83 8092 313
83 8092 314
83 8092 315
83 8092 316
83 8092 317
83 8092 318
83 8092 320
83 8092 321
83 8092 322
83 8092 323
83 8092 324
83 8092 325
83 8092 326
83 8092 327
83 8092 328
83 8092 329
83 8092 330
83 8092 331
83 8092 332
83 8092 333
83 8092 334
83 8092 335
83 8092 336
83 8092 337
83 8092 338
83 8092 339
83 8092 340
83 8092 341
83 8092 342
83 8092 343
83 8092 344
83 8092 345
83 8092 346
83 8092 347
83 8092 348
83 8092 349
83 8092 350
83 8092 351
83 8092 352
83 8092 353
83 8092 354
83 8092 355
83 8092 356
83 8092 358
83 8092 359
83 8092 360
83 8092 361
83 8092 362
83 8092 364
83 8092 365
83 8092 367
83 8092 369
83 8092 371
83 8092 372
83 8092 373
83 8092 374
83 8092 375
83 8092 376
83 8092 378
83 8092 379
83 8092 380
83 8092 381
83 8092 382
83 8092 383
83 8092 384
83 8092 385
83 8092 386
83 8092 387
83 8092 388
83 8092 389
83 8092 390
83 8092 391
83 8092 392
83 8092 393
83 8092 394
83 8092 395
83 8092 396
83 8092 397
83 8092 398
83 8092 399
83 8092 400
83 8092 401
83 8092 402
83 8092 403
83 8092 404
83 8092 405
83 8092 406
83 8092 407
83 8092 408
83 8092 409
83 8092 410
83 8092 411
83 8092 412
83 8092 413
83 8092 414
83 8092 415
83 8092 416
83 8092 417
83 8092 419
83 8092 420
83 8092 421
83 8092 422
83 8092 423
83 8092 424
83 8092 425
83 8092 426
83 8092 427
83 8092 428
83 8092 429
83 8092 430
83 8092 431
83 8092 432
83 8092 433
83 8092 434
83 8092 435
83 8092 436
83 8092 437
83 8092 438
83 8092 439
83 8092 440
83 8092 441
83 8092 442
83 8092 443
83 8092 444
83 8092 445
83 8092 446
83 8092 447
83 8092 448
83 8092 449
83 8092 450
83 8092 451
83 8092 452
83 8092 453
83 8092 454
83 8092 455
83 8092 456
83 8092 458
83 8092 459
83 8092 460
83 8092 461
83 8092 462
83 8092 463
83 8092 464
83 8092 465
83 8092 466
83 8092 467
83 8092 468
83 8092 469
83 8092 470
83 8092 471
83 8092 472
83 8092 473
83 8092 474
83 8092 475
83 8092 476
83 8092 477
83 8092 478
83 8092 479
83 8092 480
83 8092 481
83 8092 482
83 8092 483
83 8092 484

83 8092 500-599 REFRIGERATED VAN IIB

Builder: A. Gallinari, Reggio Emilia, Italy, 1967-68.
Design Code: IIE331. **Owner:** Interfrigo.
Tare Weight: 18.00 t. **Gross Laden Weight:** 36.00 t.
Maximum Speed: 60 mph. **Length:** 14020 mm (46 ft. 0 in.)
Suspension Type: Double Link. **Exchange Code:** 01.
Notes: Used on various workings to and from Europe.
Previous Number Series: 11 83 8191 000-099.

83 8092 500	83 8092 525	83 8092 550	83 8092 575
83 8092 501	83 8092 526	83 8092 551	83 8092 576
83 8092 502	83 8092 527	83 8092 552	83 8092 577
83 8092 503	83 8092 528	83 8092 553	83 8092 578
83 8092 504	83 8092 529	83 8092 554	83 8092 579
83 8092 505	83 8092 530	83 8092 555	83 8092 580
83 8092 506	83 8092 531	83 8092 556	83 8092 581
83 8092 507	83 8092 532	83 8092 557	83 8092 582
83 8092 508	83 8092 533	83 8092 558	83 8092 583
83 8092 509	83 8092 534	83 8092 559	83 8092 584
83 8092 510	83 8092 535	83 8092 560	83 8092 585
83 8092 511	83 8092 536	83 8092 561	83 8092 586
83 8092 512	83 8092 537	83 8092 562	83 8092 587
83 8092 513	83 8092 538	83 8092 563	83 8092 588
83 8092 514	83 8092 539	83 8092 564	83 8092 589
83 8092 515	83 8092 540	83 8092 565	83 8092 590
83 8092 516	83 8092 541	83 8092 566	83 8092 591
83 8092 517	83 8092 542	83 8092 567	83 8092 592
83 8092 518	83 8092 543	83 8092 568	83 8092 593
83 8092 519	83 8092 544	83 8092 569	83 8092 594
83 8092 520	83 8092 545	83 8092 570	83 8092 595
83 8092 521	83 8092 546	83 8092 571	83 8092 596
83 8092 522	83 8092 547	83 8092 572	83 8092 597
83 8092 523	83 8092 548	83 8092 573	83 8092 598
83 8092 524	83 8092 549	83 8092 574	83 8092 599

85 7390 500-560 TANK IBB

Builder: J.Meyer, Rheinfelden, Switzerland, 1979-81.
Design Code: IBE499(Ex ICE499). **Owner:** Etra.
Tare Weight: 12.60 t. **Gross Laden Weight:** 40.00 t.
Maximum Speed: 60 mph. **Length:** 10050 mm (33 ft. 0 in.)
Suspension Type: Double Link. **Exchange Code:** 23.
Notes: Used on various workings to and from Europe.
Previous Number Series: 21 85 0785 022-041/012-021. 85 7390 530-560 carry their original numbers.

85 7390 500	85 7390 508	85 7390 516	85 7390 524
85 7390 501	85 7390 509	85 7390 517	85 7390 525
85 7390 502	85 7390 510	85 7390 518	85 7390 526
85 7390 503	85 7390 511	85 7390 519	85 7390 527
85 7390 504	85 7390 512	85 7390 520	85 7390 528
85 7390 505	85 7390 513	85 7390 521	85 7390 529
85 7390 506	85 7390 514	85 7390 522	85 7390 530
85 7390 507	85 7390 515	85 7390 523	85 7390 531

85 7390 532	85 7390 540	85 7390 547	85 7390 554
85 7390 533	85 7390 541	85 7390 548	85 7390 555
85 7390 534	85 7390 542	85 7390 549	85 7390 556
85 7390 535	85 7390 543	85 7390 550	85 7390 557
85 7390 536	85 7390 544	85 7390 551	85 7390 558
85 7390 537	85 7390 545	85 7390 552	85 7390 559
85 7390 538	85 7390 546	85 7390 553	85 7390 560
85 7390 539			

85 7397 750-751 TANK IBB

Builder: J.Meyer, Rheinfelden, Switzerland, 1983.
Design Code: IBE488(Ex ICE488). **Owner:** VTG.
Tare Weight: 12.00 t. **Gross Laden Weight:** 40.00 t.
Maximum Speed: 60 mph. **Length:** 8900 mm (29 ft. 3 in.)
Suspension Type: Single Link. **Exchange Code:** 23.
Notes: Used on various workings to and from Europe.

85 7397 750 85 7397 751

85 7398 500-521 TANK IBB

Builder: J.Meyer, Rheinfelden, Switzerland, 1979.
Design Code: IBE493(Ex ICE493). **Owner:** Etra.
Tare Weight: 12.00 t. **Gross Laden Weight:** 40.00 t.
Maximum Speed: 60 mph. **Length:** 10050 mm (33 ft. 0 in.)
Suspension Type: Double Link. **Exchange Code:** 23.
Notes: Used on various workings to and from Europe.
Previous Number Series: 21 85 0785 000-011/042-051.

85 7398 500	85 7398 506	85 7398 512	85 7398 517
85 7398 501	85 7398 507	85 7398 513	85 7398 518
85 7398 502	85 7398 508	85 7398 514	85 7398 519
85 7398 503	85 7398 509	85 7398 515	85 7398 520
85 7398 504	85 7398 510	85 7398 516	85 7398 521
85 7398 505	85 7398 511		

85 7492 200-700 TANK IBB

Builder: J.Meyer, Rheinfelden, Switzerland.
Design Code: IBE366(Ex ICE366). **Owner:** SBB.
Tare Weight: 13.70 t. **Gross Laden Weight:** 36.00 t.
Maximum Speed: 60 mph. **Length:** 8900 mm (29 ft. 3 in.)
Suspension Type: Single Link. **Exchange Code:** 23.
Notes: Used on various workings to and from Europe.
Previous Number Series: 21 85 0722 554/555/589.

85 7492 200 85 7492 201 85 7492 700

85 7995 500-505 BOGIE TANK ICB

Builder: J.Meyer, Rheinfelden, Switzerland, 1982.
Design Code: ICE532. **Owner:** Etra.

Tare Weight: 24.00 t.
Gross Laden Weight: 80.00 t.
Maximum Speed: 60 mph.
Length: 16940 mm (55 ft. 7 in.)
Bogie Type: SBB.
Exchange Code: 33.
Notes: Used on various workings to and from Europe.

85 7995 500
85 7995 501
85 7995 502
85 7995 503
85 7995 504
85 7995 505

87 2380 500-999 LARGE VAN ILX

Builder: Frangeco, 1965.
Design Code: ILE304.
Owner: SNCF.
Tare Weight: 14.00 t.
Gross Laden Weight: 40.00 t.
Maximum Speed: 60 mph.
Length: 14020 mm (46 ft. 0 in.)
Suspension Type: Double Link.
Exchange Code: 21.
Notes: Used on various workings to and from Europe.
Previous Number Series: 21 87 2380 000-499.

87 2380 500
87 2380 501
87 2380 502
87 2380 503
87 2380 504
87 2380 505
87 2380 506
87 2380 507
87 2380 508
87 2380 509
87 2380 510
87 2380 511
87 2380 512
87 2380 513
87 2380 514
87 2380 515
87 2380 516
87 2380 517
87 2380 518
87 2380 519
87 2380 520
87 2380 521
87 2380 522
87 2380 523
87 2380 524
87 2380 525
87 2380 526
87 2380 527
87 2380 528
87 2380 529
87 2380 530
87 2380 531
87 2380 532
87 2380 533
87 2380 534
87 2380 535
87 2380 536
87 2380 537
87 2380 538
87 2380 539
87 2380 540
87 2380 541
87 2380 542
87 2380 543
87 2380 544
87 2380 545
87 2380 546
87 2380 547
87 2380 548
87 2380 549
87 2380 550
87 2380 551
87 2380 552
87 2380 553
87 2380 554
87 2380 555
87 2380 556
87 2380 557
87 2380 558
87 2380 559
87 2380 560
87 2380 561
87 2380 562
87 2380 563
87 2380 564
87 2380 565
87 2380 566
87 2380 567
87 2380 568
87 2380 569
87 2380 570
87 2380 571
87 2380 572
87 2380 573
87 2380 574
87 2380 575
87 2380 576
87 2380 577
87 2380 578
87 2380 579
87 2380 580
87 2380 581
87 2380 582
87 2380 583
87 2380 584
87 2380 585
87 2380 586
87 2380 587
87 2380 588
87 2380 589
87 2380 590
87 2380 591
87 2380 592
87 2380 593
87 2380 594
87 2380 595
87 2380 596
87 2380 597
87 2380 598
87 2380 599
87 2380 600
87 2380 601
87 2380 602
87 2380 603
87 2380 604
87 2380 605
87 2380 606
87 2380 607
87 2380 608
87 2380 609
87 2380 610
87 2380 611
87 2380 612
87 2380 613
87 2380 614
87 2380 615
87 2380 616
87 2380 617
87 2380 618
87 2380 619
87 2380 620
87 2380 621
87 2380 622
87 2380 623
87 2380 624
87 2380 625
87 2380 626
87 2380 627
87 2380 628
87 2380 629
87 2380 630
87 2380 631
87 2380 632
87 2380 633
87 2380 634
87 2380 635
87 2380 636
87 2380 637
87 2380 638
87 2380 639
87 2380 640
87 2380 641
87 2380 642
87 2380 643
87 2380 644
87 2380 645
87 2380 646
87 2380 647

87 2380 648
87 2380 649
87 2380 650
87 2380 651
87 2380 652
87 2380 653
87 2380 654
87 2380 655
87 2380 656
87 2380 657
87 2380 658
87 2380 659
87 2380 660
87 2380 661
87 2380 662
87 2380 663
87 2380 664
87 2380 665
87 2380 666
87 2380 667
87 2380 668
87 2380 669
87 2380 670
87 2380 671
87 2380 672
87 2380 673
87 2380 674
87 2380 675
87 2380 676
87 2380 677
87 2380 678
87 2380 679
87 2380 680
87 2380 681
87 2380 682
87 2380 683
87 2380 684
87 2380 685
87 2380 686
87 2380 687
87 2380 688
87 2380 689
87 2380 690
87 2380 691
87 2380 692
87 2380 693
87 2380 694
87 2380 695
87 2380 696
87 2380 697
87 2380 698
87 2380 699
87 2380 700
87 2380 701
87 2380 702
87 2380 703
87 2380 704
87 2380 705
87 2380 706
87 2380 707
87 2380 708
87 2380 709
87 2380 710
87 2380 711
87 2380 712
87 2380 713
87 2380 714
87 2380 715
87 2380 716
87 2380 717
87 2380 718
87 2380 719
87 2380 720
87 2380 721
87 2380 722
87 2380 723
87 2380 724
87 2380 725
87 2380 726
87 2380 727
87 2380 728
87 2380 729
87 2380 730
87 2380 731
87 2380 732
87 2380 733
87 2380 734
87 2380 735
87 2380 736
87 2380 737
87 2380 738
87 2380 739
87 2380 740
87 2380 741
87 2380 742
87 2380 743
87 2380 744
87 2380 745
87 2380 746
87 2380 747
87 2380 748
87 2380 749
87 2380 750
87 2380 751
87 2380 752
87 2380 753
87 2380 754
87 2380 755
87 2380 756
87 2380 757
87 2380 758
87 2380 759
87 2380 760
87 2380 761
87 2380 762
87 2380 763
87 2380 764
87 2380 765
87 2380 766
87 2380 767
87 2380 768
87 2380 769
87 2380 770
87 2380 771
87 2380 772
87 2380 773
87 2380 774
87 2380 775
87 2380 776
87 2380 777
87 2380 778
87 2380 779
87 2380 780
87 2380 781
87 2380 782
87 2380 783
87 2380 784
87 2380 785
87 2380 786
87 2380 787
87 2380 788
87 2380 789
87 2380 790
87 2380 791
87 2380 792
87 2380 793
87 2380 794
87 2380 795
87 2380 796
87 2380 797
87 2380 798
87 2380 799
87 2380 800
87 2380 801
87 2380 802
87 2380 803
87 2380 804
87 2380 805
87 2380 806
87 2380 807
87 2380 808
87 2380 809
87 2380 810
87 2380 811
87 2380 812
87 2380 813
87 2380 814
87 2380 815
87 2380 816
87 2380 817
87 2380 818
87 2380 819
87 2380 820
87 2380 821
87 2380 822
87 2380 823
87 2380 824
87 2380 825
87 2380 826
87 2380 827
87 2380 828
87 2380 829
87 2380 830
87 2380 831
87 2380 832
87 2380 833
87 2380 834
87 2380 835
87 2380 836
87 2380 837
87 2380 838
87 2380 839
87 2380 840
87 2380 841
87 2380 842
87 2380 843
87 2380 844
87 2380 845
87 2380 846
87 2380 847
87 2380 848
87 2380 849
87 2380 850
87 2380 851
87 2380 852
87 2380 853
87 2380 854
87 2380 855
87 2380 856
87 2380 857
87 2380 858
87 2380 859
87 2380 860
87 2380 861
87 2380 862
87 2380 863
87 2380 864
87 2380 865
87 2380 866
87 2380 867
87 2380 868
87 2380 869
87 2380 870
87 2380 871

87 2380 872	87 2380 904	87 2380 936	87 2380 968
87 2380 873	87 2380 905	87 2380 937	87 2380 969
87 2380 874	87 2380 906	87 2380 938	87 2380 970
87 2380 875	87 2380 907	87 2380 939	87 2380 971
87 2380 876	87 2380 908	87 2380 940	87 2380 972
87 2380 877	87 2380 909	87 2380 941	87 2380 973
87 2380 878	87 2380 910	87 2380 942	87 2380 974
87 2380 879	87 2380 911	87 2380 943	87 2380 975
87 2380 880	87 2380 912	87 2380 944	87 2380 976
87 2380 881	87 2380 913	87 2380 945	87 2380 977
87 2380 882	87 2380 914	87 2380 946	87 2380 978
87 2380 883	87 2380 915	87 2380 947	87 2380 979
87 2380 884	87 2380 916	87 2380 948	87 2380 980
87 2380 885	87 2380 917	87 2380 949	87 2380 981
87 2380 886	87 2380 918	87 2380 950	87 2380 982
87 2380 887	87 2380 919	87 2380 951	87 2380 983
87 2380 888	87 2380 920	87 2380 952	87 2380 984
87 2380 889	87 2380 921	87 2380 953	87 2380 985
87 2380 890	87 2380 922	87 2380 954	87 2380 986
87 2380 891	87 2380 923	87 2380 955	87 2380 987
87 2380 892	87 2380 924	87 2380 956	87 2380 988
87 2380 893	87 2380 925	87 2380 957	87 2380 989
87 2380 894	87 2380 926	87 2380 958	87 2380 990
87 2380 895	87 2380 927	87 2380 959	87 2380 991
87 2380 896	87 2380 928	87 2380 960	87 2380 992
87 2380 897	87 2380 929	87 2380 961	87 2380 993
87 2380 898	87 2380 930	87 2380 962	87 2380 994
87 2380 899	87 2380 931	87 2380 963	87 2380 995
87 2380 900	87 2380 932	87 2380 964	87 2380 996
87 2380 901	87 2380 933	87 2380 965	87 2380 997
87 2380 902	87 2380 934	87 2380 966	87 2380 998
87 2380 903	87 2380 935	87 2380 967	87 2380 999

87 2396 000-005 CURTAIN SIDED VAN IYX

Builder: Inge Trans, 1984.
Design Code: IYE540(Ex IPE540). **Owner:** Eva.
Tare Weight: 13.80 t. **Gross Laden Weight:** 40.00 t.
Maximum Speed: 60 mph. **Length:** 14020 mm (46 ft. 0 in.)
Suspension Type: Double Link. **Exchange Code:** 23.
Notes: Used on various workings to and from Europe.
Previous Number Series: 43 87 2396 000-005.

87 2396 000	87 2396 002	87 2396 004	87 2396 005
87 2396 001	87 2396 003		

87 4145 200-299 40 ft FLAT IFB

Builder: Frangeco, 1967.
Design Code: IFE342. **Owner:** SNCF.
Tare Weight: 11.50 t. **Gross Laden Weight:** 40.00 t.
Maximum Speed: 60 mph. **Length:** 13860 mm (45 ft. 5 in.)
Suspension Type: Double Link. **Exchange Code:** 21.
Notes: Used on various workings to and from Europe.

87 4145 200
87 4145 201
87 4145 202
87 4145 203
87 4145 204
87 4145 205
87 4145 206
87 4145 207
87 4145 208
87 4145 209
87 4145 210
87 4145 211
87 4145 212
87 4145 213
87 4145 214
87 4145 215
87 4145 216
87 4145 217
87 4145 218
87 4145 219
87 4145 220
87 4145 221
87 4145 222
87 4145 223
87 4145 224
87 4145 225
87 4145 226
87 4145 227
87 4145 228
87 4145 229
87 4145 230
87 4145 231
87 4145 232
87 4145 233
87 4145 234
87 4145 235
87 4145 236
87 4145 237
87 4145 238
87 4145 239
87 4145 240
87 4145 241
87 4145 242
87 4145 243
87 4145 244
87 4145 245
87 4145 246
87 4145 247
87 4145 248
87 4145 249
87 4145 250
87 4145 251
87 4145 252
87 4145 253
87 4145 254
87 4145 255
87 4145 256
87 4145 257
87 4145 258
87 4145 259
87 4145 260
87 4145 261
87 4145 262
87 4145 263
87 4145 264
87 4145 265
87 4145 266
87 4145 267
87 4145 268
87 4145 269
87 4145 270
87 4145 271
87 4145 272
87 4145 273
87 4145 274
87 4145 275
87 4145 276
87 4145 277
87 4145 278
87 4145 279
87 4145 280
87 4145 281
87 4145 282
87 4145 283
87 4145 284
87 4145 285
87 4145 286
87 4145 287
87 4145 288
87 4145 289
87 4145 290
87 4145 291
87 4145 292
87 4145 293
87 4145 294
87 4145 295
87 4145 296
87 4145 297
87 4145 298
87 4145 299

87 4176 000-099 IPA

DOUBLE DECK CAR CARRIER

Builder: Société ANF-Industrie, Blanc-Misseron, France, 1989.
Design Code: IPE695.
Owner:
Tare Weight: 14.50 t.
Gross Laden Weight: 26.50 t.
Maximum Speed: 60 mph.
Length: 15200 mm (49 ft. 10 in.)
Suspension Type:
Exchange Code: 23.
Notes: Used on various workings to and from Europe.

87 4176 000
87 4176 001
87 4176 002
87 4176 003
87 4176 004
87 4176 005
87 4176 006
87 4176 007
87 4176 008
87 4176 009
87 4176 010
87 4176 011
87 4176 012
87 4176 013
87 4176 014
87 4176 015
87 4176 016
87 4176 017
87 4176 018
87 4176 019
87 4176 020
87 4176 021
87 4176 022
87 4176 023
87 4176 024
87 4176 025
87 4176 026
87 4176 027
87 4176 028
87 4176 029
87 4176 030
87 4176 031
87 4176 032
87 4176 033
87 4176 034
87 4176 035
87 4176 036
87 4176 037
87 4176 038
87 4176 039
87 4176 040
87 4176 041
87 4176 042
87 4176 043
87 4176 044
87 4176 045
87 4176 046
87 4176 047
87 4176 048
87 4176 049
87 4176 050
87 4176 051
87 4176 052
87 4176 053
87 4176 054
87 4176 055
87 4176 056
87 4176 057
87 4176 058
87 4176 059
87 4176 060
87 4176 061
87 4176 062
87 4176 063
87 4176 064
87 4176 065
87 4176 066
87 4176 067
87 4176 068
87 4176 069
87 4176 070
87 4176 071
87 4176 072
87 4176 073
87 4176 074
87 4176 075
87 4176 076
87 4176 077
87 4176 078
87 4176 079

87 4176 080	87 4176 085	87 4176 090	87 4176 095
87 4176 081	87 4176 086	87 4176 091	87 4176 096
87 4176 082	87 4176 087	87 4176 092	87 4176 097
87 4176 083	87 4176 088	87 4176 093	87 4176 098
87 4176 084	87 4176 089	87 4176 094	87 4176 099

87 4177 000-019 IPA

DOUBLE DECK CAR CARRIER

Builder: Société ANF-Industrie, Blanc-Misseron, France, 1989.
Design Code: IPE720. **Owner:**
Tare Weight: 14.50 t. **Gross Laden Weight:** 26.50 t.
Maximum Speed: 60 mph. **Length:** 15200 mm (49 ft. 10 in.)
Suspension Type: **Exchange Code:** 23.
Notes: Used on various workings to and from Europe.

87 4177 000	87 4177 005	87 4177 010	87 4177 015
87 4177 001	87 4177 006	87 4177 011	87 4177 016
87 4177 002	87 4177 007	87 4177 012	87 4177 017
87 4177 003	87 4177 008	87 4177 013	87 4177 018
87 4177 004	87 4177 009	87 4177 014	87 4177 019

87 4246 002-021 40 ft FLAT IFR

Builder: Leeds Forge Co. Ltd., United Kingdom.
Design Code: IFE403. **Owner:** SNCF.
Tare Weight: **Gross Laden Weight:**
Maximum Speed: 60 mph. **Length:**
Bogie Type: **Exchange Code:** 31.
Notes: Not currently running on British Rail.

87 4246 002	87 4246 012	87 4246 018	87 4246 020
87 4246 008	87 4246 013	87 4246 019	87 4246 021
87 4246 011	87 4246 014		

87 4443 000 FLAT IEB

Builder: Arbel-Fauvet, Douai, France, 1984.
Design Code: IEE573(Ex IPE573). **Owner:** Société Ethyl.
Tare Weight: 10.00 t. **Gross Laden Weight:** 30.00 t.
Maximum Speed: 60 mph. **Length:** 8590 mm (28 ft. 2 in.)
Suspension Type: **Exchange Code:** 23.
Notes: Used on various workings to and from Europe.
Previous Number: 23 87 4420 000.

87 4443 000

87 4572 220-244 MULTIFRET IFA

Builder: Arbel-Fauvet, Douai, France, 1989.
Design Code: IFE706. **Owner:** SNCF.
Tare Weight: 18.30 t. **Gross Laden Weight:** 56.00 t.
Maximum Speed: 75 mph. **Length:** 19340 mm (63 ft. 5 in.)

Bogie Type: Y25.
Exchange Code: 31.
Notes: Used between Harwich & the North West.

87 4572 224
87 4572 225
87 4572 226
87 4572 227
87 4572 228
87 4572 229
87 4572 230
87 4572 231
87 4572 232
87 4572 233
87 4572 234
87 4572 235
87 4572 236
87 4572 237
87 4572 238
87 4572 239
87 4572 240
87 4572 241
87 4572 242
87 4572 243
87 4572 244

87 4737 015 CURTAIN SIDED VAN IOB

Builder: Arbel-Fauvet, Douai, France, 1983.
Design Code: IOE733.
Owner: Cargowaggon.
Tare Weight: 24.00 t.
Gross Laden Weight: 80.00 t.
Maximum Speed: 75 mph.
Length: 20590 mm (67 ft. 6 in.)
Bogie Type: Y25CSS.
Exchange Code: 33.
Notes: Used on various workings to and from Europe.
Previous Number: 33 87 4746 035.

87 4737 015

87 4739 020-024 CURTAIN SIDED VAN IUB

Builder: Arbel-Fauvet, Douai, France, 1983.
Design Code: IUE545(Ex IPE545).
Owner: Transfesa.
Tare Weight: 24.00 t.
Gross Laden Weight: 80.00 t.
Maximum Speed: 75 mph.
Length: 20590 mm (67 ft. 6 in.)
Bogie Type: Y25CS2.
Exchange Code: 83.
Notes: Used on various workings to and from Europe.
Previous Number Series: 33 87 4746 035.

87 4739 020
87 4739 021
87 4739 022
87 4729 023
87 4729 024

87 4741 000 EASILOADER IUA

Builder: Ateliers de Breton, France, 1987.
Design Code: IUE691(Ex IPE691).
Owner:
Tare Weight: 24.30 t.
Gross Laden Weight: 90.00 t.
Maximum Speed: 60 mph.
Length: 20264 mm (66 ft. 6 in.)
Bogie Type: Y25LST.
Exchange Code: 33.
Notes: Used on various workings to and from Europe.

87 4741 000

87 4741 001-012 HOODED FLAT IUA

Builder: Société ANF-Industrie, Blanc-Misseron, France, 1987.
Design Code: IUE694(Ex IPE694).
Owner: Sati.
Tare Weight: 25.00 t.
Gross Laden Weight: 90.00 t.
Maximum Speed: 60 mph.
Length: 20090 mm (65 ft. 11 in.)
Bogie Type: Y25LSD.
Exchange Code: 33.

87 4741 001	87 4741 004	87 4741 007	87 4741 010
87 4741 002	87 4741 005	87 4741 008	87 4741 011
87 4741 003	87 4741 006	87 4741 009	87 4741 012

87 4746 000-011 CURTAIN SIDED VAN IUA

Builder: Inge-Trans, 1986.
Design Code: IUE598(Ex IPE598). **Owner:** Tiphook.
Tare Weight: 24.00 t. **Gross Laden Weight:** 84.00 t.
Maximum Speed: 60 mph. **Length:** 20264 mm (66 ft. 6 in.)
Bogie Type: **Exchange Code:** 33.
Notes: On hire to Norsk Hydro. Used on various workings to and from Immingham.

87 4746 000	87 4746 003	87 4746 006	87 4746 009
87 4746 001	87 4746 004	87 4746 007	87 4746 010
87 4746 002	87 4746 005	87 4746 008	87 4746 011

87 4746 012-019 CURTAIN SIDED VAN IUA

Builder: Inge-Trans, 1986.
Design Code: IUE672(Ex IPE672). **Owner:** Tiphook.
Tare Weight: 24.00 t. **Gross Laden Weight:** 84.00 t.
Maximum Speed: 60 mph. **Length:** 20264 mm (66 ft. 6 in.)
Bogie Type: Y25CM. **Exchange Code:** 33.
Notes: On hire to Norsk Hydro. Used on various workings to and from Immingham.

87 4746 012	87 4746 014	87 4746 016	87 4746 018
87 4746 012	87 4746 015	87 4746 017	87 4746 019

87 4746 020-049 CURTAIN SIDED VAN IUA

Builder: Arbel-Fauvet, Douai, France, 1983.
Design Code: IUE545(Ex IPE545). **Owner:** Cargowaggon.
Tare Weight: 24.00 t. **Gross Laden Weight:** 80.00 t.
Maximum Speed: 75 mph. **Length:** 20590 mm (67 ft. 6 in.)
Bogie Type: Y25CSS. **Exchange Code:** 33.
Notes: Used on various workings to and from Europe.

87 4746 020	87 4746 028	87 4746 036	87 4746 043
87 4746 021	87 4746 029	87 4746 037	87 4746 044
87 4746 022	87 4746 030	87 4746 038	87 4746 045
87 4746 023	87 4746 031	87 4746 039	87 4746 046
87 4746 024	87 4746 032	87 4746 040	87 4746 047
87 4746 025	87 4746 033	87 4746 041	87 4746 048
87 4746 026	87 4746 034	87 4746 042	87 4746 049
87 4746 027			

87 5699 000 COVERED HOPPER IRB

Builder: Arbel-Fauvet, Douai, France, 1972.
Design Code: IRE384(Ex IPE384). **Owner:** Sotranda.
Tare Weight: **Gross Laden Weight:**
Maximum Speed: 60 mph. **Length:**

Bogie Type: **Exchange Code:** 33.
Notes: Used on various workings to and from Europe.
Previous Number: 21 87 0598 000.

87 5699 000

87 5699 001 COVERED HOPPER IRB

Builder: Arbel-Fauvet, Douai, France, 1974.
Design Code: IRE389(Ex IPE389). **Owner:** Slemi.
Tare Weight: 23.35 t. **Gross Laden Weight:** 80.00 t.
Maximum Speed: 60 mph. **Length:** 16040 mm (52 ft. 8 in.)
Bogie Type: Y25CSI. **Exchange Code:** 33.
Notes: Used on various workings to and from Europe.
Previous Number: 21 87 0598 001.

87 5699 001

87 5699 007-025 COVERED HOPPER IRB

Builder: Arbel-Fauvet, Douai, France, 1974-75 (a 1983).
Design Code: IRE644 (Ex IPE644) **Owner:** Lefebure.
Tare Weight: 21.85 t. **Gross Laden Weight:** 80.00 t.
Maximum Speed: 60 mph. **Length:** 16040 mm (52 ft. 8 in.)
Bogie Type: **Exchange Code:** 33.
Notes: Used on workings between St. Julien and Barry and also between Scotland or the West of England and Basel.
Previous Number Series: 21 70 0999 022/039/055/056 (007-010 only).

87 5699 007
87 5699 008
87 5699 009
87 5699 010
87 5699 011 a
87 5699 012 a
87 5699 013 a
87 5699 014 a
87 5699 015 a
87 5699 016 a
87 5699 017 a
87 5699 018 a
87 5699 019 a
87 5699 020 a
87 5699 021 a
87 5699 022 a
87 5699 023 a
87 5699 024 a
87 5699 025 a

87 6094 000-049 HIGH OPEN IOB

Buildor:
Design Code: IOE390. **Owner:** SNCF.
Tare Weight: 10.50 t. **Gross Laden Weight:** 40.00 t.
Maximum Speed: 60 mph. **Length:** 8892 mm (29 ft. 2 in.)
Suspension Type: Double Link. **Exchange Code:** 21.
Notes: Used on various workings to and from Europe.
Previous Number Series: 21 87 6190 000-049.

87 6094 000
87 6094 001
87 6094 002
87 6094 003
87 6094 004
87 6094 005
87 6094 006
87 6094 007
87 6094 008
87 6094 009
87 6094 010
87 6094 012
87 6094 013
87 6094 014
87 6094 015
87 6094 016
87 6094 017
87 6094 018
87 6094 019
87 6094 020
87 6094 021
87 6094 022
87 6094 023
87 6094 024
87 6094 025
87 6094 026
87 6094 027
87 6094 028
87 6094 029
87 6094 030
87 6094 031
87 6094 032
87 6094 033
87 6094 034
87 6094 035
87 6094 036

High Open 21 87 6094 006 at Hoo Junction on 23rd June 1983. *(R. Wallace)*

Tank 33 87 7898 041 at Hoo Junction on 25th February 1990. *(R. Wallace)*

87 6094 037	87 6094 041	87 6094 044	87 6094 047
87 6094 038	87 6094 042	87 6094 045	87 6094 048
87 6094 039	87 6094 043	87 6094 046	87 6094 049
87 6094 040			

87 7190 000-004 TANK IBR

Builder:
Design Code: IBE347 (Ex ICE347). **Owner:** Simotra.
Tare Weight: **Gross Laden Weight:**
Maximum Speed: 60 mph. **Length:**
Suspension Type: **Exchange Code:** 23.
Notes: Not currently operating on British Rail.
Previous Number Series: 21 87 0782 077-081.

87 7190 000	87 7190 002	87 7190 003	87 7190 004
87 7190 001			

87 7190 005-006 TANK IBB

Builder:
Design Code: IBE349 (Ex ICE349). **Owner:** Simotra.
Tare Weight: **Gross Laden Weight:**
Maximum Speed: 60 mph. **Length:**
Suspension Type: **Exchange Code:** 23.
Notes: Used on various workings to and from Europe.
Previous Number Series: 21 87 0782 082-083.

87 7190 005	87 7190 006

87 7190 500-509 TANK IBB

Builder: Arbel-Fauvet, Douai, France.
Design Code: IBE315 (Ex ICE315)[a IBE316 (Ex ICE316)].
Owner: Ermewa. **Tare Weight:** 10.24 t (a 10.30 t).
Gross Laden Weight: 36.00 t (a 40.00 t). **Maximum Speed:** 50 mph.
Length: 8340 mm (27 ft 4 in).
Suspension Type: Double Link. **Exchange Code:** 23.
Notes: 504 & 506 are used on various workings to and from Europe. The remainder are not currently operating on British Rail.
Previous Number Series: 21 87 0780 010/012-014/016/019.

87 7190 500	87 7190 503	87 7190 506	87 7190 509 a
87 7190 502 a	87 7190 504		

87 7191 002-003 TANK IBB

Builder: Arbel-Fauvet, Douai, France, 1959.
Design Code: IBE619. **Owner:** Société Ethyl.
Tare Weight: **Gross Laden Weight:**
Maximum Speed: 60 mph. **Length:**
Suspension Type: **Exchange Code:** 23.
Notes: Used on various workings to and from Europe.

Previous Number Series: 21 87 0782 054/056.

87 7191 002 87 7191 003

87 7191 020 TANK IBB

Builder: Arbel-Fauvet, Douai, France.
Design Code: IBE272.
Owner: Solvay.
Tare Weight: 10.68 t.
Gross Laden Weight: 40.00 t.
Maximum Speed: 50 mph.
Length: 8840 mm (29 ft 0 in).
Suspension Type: Double Link.
Exchange Code: 23.
Notes: Not currently operating on British Rail.
Previous Number: 21 87 0782 064.

87 7191 020

87 7191 021-023 TANK IBX

Builder: Arbel-Fauvet, Douai, France.
Design Code: IBE318 (Ex ICE318)[a IBE279 (Ex ICE279).
Owner: Solvay.
Tare Weight: 10.50 t (a 10.79 t).
Gross Laden Weight: 40.00 t.
Maximum Speed: 50 mph.
Length: 9140 mm (30 ft 0 in)[a 9340 mm 30 ft. 8 in).
Suspension Type: Double Link.
Exchange Code: 23.
Notes: 023 is used on various workings to and from Europe. The remainder are not currently operating on British Rail.
Previous Number Series: 21 87 0782 065-067.

87 7191 021 87 7191 022 a 87 7191 023

87 7191 024 TANK IBB

Builder: Arbel-Fauvet, Douai, France.
Design Code: IBE627 (Ex ICE627).
Owner: Solvay.
Tare Weight:
Gross Laden Weight:
Maximum Speed: 60 mph.
Length:
Suspension Type:
Exchange Code: 23.
Notes: Not currently operating on British Rail.
Previous Number: 21 87 0782 068.

87 7191 024

87 7191 025-034 TANK IBB

Builder: Ateliers de Provence, Miramas, France.
Design Code: IBE477 (Ex ICE477)[a IBE478 (Ex ICE478).
Owner: Europrail.
Tare Weight: 11.50 t (a 10.50 t).
Gross Laden Weight: 40.00 t.
Maximum Speed: 50 mph.
Length: 9040 mm (29 ft 8 in).
Exchange Code: 23.
Suspension Type: Double Link (a Single Limk).
Notes: Not currently operating on British Rail.
Previous Number Series: 21 87 0782 085-094.

87 7191 025
87 7191 026
87 7191 027
87 7191 028 a
87 7191 029 a
87 7191 030 a
87 7191 031 a
87 7191 032 a
87 7191 033 a
87 7191 034 a

87 7191 500 TANK IBB

Builder: Arbel-Fauvet, Douai, France.
Design Code: IBE207 (Ex ICE207).
Tare Weight: 11.20 t.
Maximum Speed: 50 mph.
Suspension Type: Single Limk.
Owner: Ugilor.
Gross Laden Weight: 36.00 t.
Length: 8590 mm (28 ft 2 in).
Exchange Code: 23.
Notes: Not currently operating on British Rail.
Previous Number: 21 87 0782 037.

87 7191 500

87 7287 000 TANK IBB

Builder:
Design Code: IBE214 (Ex ICE214).
Tare Weight:
Maximum Speed: 60 mph.
Suspension Type:
Owner: Kuhlmann.
Gross Laden Weight:
Length:
Exchange Code: 23.
Notes: Used on various workings to and from Europe.
Previous Number: 21 87 0782 076.

87 7287 000

87 7287 001-015 TANK IBB

Builder:
Owner: Société Ethyl.
Design Code: IBE619 (Ex ICE619)[a IBE660 (Ex ICE660).
Tare Weight:
Maximum Speed: 60 mph.
Suspension Type:
Gross Laden Weight:
Length:
Exchange Code: 23.
Notes: IBE660 is coded IBR. Used on various workings to and from Europe.
Previous Number Series: 21 87 0782 043/044/046/047/049/051/055/058/061.

87 7287 001
87 7287 002
87 7287 004
87 7287 005 a
87 7287 007
87 7287 009
87 7287 011
87 7287 013
87 7287 015

87 7289 000 TANK IBB

Builder: Ers Fernard Rolland.
Design Code: IBE462 (Ex ICE462).
Tare Weight:
Maximum Speed: 60 mph.
Suspension Type:
Owner: Société Ethyl.
Gross Laden Weight:
Length:
Exchange Code: 23.
Notes: Used on various workings to and from Europe.
Previous Number: 21 87 0782 084.

87 7289 000

87 7390 005-007 TANK IBX

Builder: Arbel-Fauvet, Douai, France.
Design Code: IBE327 (Ex ICE327) **Owner:** Société Metro.
Tare Weight: 12.88 t. **Gross Laden Weight:** 40.00 t.
Maximum Speed: 60 mph. **Length:** 10540 mm (34 ft. 7 in.)
Suspension Type: Double Link. **Exchange Code:** 23.
Notes: Used on various workings to and from Europe.
Previous Number Series: 21 87 0785 010-012.

87 7390 005	87 7390 006	87 7390 007

87 7390 500 TANK IBQ

Builder:
Design Code: IBE116 (Ex ICE116). **Owner:** Dubonnet.
Tare Weight: 9.35 t. **Gross Laden Weight:** 30.00 t.
Maximum Speed: 50 mph. **Length:** 7780 mm (25 ft. 10 in.)
Suspension Type: Single Link. **Exchange Code:** 23.
Notes: Not currently operating on British Rail.
Previous Number: 21 87 0785 501.

87 7390 500

87 7390 501-518 TANK IBB

Builder: Ateliers de Joigny, France.
Design Code: IBE360 (Ex ICE360)[a IBE361 (Ex ICE36100, b IBE362 (Ex ICE362)].
Owner: Ermewa (a VTG, b TSL). **Tare Weight:** 10.85 t (a 12.54 t, b 11.00 t).
Gross Laden Weight: 36.35 t (a & b 40.00 t).
Maximum Speed: 60 mph.
Length: 8340 mm (27 ft. 4 in.)[b 9040 mm (29 ft 8 in).
Suspension Type: Single Link. **Exchange Code:** 23.
Notes: Used on various workings to and from Europe.
Previous Number Series: 21 87 0785 502-509/513/515/517/514/516/518-520/510/511.

87 7390 501	87 7390 505	87 7390 509	87 7390 513
87 7390 502	87 7390 506	87 7390 510	87 7390 514 a
87 7390 503	87 7390 507 b	87 7390 511	87 7390 517
87 7390 504	87 7390 508	87 7390 512	87 7390 518

87 7391 000 TANK IBB

Builder: C.F.M.F., France, 1980.
Design Code: IBE484 (Ex ICE484). **Owner:** CFPM.
Tare Weight: **Gross Laden Weight:**
Maximum Speed: 60 mph. **Length:**
Suspension Type: **Exchange Code:** 23.
Notes: Not currently operating on British Rail.
Previous Number: 21 87 0785 013.

87 7391 000

87 7391 001-004 TANK IBB

Builder: Lormafer.
Design Code: IBE373 (Ex ICE373). **Owner:** Algeco.
Tare Weight: 12.60 t. **Gross Laden Weight:** 40.00 t.
Maximum Speed: 60 mph. **Length:** 12040 mm (39 ft 6 in).
Suspension Type: Double Link. **Exchange Code:** 23.
Notes: Used on various workings to and from Europe.
Previous Number Series: 21 87 0785 005/007/009/006.

87 7391 001 87 7391 002 87 7391 003 87 7391 004

87 7395 000 TANK IBB

Builder: Arbel-Fauvet, Douai, France.
Design Code: IBE338 (Ex ICE338). **Owner:** Simotra.
Tare Weight: 12.65 t. **Gross Laden Weight:** 40.00 t.
Maximum Speed: 60 mph. **Length:** 9840 mm (32 ft 3 in).
Suspension Type: Double Link. **Exchange Code:** 23.
Notes: Not currently operating on British Rail.
Previous Number: 21 87 0085 500.

87 7395 000

87 7397 000-002 TANK IBB

Builder: C.F.M.F., France.
Design Code: IBE309 (Ex ICE309). **Owner:** SNCF.
Tare Weight: 12.80 t. **Gross Laden Weight:** 40.00 t.
Maximum Speed: 60 mph. **Length:** 9240 mm (30 ft 4 in).
Suspension Type: Double Link. **Exchange Code:** 23.
Notes: Not currently operating on British Rail.
Previous Number Series: 21 87 0785 000-002.

87 7397 000 87 7397 001 87 7397 002

87 7397 003-004 TANK IBB

Builder: Arbel-Fauvet, Douai, France.
Design Code: IBE364 (Ex ICE364). **Owner:** Selmi.
Tare Weight: **Gross Laden Weight:**
Maximum Speed: 60 mph. **Length:**
Suspension Type: **Exchange Code:** 23.
Notes: Used on various workings to and from Europe.
Previous Number Series: 21 87 0785 003-004.

87 7397 003 87 7397 004

87 7397 500 TANK ICB

Builder: Arbel-Fauvet, Douai, France.
Design Code: IBE081 (Ex ICE081). **Owner:** TSL.

Tare Weight: 12.20 t.
Gross Laden Weight: 40.00 t.
Maximum Speed: 60 mph.
Length: 8340 mm (27 ft. 4 in.)
Suspension Type: Double Link.
Exchange Code: 23.
Notes: Not currently operating on British Rail.
Previous Number: 21 87 0785 500.

87 7397 500

87 7490 500 TANK IBB

Builder: Ateliers de Joigny, France.
Design Code: IBE360 (Ex ICE360).
Owner: TSL.
Tare Weight: 10.85 t.
Gross Laden Weight: 36.00 t.
Maximum Speed: 60 mph.
Length: 8340 mm (27 ft. 4 in.)
Suspension Type: Double Link.
Exchange Code: 23.
Notes: Used on various workings to and from Europe.
Previous Number: 21 87 0785 512.

87 7490 500

87 7491 000 TANK IBB

Builder: Arbel-Fauvet, Douai, France.
Design Code: IBE492 (Ex ICE492).
Owner: Logemafer.
Tare Weight: 14.00 t.
Gross Laden Weight: 40.00 t.
Maximum Speed: 60 mph.
Length: 9340 mm (30 ft. 8 in.)
Suspension Type: Double Link.
Exchange Code: 23.
Notes: Used on various workings to and from Europe.
Previous Number: 21 87 0785 014.

87 7491 000

87 7890 500-514 TANK ICB

Builder: Arbel-Fauvet, Douai, France, 1975.
Design Code: ICE457.
Owner: TSL/CAIB.
Tare Weight: 18.60 t.
Gross Laden Weight: 80.00 t.
Maximum Speed: 60 mph.
Length: 14700 mm (48 ft. 3 in.)
Bogie Type: Y25CS2.
Exchange Code: 33.
Notes: Used on various workings to and from Europe.
Previous Number Series: 21 87 0798 887-901.

87 7890 500	87 7890 504	87 7890 508	87 7890 512
87 7890 501	87 7890 505	87 7890 509	87 7890 513
87 7890 502	87 7890 506	87 7890 510	87 7890 514
87 7890 503	87 7890 507	87 7890 511	

87 7890 515-519 TANK ICX

Builder: Arbel-Fauvet, Douai, France, 1981.
Design Code: ICE456(a ICE659).
Owner: Ermewa.
Tare Weight: 22.77 t.
Gross Laden Weight: 80.00 t.
Maximum Speed: 60 mph.
Length: 14840 mm (48 ft. 8 in.)

Bogie Type: Y21CSE. **Exchange Code:** 34.
Notes: ICE659 is coded ICB. Used on various workings to and from Europe.
Previous Number Series: 21 87 0798 902-906.

87 7890 515	87 7890 517 a	87 7890 518	87 7890 519
87 7890 516			

87 7890 520-554 TANK ICB

Builder: Arbel-Fauvet, Douai, France, 1974-75.
Design Code: ICE446. **Owner:** TSL/CAIB.
Tare Weight: 18.40 t. **Gross Laden Weight:** 80.00 t.
Maximum Speed: 60 mph. **Length:** 14700 mm (48 ft. 3 in.)
Bogie Type: Y25CS2. **Exchange Code:** 33.
Notes: Used on various workings to and from Europe.
Previous Number Series: 21 87 0798 911-945.

87 7890 520	87 7890 529	87 7890 538	87 7890 547
87 7890 521	87 7890 530	87 7890 539	87 7890 548
87 7890 522	87 7890 531	87 7890 540	87 7890 549
87 7890 523	87 7890 532	87 7890 541	87 7890 550
87 7890 524	87 7890 533	87 7890 542	87 7890 551
87 7890 525	87 7890 534	87 7890 543	87 7890 552
87 7890 526	87 7890 535	87 7890 544	87 7890 553
87 7890 527	87 7890 536	87 7890 545	87 7890 554
87 7890 528	87 7890 537	87 7890 546	

87 7890 555-564 TANK ICB

Builder: Arbel-Fauvet, Douai, France, 1974.
Design Code: ICE428. **Owner:** TSL.
Tare Weight: 19.50 t. **Gross Laden Weight:** 80.00 t.
Maximum Speed: 60 mph. **Length:** 14700 mm (48 ft. 3 in.)
Bogie Type: Y25CS2. Exchange Code: 33.
Notes: Used on various workings to and from Europe.
Previous Number Series: 21 87 0798 968-977.

87 7890 555	87 7890 558	87 7890 561	87 7890 563
87 7890 556	87 7890 559	87 7890 562	87 7890 564
87 7890 557	87 7890 560		

87 7890 565-584 TANK ICB

Builder: Arbel-Fauvet, Douai, France.
Design Code: ICE429. **Owner:** TSL.
Tare Weight: 18.70 t. **Gross Laden Weight:** 80.00 t.
Maximum Speed: 60 mph. **Length:** 13800 mm (45 ft. 3 in.)
Bogie Type: Y25CS2. **Exchange Code:** 33.
Notes: Used on various workings to and from Europe.
Previous Number Series: 21 87 0798 980-999.

87 7890 565	87 7890 568	87 7890 571	87 7890 574
87 7890 566	87 7890 569	87 7890 572	87 7890 575
87 7890 567	87 7890 570	87 7890 573	87 7890 576

87 7890 577 87 7890 578 87 7890 579 87 7890 580 87 7890 581 87 7890 582 87 7890 583 87 7890 584

87 7890 585-588 TANK ICX

Builder: C.F.M.F., France, 1981.
Design Code: ICE454.
Owner: Simotra.
Tare Weight: 22.25 t.
Gross Laden Weight: 80.00 t.
Maximum Speed: 60 mph.
Length: 14480 mm (47 ft. 6 in.)
Bogie Type: Y21CSE.
Exchange Code: 34.
Notes: Used on various workings to and from Europe.
Previous Number Series: 24 87 0798 907-910.

87 7890 585 87 7890 586 87 7890 587 87 7890 588

87 7890 589-598 TANK ICB

Builder: Arbel-Fauvet, Douai, France, 1974-75.
Design Code: ICE446.
Owner: TSL.
Tare Weight: 18.40 t.
Gross Laden Weight: 80.00 t.
Maximum Speed: 60 mph.
Length: 14700 mm (48 ft. 3 in.)
Bogie Type: Y25CS2.
Exchange Code: 33.
Notes: Used on various workings to and from Europe.
Previous Number Series: 21 87 0798 946-955.

87 7890 589 87 7890 590 87 7890 591 87 7890 592 87 7890 593 87 7890 594 87 7890 595 87 7890 596 87 7890 597 87 7890 598

87 7890 599-610 TANK ICB

Builder: C.F.M.F., France.
Design Code: ICE440.
Owner: Fert.
Tare Weight: 17.50 t.
Gross Laden Weight: 80.00 t.
Maximum Speed: 60 mph.
Length: 13730 mm (45 ft. 1 in.)
Bogie Type: Y25CS2.
Exchange Code: 33.
Notes: Used on various workings to and from Europe.
Previous Number Series: 21 87 0798 956-967.

87 7890 599 87 7890 600 87 7890 601 87 7890 602 87 7890 603 87 7890 604 87 7890 605 87 7890 606 87 7890 607 87 7890 608 87 7890 609 87 7890 610

87 7890 611-612 TANK ICB

Builder: C.F.M.F., France.
Design Code: ICE441.
Owner: Fert.
Tare Weight: 18.70 t.
Gross Laden Weight: 80.00 t.
Maximum Speed: 60 mph.
Length: 13730 mm (45 ft. 1 in.)
Bogie Type: Y25CS2.
Exchange Code: 33.
Notes: Used on various workings to and from Europe.
Previous Number Series: 21 87 0798 978-979.

87 7890 611 87 7890 612

87 7890 613-616 TANK ICB

Builder: C.F.M.F., France, 1981.
Design Code: ICE432.
Owner: Transcit.
Tare Weight: 20.00 t.
Gross Laden Weight: 80.00 t.
Maximum Speed: 60 mph.
Length: 14480 mm (47 ft. 6 in.)
Bogie Type: Y25CS2.
Exchange Code: 33.
Notes: Used on various workings to and from Europe.

87 7890 613	87 7890 614	87 7890 615	87 7890 616

87 7895 000-006 TANK ICB

Builder: Arbel-Fauvet, Douai, France, 1972.
Design Code: ICE394.
Owner: Sotranda.
Tare Weight: 23.00 t.
Gross Laden Weight: 80.00 t.
Maximum Speed: 60 mph.
Length: 18640 mm (61 ft. 2 in.)
Bogie Type: Y25C.
Exchange Code: 33.
Notes: Used on various workings to and from Europe.
Previous Number Series: 21 87 0798 000-006.

87 7895 000	87 7895 002	87 7895 004	87 7895 006
87 7895 001	87 7895 003	87 7895 005	

87 7896 000 TANK ICA

Builder: C.F.M.F., France, 1979.
Design Code: ICE507.
Owner: Simotra.
Tare Weight: 21.30 t.
Gross Laden Weight: 80.00 t.
Maximum Speed: 60 mph.
Length: 15110 mm (49 ft. 7 in.)
Bogie Type: Y25CS2.
Exchange Code: 33.
Notes: Used on various workings to and from Europe.
Previous Number: 21 87 0098 026.

87 7896 000

87 7896 001-007 TANK ICB

Builder: C.F.M.F., France, 1981.
Design Code: ICE525.
Owner: Simotra.
Tare Weight: 22.30 t.
Gross Laden Weight: 80.00 t.
Maximum Speed: 60 mph.
Length: 17680 mm (58 ft. 0 in.)
Bogie Type: Y25CS2.
Exchange Code: 33.
Notes: Used on various workings to and from Europe.

87 7896 001	87 7896 003	87 7896 005	87 7896 007
87 7896 002	87 7896 004	87 7896 006	

87 7896 008-011 TANK ICA

Builder: C.F.M.F., France, 1982.
Design Code: ICE533.
Owner: Simotra.
Tare Weight: 19.90 t.
Gross Laden Weight: 80.00 t.
Maximum Speed: 60 mph.
Length: 13730 mm (45 ft. 1 in.)
Bogie Type: Y25CS2.
Exchange Code: 33.
Notes: Used on various workings to and from Europe.

87 7896 008
87 7896 009
87 7896 010
87 7896 011

87 7896 012-016 TANK ICA

Builder: Arbel-Fauvet, Douai, France, 1983.
Design Code: ICE541.
Owner: Loca.
Tare Weight: 19.80 t.
Gross Laden Weight: 80.00 t.
Maximum Speed: 60 mph.
Length: 12500 mm (41 ft. 0 in.)
Bogie Type: Y25CS2 or Y25CST.
Exchange Code: 33.
Notes: Used on various workings to and from Europe.

87 7896 012
87 7896 013
87 7896 014
87 7896 015
87 7896 016

87 7898 000-099 TANK ICA

Builder: Arbel-Fauvet, Douai, France, 1989.
Design Code: ICE719.
Owner:
Tare Weight: 21.45 t.
Gross Laden Weight: 90.00 t.
Maximum Speed: 60 mph.
Length: 14460 mm (47 ft. 5 in.)
Bogie Type: Y25.
Exchange Code: 33.
Notes: Used on various workings to and from Europe.

87 7898 000
87 7898 001
87 7898 002
87 7898 003
87 7898 004
87 7898 005
87 7898 006
87 7898 007
87 7898 008
87 7898 009
87 7898 010
87 7898 011
87 7898 012
87 7898 013
87 7898 014
87 7898 015
87 7898 016
87 7898 017
87 7898 018
87 7898 019
87 7898 020
87 7898 021
87 7898 022
87 7898 023
87 7898 024
87 7898 025
87 7898 026
87 7898 027
87 7898 028
87 7898 029
87 7898 030
87 7898 031
87 7898 032
87 7898 033
87 7898 034
87 7898 035
87 7898 036
87 7898 037
87 7898 038
87 7898 039
87 7898 044
87 7898 045
87 7898 047
87 7898 048
87 7898 049
87 7898 050
87 7898 054
87 7898 060
87 7898 061
87 7898 062
87 7898 063
87 7898 064
87 7898 065
87 7898 066
87 7898 067
87 7898 068
87 7898 069
87 7898 070
87 7898 071
87 7898 072
87 7898 073
87 7898 074
87 7898 075
87 7898 076
87 7898 077
87 7898 078
87 7898 079
87 7898 080
87 7898 081
87 7898 082
87 7898 083
87 7898 084
87 7898 085
87 7898 086
87 7898 087
87 7898 088
87 7898 089
87 7898 090
87 7898 091
87 7898 092
87 7898 093
87 7898 094
87 7898 095
87 7898 096
87 7898 097
87 7898 098
87 7898 099

87 7899 000-002 TANK ICX

Builder: C.F.M.F., France, 1982.
Design Code: ICE530.
Tare Weight: 21.20 t.
Maximum Speed: 60 mph.
Bogie Type: Y21CSe.
Owner: CAIB.
Gross Laden Weight: 80.00 t.
Length: 16170 mm (53 ft. 0 in.)
Exchange Code: 33 (a 34).
Notes: Used on various workings to and from Europe.

87 7899 000 a
87 7899 001
87 7899 002

87 7899 003-009 TANK ICX

Builder: Arbel-Fauvet, Douai, France, 1982.
Design Code: ICE539.
Tare Weight: 22.15 t.
Maximum Speed: 60 mph.
Bogie Type: Y25CS2.
Owner: Ermewa.
Gross Laden Weight: 80.00 t.
Length: 15540 mm (51 ft. 0 in.)
Exchange Code: 33.
Notes: Used on various workings to and from Europe.

87 7899 003
87 7899 004
87 7899 005
87 7899 006
87 7899 007
87 7899 008
87 7899 009

87 7899 010-014 TANK ICX

Builder: Arbel-Fauvet, Douai, France, 1982.
Design Code: ICE536.
Tare Weight: 22.50 t.
Maximum Speed: 60 mph.
Bogie Type: Y21CSE.
Owner: Ermewa.
Gross Laden Weight: 80.00 t.
Length: 14740 mm (48 ft. 4 in.)
Exchange Code: 34.
Notes: Used on various workings to and from Europe.

87 7899 010
87 7899 011
87 7899 012
87 7899 013
87 7899 014

87 7992 000-015 TANK ICA

Builder: C.F.M.F., France, 1979.
Design Code: ICE496.
Tare Weight: 21.70 t.
Maximum Speed: 60 mph.
Bogie Type: Y25CS2.
Owner: Nacco.
Gross Laden Weight: 80.00 t.
Length: 16540 mm (54 ft. 3 in.)
Exchange Code: 33.
Notes: Used on various workings between Ellesmere Port and Europe.
Previous Number Series: 21 87 0798 007-022.

87 7992 000
87 7992 001
87 7992 002
87 7992 003
87 7992 004
87 7992 005
87 7992 006
87 7992 007
87 7992 008
87 7992 009
87 7992 010
87 7992 011
87 7992 012
87 7992 013
87 7992 014
87 7992 015

43 87 9196 015 at Warrington on 18th March 1984. *(R. Wallace)*

Large Sliding Roof Van 21 88 5799 at Hoo Junction on 30th May 1987. *(R. Wallace)*

87 7994 000-009 TANK ICA

Builder: Société ANF-Industrie, Blanc Misseron, France, 1987.
Design Code: ICE677.
Owner: Simotra.
Tare Weight: 25.50 t.
Gross Laden Weight: 90.00 t.
Maximum Speed: 60 mph.
Length: 17900 mm (58 ft. 9 in.)
Bogie Type: Y25LS.
Exchange Code: 33.
Notes: Used on various workings to and from Europe.

87 7994 000	87 7994 003	87 7994 006	87 7994 008
87 7994 001	87 7994 004	87 7994 007	87 7994 009
87 7994 002	87 7994 005		

87 7994 010-029 TANK ICA

Builder: Arbel-Fauvet, Douai, France, 1987.
Design Code: ICE698.
Owner: VTG.
Tare Weight: 27.30 t.
Gross Laden Weight: 90.00 t.
Maximum Speed: 60 mph.
Length: 18900 mm (62 ft. 0 in.)
Bogie Type:
Exchange Code: 33.
Notes: Not currently operating on British Rail.

87 7994 010	87 7994 015	87 7994 020	87 7994 025
87 7994 011	87 7994 016	87 7994 021	87 7994 026
87 7994 012	87 7994 017	87 7994 022	87 7994 027
87 7994 013	87 7994 018	87 7994 023	87 7994 028
87 7994 014	87 7994 019	87 7994 024	87 7994 029

87 7995 000-002 TANK ICA

Builder: C.F.M.F., France, 1979.
Design Code: ICE498.
Owner: CFPM.
Tare Weight: 20.30 t.
Gross Laden Weight: 80.00 t.
Maximum Speed: 60 mph.
Length: 15440 mm (47 ft. 4 in.)
Bogie Type: Y25CS2.
Exchange Code: 33.
Notes: Not currently operating on British Rail.
Previous Number Series: 21 87 0798 023-025.

87 7995 000	87 7995 001	87 7995 002

87 7996 000-007 TANK ICA

Builder: C.F.M.F., France, 1979.
Design Code: ICE510.
Owner: Simotra.
Tare Weight: 21.50 t.
Gross Laden Weight: 80.00 t.
Maximum Speed: 60 mph.
Length: 15440 mm (47 ft. 4 in.)
Bogie Type: Y25CS2.
Exchange Code: 33.
Notes: Used on workings between Ellesmere Port and Europe.
Previous Number Series: 21 87 0798 028-035.

87 7996 000	87 7996 002	87 7996 004	87 7996 006
87 7996 001	87 7996 003	87 7996 005	87 7996 007

87 7996 008-014 TANK ICB

Builder: C.F.M.F., France, 1980.
Design Code: ICE513.
Tare Weight: 21.00 t.
Maximum Speed: 60 mph.
Bogie Type: Y25CS2.
Owner: Simotra.
Gross Laden Weight: 80.00 t.
Length: 15680 mm (51 ft. 5 in.)
Exchange Code: 33.
Notes: Used on workings between Ellesmere Port and Europe.
Previous Number Series: 21 87 0798 036-042.

87 7996 008	87 7996 010	87 7996 012	87 7996 014
87 7996 009	87 7996 011	87 7996 013	

87 7996 015-029 TANK ICB

Builder: C.F.M.F., France, 1981.
Design Code: ICE522.
Tare Weight: 22.30 t.
Maximum Speed: 60 mph.
Bogie Type: Y25CS2.
Owner: TSL.
Gross Laden Weight: 80.00 t.
Length: 15680 mm (51 ft. 5 in.)
Exchange Code: 33.
Notes: Used on workings between Ellesmere Port and Spondon and also between Ellesmere Port and Europe.

87 7996 015	87 7996 019	87 7996 023	87 7996 027
87 7996 016	87 7996 020	87 7996 024	87 7996 028
87 7996 017	87 7996 021	87 7996 025	87 7996 029
87 7996 018	87 7996 022	87 7996 026	

87 7996 030-039 TANK ICB

Builder: C.F.M.F., France, 1981.
Design Code: ICE516.
Tare Weight: 21.20 t.
Maximum Speed: 60 mph.
Bogie Type: Y25CS2.
Owner: Simotra.
Gross Laden Weight: 80.00 t.
Length: 15680 mm (51 ft. 5 in.)
Exchange Code: 33.
Notes: Used on workings between Sittingbourne and Europe.

87 7996 030	87 7996 033	87 7996 036	87 7996 038
87 7996 031	87 7996 034	87 7996 037	87 7996 039
87 7996 032	87 7996 035		

87 7996 040-045 TANK ICB

Builder: Arbel-Fauvet, Douai, France, 1983.
Design Code: ICE549.
Tare Weight: 29.00 t.
Maximum Speed: 60 mph.
Bogie Type: Y25CS2.
Owner: Metaux Spéciale.
Gross Laden Weight: 80.00 t.
Length: 16490 mm (54 ft. 1 in.)
Exchange Code: 33.
Notes: Used on various workings to and from Europe.

87 7996 040	87 7996 042	87 7996 044	87 7996 045
87 7996 041	87 7996 043		

87 7996 046-047 TANK ICA

Builder: Simotra, France, 1983.
Design Code: ICE560.
Tare Weight: 20.30 t.
Maximum Speed: 75 mph.
Bogie Type: Y25CS2.
Owner: Simotra.
Gross Laden Weight: 80.00 t.
Length: 15440 mm (49 ft. 11 in.)
Exchange Code: 33.
Notes: Used on workings between Sittingbourne and Europe.

87 7996 046 87 7996 047

87 7996 048-053 TANK ICA

Builder: C.F.M.F., France, 1984.
Design Code: ICE582.
Tare Weight: 20.30 t.
Maximum Speed: 60 mph.
Bogie Type: Y25CS2.
Owner: Hauser.
Gross Laden Weight: 80.00 t.
Length: 15440 mm (49 ft. 11 in.)
Exchange Code: 33.
Notes: Used on various workings to and from Europe.

87 7996 048
87 7996 049
87 7996 050
87 7996 051
87 7996 052
87 7996 053

87 9192 000 COVERED HOPPER ISB

Builder: Arbel-Fauvet, Douai, France, 1972.
Design Code: ISE426 (Ex IPE426).
Tare Weight: 14.80 t.
Maximum Speed: 60 mph.
Suspension Type: Double Link.
Owner: Sotrampa.
Gross Laden Weight: 40.00 t.
Length: 11140 mm (36 ft. 7 in.)
Exchange Code: 23.
Notes: Used on various workings to and from Europe.
Previous Number: 21 87 0985 000.

87 9192 000

87 9192 001 COVERED TWIN HOPPER ISB

Builder: Simotra, France, 1959.
Design Code: ISE480 (Ex IPE480).
Tare Weight: 11.00 t.
Maximum Speed: 60 mph.
Suspension Type: Single Link.
Owner: CNC.
Gross Laden Weight: 40.00 t.
Length: 8340 mm (27 ft. 4 in.)
Exchange Code: 23.
Notes: Used on various workings to and from Europe.
Previous Number: 21 87 0985 001.

87 9192 001

87 9195 000 SPECIAL COVERED FLAT ITX

Builder: Ateliers de Breton, France, 1982.
Design Code: ITE537.
Tare Weight: 15.50 t.
Owner: Transfesa.
Gross Laden Weight: 40.00 t.

Maximum Speed: 60 mph.
Suspension Type: Double Link.
Length: 13970 mm (45 ft. 10 in.)
Exchange Code: 43.
Notes: Used on various workings to and from Europe.

87 9195 000

87 9196 000-019 MEDIUM FLAT ITX

Builder: Ateliers de Breton, France, 1982.
Design Code: ITE542.
Tare Weight: 14.90 t.
Maximum Speed: 75 mph.
Suspension Type: Double Link.
Owner: Transfesa.
Gross Laden Weight: 40.00 t.
Length: 13850 mm (45 ft. 5 in.)
Exchange Code: 43.
Notes: Used on various workings to and from Europe.

87 9196 000	87 9196 005	87 9196 010	87 9196 015
87 9196 001	87 9196 006	87 9196 011	87 9196 016
87 9196 002	87 9196 007	87 9196 012	87 9196 017
87 9196 003	87 9196 008	87 9196 013	87 9196 018
87 9196 004	87 9196 009	87 9196 014	87 9196 019

87 9196 020-024 MEDIUM FLAT ITX

Builder: Ateliers de Breton, France, 1983.
Design Code: ITE543.
Tare Weight: 15.10 t.
Maximum Speed: 75 mph.
Suspension Type: Double Link.
Owner: Transfesa.
Gross Laden Weight: 40.00 t.
Length: 14100 mm (46 ft. 3 in.)
Exchange Code: 43.
Notes: Used on various workings to and from Europe.

87 9196 020	87 9196 022	87 9196 023	87 9196 024
87 9196 021			

87 9382 000-021 COVERED HOPPER IRB

Builder: Arbel-Fauvet, Douai, France, 1974-5.
Design Code: IRE453 (Ex IPE453).
Tare Weight: 23.11 t.
Maximum Speed: 60 mph.
Bogie Type: Y25CS2.
Owner: Polybulk.
Gross Laden Weight: 80.00 t.
Length: 18288 mm (60 ft. 0 in.)
Exchange Code: 33.
Notes: Used on various workings to and from Europe.
Previous Number Series: 21 87 0998 000-021.

87 9382 000	87 9382 006	87 9382 012	87 9382 017
87 9382 001	87 9382 007	87 9382 013	87 9382 018
87 9382 002	87 9382 008	87 9382 014	87 9382 019
87 9382 003	87 9382 009	87 9382 015	87 9382 020
87 9382 004	87 9382 010	87 9382 016	87 9382 021
87 9382 005	87 9382 011		

87 9384 000-002 COVERED HOPPER IRB

Builder: Arbel-Fauvet, Douai, France, 1974-5.
Design Code: IRE442 (Ex IPE442). **Owner:**
Tare Weight: 21.00 t. **Gross Laden Weight:** 80.00 t.
Maximum Speed: 60 mph. **Length:** 18288 mm (60 ft. 0 in.)
Bogie Type: Y25C. **Exchange Code:** 33.
Notes: Used on various workings to and from Europe.
Previous Number Series: 33 88 9380 105/107/109.

87 9384 000	87 9384 001	87 9384 002

87 9985 000-007 NUCLEAR FLASK IQB

Builder: Arbel-Fauvet, Douai, France, 1981.
Design Code: IQE475. **Owner:** Nuclear Transport.
Tare Weight: 47.44 t. **Gross Laden Weight:** 153.00 t.
Maximum Speed: 60 mph. **Length:** 20700 mm (67 ft. 11 in.)
Bogie Type: Y11M (four bogies). **Exchange Code:** 33.
Notes: Used on workings between Sellafield and Europe.
Previous Number Series: 21 87 0998 991-993/995-999.

87 9985 000	87 9985 002	87 9985 004	87 9985 006
87 9985 001	87 9985 003	87 9985 005	87 9985 007

87 9988 000-004 GLASS TRESTLE WELL IDB

Builder:
Design Code: IDE439 (Ex IXE439). **Owner:** SNCF.
Tare Weight: 21.00 t. **Gross Laden Weight:** 80.00 t.
Maximum Speed: 60 mph. **Length:** 15240 mm (50 ft. 0 in.)
Bogie Type: **Exchange Code:** 31.
Notes: Not currently operating on British Rail.
Previous Number Series: 31 87 9380 000-004.

87 9988 000	87 9988 002	87 9988 003	87 9988 004
87 9988 001			

87 9989 000-004 SPECIAL WELL IDB

Builder:
Design Code: IDE393 (Ex IXE393). **Owner:** SNCF.
Tare Weight: 27.00 t. **Gross Laden Weight:** 66.00 t.
Maximum Speed: 60 mph. **Length:** 18040 mm (59 ft. 2 in.)
Bogie Type: Y27E. **Exchange Code:** 31.
Notes: Used on various workings to and from Europe.
Previous Number Series: 21 87 9397 995-999.

87 9989 000	87 9989 002	87 9989 003	87 9989 004
87 9989 001			

88 2140 000-189 MEDIUM VAN IMX

Builder:
Design Code: IME035.
Tare Weight: 12.08 t.
Maximum Speed: 60 mph.
Suspension Type: Single Link.
Notes: Not currently operating on British Rail.
Owner: SNCB.
Gross Laden Weight: 32.00 t.
Length: 12585 mm (41 ft. 3 in.)
Exchange Code: 21.

88 2140 000	88 2140 013	88 2140 030	88 2140 041
88 2140 003	88 2140 014	88 2140 031	88 2140 043
88 2140 004	88 2140 015	88 2140 034	88 2140 044
88 2140 005	88 2140 019	88 2140 036	88 2140 045
88 2140 007	88 2140 024	88 2140 037	88 2140 047
88 2140 010	88 2140 025	88 2140 039	88 2140 048
88 2140 011	88 2140 026	88 2140 040	88 2140 189
88 2140 012	88 2140 028		

88 2140 201-224 IMX
MEDIUM VAN, END DOOR

Builder:
Design Code: IME036.
Tare Weight: 12.08 t.
Maximum Speed: 60 mph.
Suspension Type: Single Link.
Notes: Not currently operating on British Rail.
Owner: SNCB
Gross Laden Weight: 32.00 t.
Length: 12585 mm (41 ft. 3 in.)
Exchange Code: 21.

88 2140 201	88 2140 208	88 2140 214	88 2140 220
88 2140 202	88 2140 212	88 2140 218	88 2140 223
88 2140 204	88 2140 213	88 2140 219	88 2140 224
88 2140 206			

88 2140 406-422 MEDIUM VAN IMX

Builder:
Design Code: IME037.
Tare Weight: 12.00 t.
Maximum Speed: 60 mph.
Suspension Type: Single Link.
Notes: Not currently operating on British Rail.
Owner: SNCB.
Gross Laden Weight: 32.00 t.
Length: 12585 mm (41 ft. 3 in.)
Exchange Code: 21.

88 2140 406	88 2140 409	88 2140 414	88 2140 418
88 2140 407	88 2140 412	88 2140 415	88 2140 421
88 2140 408	88 2140 413	88 2140 417	88 2140 422

88 2380 000-199 LARGE VAN ILB

Builder: Arbel-Fauvet, Douai, France, 1973.
Design Code: ILE423.
Tare Weight: 14.60 t.
Maximum Speed: 60 mph.
Suspension Type:
Owner: SNCB.
Gross Laden Weight: 40.00 t.
Length: 12780 mm (41 ft. 11 in.)
Exchange Code: 21.

Notes: Used on various workings to and from Europe.
Previous Number Series: 21 88 2140 700-899.

88 2380 000
88 2380 001
88 2380 002
88 2380 003
88 2380 004
88 2380 005
88 2380 006
88 2380 007
88 2380 008
88 2380 009
88 2380 010
88 2380 011
88 2380 012
88 2380 013
88 2380 014
88 2380 015
88 2380 016
88 2380 017
88 2380 018
88 2380 019
88 2380 020
88 2380 021
88 2380 022
88 2380 023
88 2380 024
88 2380 025
88 2380 026
88 2380 027
88 2380 028
88 2380 029
88 2380 030
88 2380 031
88 2380 032
88 2380 033
88 2380 034
88 2380 035
88 2380 036
88 2380 037
88 2380 038
88 2380 039
88 2380 040
88 2380 041
88 2380 042
88 2380 043
88 2380 044
88 2380 045
88 2380 046
88 2380 047
88 2380 048
88 2380 049
88 2380 050
88 2380 051
88 2380 052
88 2380 053
88 2380 054
88 2380 055
88 2380 056
88 2380 057
88 2380 058
88 2380 059
88 2380 060
88 2380 061
88 2380 062
88 2380 063
88 2380 064
88 2380 065
88 2380 066
88 2380 067
88 2380 068
88 2380 069
88 2380 070
88 2380 071
88 2380 072
88 2380 073
88 2380 074
88 2380 075
88 2380 076
88 2380 077
88 2380 078
88 2380 079
88 2380 080
88 2380 081
88 2380 082
88 2380 083
88 2380 084
88 2380 085
88 2380 086
88 2380 087
88 2380 088
88 2380 089
88 2380 090
88 2380 091
88 2380 092
88 2380 093
88 2380 094
88 2380 095
88 2380 096
88 2380 097
88 2380 098
88 2380 099
88 2380 100
88 2380 101
88 2380 102
88 2380 103
88 2380 104
88 2380 105
88 2380 106
88 2380 107
88 2380 108
88 2380 109
88 2380 110
88 2380 111
88 2380 112
88 2380 113
88 2380 114
88 2380 115
88 2380 116
88 2380 117
88 2380 118
88 2380 119
88 2380 120
88 2380 121
88 2380 122
88 2380 123
88 2380 124
88 2380 125
88 2380 126
88 2380 127
88 2380 128
88 2380 129
88 2380 130
88 2380 131
88 2380 132
88 2380 133
88 2380 134
88 2380 135
88 2380 136
88 2380 137
88 2380 138
88 2380 139
88 2380 140
88 2380 141
88 2380 142
88 2380 143
88 2380 144
88 2380 145
88 2380 146
88 2380 147
88 2380 148
88 2380 149
88 2380 150
88 2380 151
88 2380 152
88 2380 153
88 2380 154
88 2380 155
88 2380 156
88 2380 157
88 2380 158
88 2380 159
88 2380 160
88 2380 161
88 2380 162
88 2380 163
88 2380 164
88 2380 165
88 2380 166
88 2380 167
88 2380 168
88 2380 169
88 2380 170
88 2380 171
88 2380 172
88 2380 173
88 2380 174
88 2380 175
88 2380 176
88 2380 177
88 2380 178
88 2380 179
88 2380 180
88 2380 181
88 2380 182
88 2380 183
88 2380 184
88 2380 185
88 2380 186
88 2380 187
88 2380 188
88 2380 189
88 2380 190
88 2380 191
88 2380 192
88 2380 193
88 2380 194
88 2380 195
88 2380 196
88 2380 197
88 2380 198
88 2380 199

88 2390 000-097 LARGE VAN ILX

Builder: Brugeiose et Nivelles, Bruges, Belgium.
Design Code: ILE266.
Owner: SNCB.
Tare Weight: 15.50 t.
Gross Laden Weight: 40.00 t.
Maximum Speed: 60 mph.
Length: 13990 mm (45 ft. 11 in.)
Suspension Type: Double Link.
Exchange Code: 21.
Notes: Used on various workings to and from Europe.
Previous Number Series: 21 88 2140 600-697.

88 2390 000
88 2390 001
88 2390 002
88 2390 003
88 2390 004
88 2390 005
88 2390 006
88 2390 007
88 2390 008
88 2390 009
88 2390 010
88 2390 011
88 2390 012
88 2390 013
88 2390 014
88 2390 015
88 2390 016
88 2390 017
88 2390 018
88 2390 019
88 2390 020
88 2390 021
88 2390 022
88 2390 023
88 2390 024
88 2390 025
88 2390 026
88 2390 027
88 2390 028
88 2390 029
88 2390 030
88 2390 031
88 2390 032
88 2390 033
88 2390 034
88 2390 036
88 2390 037
88 2390 038
88 2390 039
88 2390 040
88 2390 041
88 2390 042
88 2390 043
88 2390 044
88 2390 045
88 2390 046
88 2390 047
88 2390 048
88 2390 049
88 2390 050
88 2390 051
88 2390 052
88 2390 053
88 2390 054
88 2390 055
88 2390 056
88 2390 057
88 2390 058
88 2390 059
88 2390 060
88 2390 061
88 2390 062
88 2390 063
88 2390 064
88 2390 065
88 2390 066
88 2390 067
88 2390 068
88 2390 069
88 2390 070
88 2390 071
88 2390 072
88 2390 073
88 2390 074
88 2390 075
88 2390 076
88 2390 077
88 2390 078
88 2390 079
88 2390 080
88 2390 081
88 2390 082
88 2390 083
88 2390 084
88 2390 085
88 2390 086
88 2390 087
88 2390 088
88 2390 089
88 2390 090
88 2390 091
88 2390 092
88 2390 093
88 2390 094
88 2390 095
88 2390 096
88 2390 097

88 4053 000-064 40 ft FLAT IFR

Builder: Arbel-Fauvet, Douai, France.
Design Code: IFE004.
Owner: SNCB.
Tare Weight:
Gross Laden Weight:
Maximum Speed: 60 mph.
Length:
Suspension Type:
Exchange Code: 21.
Notes: Used on various workings to and from Europe.
Previous Number Series: 21 88 4040 000-044/050-065/080-083.

88 4053 000
88 4053 001
88 4053 002
88 4053 003
88 4053 004
88 4053 005
88 4053 006
88 4053 007
88 4053 008
88 4053 009
88 4053 010
88 4053 011
88 4053 012
88 4053 013
88 4053 014
88 4053 015
88 4053 016
88 4053 017
88 4053 018
88 4053 019
88 4053 020
88 4053 022
88 4053 023
88 4053 024
88 4053 025
88 4053 026
88 4053 027
88 4053 028
88 4053 029
88 4053 030
88 4053 031
88 4053 032
88 4053 033
88 4053 034
88 4053 035
88 4053 036

88 4053 036
88 4053 037
88 4053 038
88 4053 039
88 4053 040
88 4053 041
88 4053 042
88 4053 043
88 4053 044
88 4053 045
88 4053 046
88 4053 047
88 4053 048
88 4053 049
88 4053 050
88 4053 051
88 4053 052
88 4053 053
88 4053 054
88 4053 055
88 4053 056
88 4053 057
88 4053 058
88 4053 059
88 4053 060
88 4053 061
88 4053 062
88 4053 063
88 4053 064

88 4140 100-199 40 ft FLAT IFB

Builder:
Design Code: IFE648(a IFE276). **Owner:** SNCB.
Tare Weight: 12.00 t(a 12.40 t) **Gross Laden Weight:** 39.50 t(a 40.00 t)
Maximum Speed: 60 mph.
Length: 13716 mm (45 ft. 0 in.)[a 13860 mm (45 ft 5 in.)].
Suspension Type: Double Link. **Exchange Code:** 21.
Notes: IFE276 are coded IFX. Used on various workings to and from Europe.

88 4140 100
88 4140 101 a
88 4140 102
88 4140 103
88 4140 104
88 4140 105
88 4140 106
88 4140 107
88 4140 108
88 4140 109
88 4140 110
88 4140 111
88 4140 112
88 4140 113
88 4140 114
88 4140 115
88 4140 116
88 4140 117
88 4140 118
88 4140 119
88 4140 120
88 4140 121
88 4140 122
88 4140 123
88 4140 124
88 4140 125
88 4140 126
88 4140 127
88 4140 128
88 4140 129
88 4140 130
88 4140 131
88 4140 132
88 4140 133
88 4140 134
88 4140 135
88 4140 136 a
88 4140 137
88 4140 138 a
88 4140 139
88 4140 140
88 4140 141 a
88 4140 142
88 4140 143 a
88 4140 144
88 4140 145
88 4140 146
88 4140 147
88 4140 148
88 4140 149
88 4140 150
88 4140 151
88 4140 152 a
88 4140 153
88 4140 154 a
88 4140 155
88 4140 156
88 4140 157 a
88 4140 158 a
88 4140 159 a
88 4140 160 a
88 4140 161 a
88 4140 162 a
88 4140 164
88 4140 165
88 4140 166 a
88 4140 167 a
88 4140 168 a
88 4140 169 a
88 4140 170 a
88 4140 171 a
88 4140 172 a
88 4140 173 a
88 4140 174 a
88 4140 175 a
88 4140 176 a
88 4140 177 a
88 4140 178 a
88 4140 179 a
88 4140 180 a
88 4140 181 a
88 4140 182 a
88 4140 183 a
88 4140 184 a
88 4140 185 a
88 4140 186 a
88 4140 187
88 4140 188 a
88 4140 189 a
88 4140 190 a
88 4140 191
88 4140 192 a
88 4140 193 a
88 4140 194
88 4140 195 a
88 4140 196 a
88 4140 197 a
88 4140 198 a
88 4140 199 a

88 4140 200-299 40 ft FLAT IFB

Builder: C.W. Gentbrugge, Belgium.
Design Code: IFE464. **Owner:** SNCB.
Tare Weight: 13.67 t. **Gross Laden Weight:** 39.00 t.
Maximum Speed: 60 mph. **Length:** 13712 mm (45 ft. 0 in.).
Suspension Type: Double Link. **Exchange Code:** 21.
Notes: Used on various workings to and from Europe.

88 4140 200
88 4140 201
88 4140 202
88 4140 203

88 4140 204
88 4140 205
88 4140 206
88 4140 207
88 4140 208
88 4140 209
88 4140 210
88 4140 211
88 4140 212
88 4140 213
88 4140 214
88 4140 215
88 4140 216
88 4140 217
88 4140 218
88 4140 219
88 4140 220
88 4140 221
88 4140 222
88 4140 223
88 4140 224
88 4140 225
88 4140 226
88 4140 227
88 4140 228
88 4140 229
88 4140 230
88 4140 231
88 4140 232
88 4140 233
88 4140 234
88 4140 235
88 4140 236
88 4140 237
88 4140 238
88 4140 239
88 4140 240
88 4140 241
88 4140 242
88 4140 243
88 4140 244
88 4140 245
88 4140 246
88 4140 247
88 4140 248
88 4140 249
88 4140 250
88 4140 251
88 4140 252
88 4140 253
88 4140 254
88 4140 255
88 4140 256
88 4140 257
88 4140 258
88 4140 259
88 4140 260
88 4140 261
88 4140 262
88 4140 263
88 4140 264
88 4140 265
88 4140 266
88 4140 267
88 4140 268
88 4140 269
88 4140 270
88 4140 271
88 4140 273
88 4140 274
88 4140 275
88 4140 276
88 4140 277
88 4140 278
88 4140 279
88 4140 280
88 4140 281
88 4140 282
88 4140 283
88 4140 284
88 4140 285
88 4140 286
88 4140 287
88 4140 288
88 4140 289
88 4140 290
88 4140 291
88 4140 292
88 4140 293
88 4140 294
88 4140 295
88 4140 296
88 4140 297
88 4140 298
88 4140 299

88 5799 000-049 ILB

LARGE VAN, SLIDING ROOF

Builder: C.W. Gentbrugge, Belgium, 1977.
Design Code: ILE479.
Owner: SNCB.
Tare Weight: 14.50 t.
Gross Laden Weight: 40.00 t.
Maximum Speed: 60 mph.
Length: 14020 mm (46 ft. 0 in.).
Suspension Type: Double Link.
Exchange Code: 21.
Notes: Used on various workings to and from Europe.

88 5799 000
88 5799 001
88 5799 002
88 5799 003
88 5799 004
88 5799 005
88 5799 006
88 5799 007
88 5799 008
88 5799 009
88 5799 010
88 5799 011
88 5799 012
88 5799 013
88 5799 014
88 5799 015
88 5799 016
88 5799 017
88 5799 018
88 5799 019
88 5799 020
88 5799 021
88 5799 022
88 5799 023
88 5799 024
88 5799 025
88 5799 026
88 5799 027
88 5799 028
88 5799 029
88 5799 030
88 5799 031
88 5799 032
88 5799 033
88 5799 034
88 5799 035
88 5799 036
88 5799 037
88 5799 038
88 5799 039
88 5799 040
88 5799 041
88 5799 042
88 5799 043
88 5799 044
88 5799 045
88 5799 046
88 5799 047
88 5799 048
88 5799 049

88 6094 000-019 OPEN HIGH IOB

Builder: Waggonfabrik Uerdingen, Krefeld, West Germany, 1971.
Design Code: IOE377.
Owner: SNCB.
Tare Weight: 12.00 t.
Gross Laden Weight: 40.00 t.
Maximum Speed: 60 mph.
Length: 10000 mm (32 ft. 10 in.).

Suspension Type: Eight leaf plates. **Exchange Code:** 21.
Notes: Used on various workings to and from Europe.
Previous Number Series: 21 88 6190 000-019.

88 6094 000	88 6094 005	88 6094 010	88 6094 015
88 6094 001	88 6094 006	88 6094 011	88 6094 016
88 6094 002	88 6094 007	88 6094 012	88 6094 017
88 6094 003	88 6094 008	88 6094 013	88 6094 018
88 6094 004	88 6094 009	88 6094 014	88 6094 019

88 7194 000 TANK IBP

Builder: Frères Cobert, Belgium.
Design Code: IBE174 (Ex ICE174). **Owner:** Solvay.
Tare Weight: 12.37 t. **Gross Laden Weight:** 37.00 t.
Maximum Speed: 50 mph. **Length:** 7740 mm (25 ft. 5 in.)
Suspension Type: Single Link. **Exchange Code:** 23.
Notes: Used on various workings to and from Europe.
Previous Number: 21 88 0780 000.

88 7194 000

88 7499 000-009 TANK IBB

Builder: S.A.T.I., Antwerp, Belgium, 1984.
Design Code: IBE425 (Ex ICE 425). **Owner:** CAIB.
Tare Weight: 12.00 t. **Gross Laden Weight:** 40.00 t.
Maximum Speed: 60 mph. **Length:** 8820 mm (28 ft. 11 in.)
Suspension Type: Double Link. **Exchange Code:** 23.
Notes: Used on various workings to and from Europe.

88 7499 000	88 7499 004	88 7499 007	88 7499 009
88 7499 001	88 7499 005	88 7499 008	

88 8089 980-992 REFRIGERATED VAN IIX

Builder: Brugeoise et Nivelles, Bruges, Belgium.
Design Code: IIE300. **Owner:** Interfrigo.
Tare Weight: 17.00 t. **Gross Laden Weight:** 36.00 t.
Maximum Speed: 60 mph. **Length:** 14020 mm (46 ft. 0 in.)
Suspension Type: Single Link. **Exchange Code:** 04.
Notes: Not currently operating on British Rail.
Previous Number Series: 14 88 0888 983/985/988-998.

88 8089 980	88 8089 984	88 8089 987	88 8089 990
88 8089 981	88 8089 985	88 8089 988	88 8089 991
88 8089 982	88 8089 986	88 8089 989	88 8089 992
88 8089 983			

88 8091 002-008 REFRIGERATED VAN IIX

Builder: Brugeoise et Nivelles, Bruges, Belgium, 1981.
Design Code: IIE326. **Owner:** Interfrigo.

Tare Weight: 16.70 t. **Gross Laden Weight:** 36.00 t.
Maximum Speed: 75 mph. **Length:** 14040 mm (46 ft. 1 in.)
Suspension Type: Double Link. **Exchange Code:** 04.
Notes: Not currently operating on British Rail.
Previous Number Series: 14 88 0891 991-997.

88 8091 002	88 8091 004	88 8091 006	88 8091 008
88 8091 003	88 8091 005	88 8091 007	

88 8092 000-199 REFRIGERATED VAN IIX

Builder: Brugeoise & Nivelles, Bruges, Belgium.
Design Code: IIE299. **Owner:** Interfrigo.
Tare Weight: 18.60 t. **Gross Laden Weight:** 40.00 t.
Maximum Speed: 60 mph. **Length:** 14040 mm (46 ft. 1 in.)
Suspension Type: Double Link. **Exchange Code:** 04.
Notes: Not currently operating on British Rail.
Previous Number Series: 14 88 0888 000-199.

88 8092 000	88 8092 036	88 8092 072	88 8092 108
88 8092 001	88 8092 037	88 8092 073	88 8092 109
88 8092 002	88 8092 038	88 8092 074	88 8092 110
88 8092 003	88 8092 039	88 8092 075	88 8092 111
88 8092 004	88 8092 040	88 8092 076	88 8092 112
88 8092 005	88 8092 041	88 8092 077	88 8092 113
88 8092 006	88 8092 042	88 8092 078	88 8092 114
88 8092 007	88 8092 043	88 8092 079	88 8092 115
88 8092 008	88 8092 044	88 8092 080	88 8092 116
88 8092 009	88 8092 045	88 8092 081	88 8092 117
88 8092 010	88 8092 046	88 8092 082	88 8092 118
88 8092 011	88 8092 047	88 8092 083	88 8092 119
88 8092 012	88 8092 048	88 8092 084	88 8092 120
88 8092 013	88 8092 049	88 8092 085	88 8092 121
88 8092 014	88 8092 050	88 8092 086	88 8092 122
88 8092 015	88 8092 051	88 8092 087	88 8092 123
88 8092 016	88 8092 052	88 8092 088	88 8092 124
88 8092 017	88 8092 053	88 8092 089	88 8092 125
88 8092 018	88 8092 054	88 8092 090	88 8092 126
88 8092 019	88 8092 055	88 8092 091	88 8092 127
88 8092 020	88 8092 056	88 8092 092	88 8092 128
88 8092 021	88 8092 057	88 8092 093	88 8092 129
88 8092 022	88 8092 058	88 8092 094	88 8092 130
88 8092 023	88 8092 059	88 8092 095	88 8092 131
88 8092 024	88 8092 060	88 8092 096	88 8092 132
88 8092 025	88 8092 061	88 8092 097	88 8092 133
88 8092 026	88 8092 062	88 8092 098	88 8092 134
88 8092 027	88 8092 063	88 8092 099	88 8092 135
88 8092 028	88 8092 064	88 8092 100	88 8092 136
88 8092 029	88 8092 065	88 8092 101	88 8092 137
88 8092 030	88 8092 066	88 8092 102	88 8092 138
88 8092 031	88 8092 067	88 8092 103	88 8092 139
88 8092 032	88 8092 068	88 8092 104	88 8092 140
88 8092 033	88 8092 069	88 8092 105	88 8092 141
88 8092 034	88 8092 070	88 8092 106	88 8092 142
88 8092 035	88 8092 071	88 8092 107	88 8092 143

88 8092 144	88 8092 158	88 8092 172	88 8092 186
88 8092 145	88 8092 159	88 8092 173	88 8092 187
88 8092 146	88 8092 160	88 8092 174	88 8092 188
88 8092 147	88 8092 161	88 8092 175	88 8092 189
88 8092 148	88 8092 162	88 8092 176	88 8092 190
88 8092 149	88 8092 163	88 8092 177	88 8092 191
88 8092 150	88 8092 164	88 8092 178	88 8092 192
88 8092 151	88 8092 165	88 8092 179	88 8092 193
88 8092 152	88 8092 166	88 8092 180	88 8092 194
88 8092 153	88 8092 167	88 8092 181	88 8092 195
88 8092 154	88 8092 168	88 8092 182	88 8092 196
88 8092 155	88 8092 169	88 8092 183	88 8092 197
88 8092 156	88 8092 170	88 8092 184	88 8092 198
88 8092 157	88 8092 171	88 8092 185	88 8092 199

88 9282 000-009 COVERED HOPPER IRB

Builder: Arbel-Fauvet, Douai, France, 1974.
Design Code: IRE442 (Ex IPE442). **Owner:** CAIB.
Tare Weight: 21.00 t. **Gross Laden Weight:** 80.00 t.
Maximum Speed: 60 mph. **Length:** 18288 mm (60 ft. 0 in.)
Bogie Type: Y25C. **Exchange Code:** 33.
Notes: Used on various workings to and from Europe.
Previous Number Series: 33 87 9282 000-009.

88 9282 000	88 9282 003	88 9282 006	88 9282 008
88 9282 001	88 9282 004	88 9282 007	88 9282 009
88 9282 002	88 9282 005		

88 9380 000-110 COVERED HOPPER IRB

Builder: Arbel-Fauvet, Douai, France, 1974-75.
Design Code: IRE442 (Ex IPE442). **Owner:** TSL.
Tare Weight: 21.00 t. **Gross Laden Weight:** 80.00 t.
Maximum Speed: 60 mph. **Length:** 18288 mm (60 ft. 0 in.)
Bogie Type: Y25C. **Exchange Code:** 33.
Notes: Used on various workings to and from Europe.
Previous Number Series: 21 88 0998 000-110 series.

88 9380 000	88 9380 032	88 9380 045	88 9380 064
88 9380 004	88 9380 033	88 9380 046	88 9380 065
88 9380 005	88 9380 034	88 9380 047	88 9380 066
88 9380 006	88 9380 035	88 9380 054	88 9380 067
88 9380 009	88 9380 036	88 9380 055	88 9380 068
88 9380 010	88 9380 037	88 9380 056	88 9380 100
88 9380 011	88 9380 038	88 9380 057	88 9380 101
88 9380 012	88 9380 039	88 9380 058	88 9380 102
88 9380 013	88 9380 040	88 9380 059	88 9380 103
88 9380 015	88 9380 041	88 9380 060	88 9380 104
88 9380 016	88 9380 042	88 9380 061	88 9380 106
88 9380 019	88 9380 043	88 9380 062	88 9380 108
88 9380 020	88 9380 044	88 9380 063	88 9380 110
88 9380 029			